NATIVE FASCISM IN THE SUCCESSOR STATES
1918-1945

Edited by
Peter F. Sugar

Santa Barbara, California
1971

Library of Congress Catalog Card No.
71-149636
SBN Paperbound Edition 0-87436-074-9
Clothbound Edition 0-87436-073-0

American Bibliographical Center—Clio Press
Riviera Campus, 2040 Alameda Padre Serra
Santa Barbara, California 93103

Preface

In the spring of 1966 several European scholars from Western and Eastern Europe visited the United States to participate in an international conference devoted to "The Nationality Problem in the Habsburg Monarchy in the Nineteenth Century: A Critical Appraisal." Taking advantage of the presence of these renowned experts in our country, the Graduate School of the University of Washington agreed to sponsor a conference dealing with the history of the Habsburg monarchy's Successor States. From the various topics that were discussed by the organizers of this second conference, held in Seattle on April 11-13, 1966, that of Fascism was selected because this movement played a significant role in all the states under consideration and because it is still of relevance and interest.

The organizer of the Seattle conference and the twelve scholars who presented papers use the expression, Fascism, in its widest possible sense, to denote all those movements that went beyond the conservatism and the traditional royal or military dictatorships that represented the extreme right wing philosophies and actions in East-Central Europe prior to the first World War and during the period between the two world-wide conflagrations. The term, as used by the authors of this volume, includes movements that are similar to Mussolini's Italian fascism and to national socialism in its German form. The main task of the contributors was to draw the line dividing these movements from those that belonged to the "traditional right" of the six states surveyed by them.

The twelve scholars—four from Eastern and two from Western Europe, one from Canada, and five from the United States—were paired with one European and one American discussing each of the six Successor States. Each of these—Austria, Czechoslovakia, Hungary, Poland, Romania, and Yugoslavia—was, therefore, investigated from two different points of view. The presentations of the lecturers differed sharply in length and emphasis as well as in scholarly apparatus if not in value. Some of them included footnotes with the texts of their lectures, one scholar attached a bibliography to his paper, while the majority followed the request of the organizers and submitted only their lectures. Your editor decided to keep this variety unchanged although it detracts from the uniformity of the presentation. His decision to do this was dictated by two considerations: The additional information supplied by the footnotes and the bibliography will help those interested in additional reading material; the omission of editorial changes over and above those that had to be introduced retains something of the flavor of the very exciting confrontation of scholars that characterized the discussions at the conference.

No preface is complete without the editor's acknowledgment of the efforts of those whose help made the volume that he has assembled possible. I would like to thank, first of all, the twelve scholars whose papers are included in this book. I wish to express my special gratitude to Professor Henryk Wereszycki of Krakow who, although prevented at the last moment from attending our conference, produced the thoughtful paper included among our essays, and to Professor Fritz Fellner of Salzburg who consented to replace another Austrian scholar, originally scheduled to read a paper, and produced his contribution in three hectic days of hard work.

The Graduate School of the University of Washington not only made the conference possible by underwriting its expenses, but also contributed to the production of this volume by paying for the transcribing of tapes and the editorial and typing costs. To Dean Joseph L. McCarthy and his colleagues at the Graduate School all of us involved in this venture owe sincere thanks.

Table of Contents

I
Introduction

Lyman H. Legters

Introduction

Lyman H. Legters

The continued outpouring of research and reflection on the phenomenon called fascism testifies to those profoundly disruptive forces that have, in the twentieth century, given rise to and been intensified by the many fascist movements seeking political power and by the few that have actually attained it. This volume joins an immense scholarly literature on fascism; yet no special justification is required for adding to this body of scholarship so long as the nature and origins of fascism, and of the devastation wrought under its banner, remain imperfectly understood.

A sampling and characterization of the literature may help to place the present collection of essays in its proper context. This book resembles three other collections of essays that have appeared in the past five years. The first issue of the *Journal of Contemporary History* appeared in 1966 and contained a symposium of essays on different national versions of fascist movements, along with two more general articles on the nature of fascism.[1] In 1965, Hans Rogger and Eugen Weber edited a set of essays on *The European Right*, conceived somewhat more broadly than studies of fascism per se but with fascist-like movements and regimes as the primary subject matter.[2] In 1966-67, the University of Reading conducted a series of lectures and seminars that appeared as a book under the editorship of S. J. Woolf, entitled *European Fascism*, containing another set of national studies along with three synthesizing essays.[3]

Neither Mr. Sugar's collection of studies nor the three mentioned above make any claim to comprehensiveness, but they all seek to present enough cases to afford a basis for comparison. Only the present book confines itself to a single European region where, owing to similarities in the degree of social integration and economic development, the traits of native fascist movements might be expected to disclose a relatively homogeneous regional style or function. Indeed, the editor calls attention to some such possibilities in his concluding remarks. East-Central Europe was represented in the other volumes (Romania, Austria, and Russia in the *Journal of Contemporary History*; Germany, Austria, Hungary, Finland, Russia, and Romania in *The European Right*; and Germany, Austria, Hungary, Romania, Poland, and Finland in *European Fascism*), and the degree of duplication between these and Sugar's collection should be viewed not as redundancy but as a welcome opportunity for critical comparison. Of course some dubiety always accompanies mere side-by-side placement as a method of comparative study, but it seems to me that Sugar has improved appreciably on the usual symposium technique by providing two more or less contrasting views—one North American and one from the area under investigation—for each national case.

I am also impressed, not only in the present volume but also in the other symposia mentioned and in such recent historical works as those by F. L. Carsten and Ernst Nolte,[4] by the enlargement of purview that has overtaken our effort to understand fascism. Without denying the importance of earlier scholarship, the bulk of it was confined to those fascist movements that successfully took power.[5] It is important, I think, that we are now witnessing a much fuller realization of fascism's pervasiveness in interwar Europe (if not also elsewhere) and the incipient attempt, made possible by the abandonment of such parochial explanatory devices as "national character," to comprehend the nature of fascism in its widest sense.[6]

It would be impossible in the space available here to attempt a survey of the literature of fascism. But it is necessary to mention at least the principal categories of investigation, beyond the studies of particular regimes or movements, which have contributed in like fashion to a grasp of fascism as a concept.

The study of totalitarianism[7] springs to mind as one such category, though I am not certain that the attendant concentration on similarities between fascism and communism has not obscured as much as it has illuminated. A related field of inquiry, the analysis of dictatorship as a phenomenon,[8] may in fact tell us as much about the nature of fascism. In any case, both bodies of literature aspire to a theoretical sophistication exceeding the possibilities of inquiries into particular fascist movements.

Another approach that must not be overlooked is that of psychological analysis, the variety of which defies summary.[9] But it too, like some sociological inquiries that will be mentioned below, aims at a comprehensive theory accounting for the appeal of fascism.

The history of ideas includes some of the most simple-minded as well as some of the most urbane scholarly efforts to discern the roots of "fascistoid" thought and behavior. Judging from the attempts to identify intellectual lineages culminating in fascism, intellectual history is more helpful when it concentrates not on the alleged antecedents of fascist thinking but rather on particular strains of thought that, by indirection, illuminate an intellectual climate that has proven favorable to the flowering of fascism.[10]

Taking the literature of fascism as a whole, there are some conceptual distinctions that apply to large sections of it, including some of the essays in this volume. The most general observation about this body of scholarship is that far too little attention has been paid to the stages through which any social movement is likely to pass. Relatively few studies of fascist phenomena give explicit recognition to the shifts in character that inevitably occur when an idea or programmatic goal or ideological construct is translated into an organized movement or political party striving to win power and when, in turn, that movement or party secures power and becomes a regime. Much that seems puzzling about the relation between ideas or ideologies and organized political groups would disappear with the simple acknowledgment that each of the three stages poses different requirements. The thinker or ideologue or demagogue is concerned initially only with the presentation of a set of ideas that will gain adherents to his cause. When he or a successor becomes the leader of a party or movement, his ideology is invariably adjusted to strategic and tactical requirements, such as the need to preserve the movement and to enlarge it through appeals to other groups of potential supporters. Most movements fail to advance beyond this stage, of course; they either make an unsuccessful attempt to take power and lose their momentum or they dilute their objectives in order to register modest gains within the existing structure and lose their integrity as dissident forces. But when a party succeeds in winning power, whether by legal or extralegal means, it undergoes a still more basic transition. The responsibilities and opportunities that accompany rule introduce additional strategic and tactical factors that further weaken whatever coherence the original doctrine or program may have had. It is thus misleading automatically to label as opportunism the attenuations of ideological programs that necessarily accompany the transitions from one stage to another. While many studies of fascist doctrines, movements, and regimes escape the trap of confusing one stage with another, rather fewer of them avoid misleading interpretation by giving express recognition to the natural differences between one stage and another. Any responsible account of Italian fascism or German national socialism from inception to demise will discern discontinuities as well as continuities from one stage to another. What is crucial, however, is that the opportunism that was endemic in both movements be recognized without making it responsible for the alterations that afflict all social movements upon acquiring power. A consequence of this observation for East Central Europe is that for the most part the native fascist movements there remained in the second stage except where enthroned by German occupation; one can therefore draw certain conclusions about the characteristics of fascist movements in that region but with very little assurance about the regimes that might have eventuated and with little assistance to be gained from comparisons with Italian or German fascism in power.

The foregoing observation applies equally to fascist and communist movements. But in the matter of doctrinal or ideological coherence, the two phenomena are not to be compared. The study of totalitarianism has taught us to see pronounced likenesses between communist and fascist regimes, but it does not follow that the role of ideology is the same in the two types of social movement. The Marxist tradition is readily susceptible to treatment as intellectual history, so long as sociopolitical conditioning factors are not ignored. But fascism does not so readily yield to the conventions of rational analysis of ideas.

This does not mean that fascism lacks the "intellectual origins" of George Mosse's subtitle[11] or that its ideas, including the preference for slogans over rational discourse, fall outside the realm of intellectual history. Just as Marxism can be analyzed as a Christian heresy because it shifts the millennium into historical time as an attainable human goal, so might fascism be interpreted as a Marxist heresy by reason of its denigration of coherent social theory in favor of the immanent values embodied in the movement itself. Marxism short-circuits the Last Judgment, so to speak, and fascism short-circuits rational striving for the millennial goal. This remains a study of ideas, but of a peculiarly slippery kind. As a standard text in political theory states, "the fascist philosophy was no doubt a vulgarization and a caricature, but like all caricatures it resembled something real."[12] Or as Arthur Koestler has written, "The secret of Fascism is the revival of archaic beliefs in an ultra-modern setting."[13] All of which merely amounts to saying that the intellectual study of fascism is a tricky business, for the scholar is always tempted to impose on his subject an order and a coherence and perhaps even an intellectual quality that it does not in fact possess. This temptation is the second major pitfall that has rendered a goodly share of the literature on fascism misleading.

Sir Isaiah Berlin's characterization of political ideas in the twentieth century, as distinguished from those of earlier ages, forms a highly pertinent warning about this pitfall. Skeptics of an earlier time did not doubt the importance of the basic political questions but only the possibility of attaining final solutions.

> It was left to the twentieth century to do something more drastic than this. For the first time it was now conceived that the most effective way of dealing with questions, particularly those recurrent issues which had perplexed and often tormented original and honest minds in every generation, was not by employing the tools of reason, still less those of the more mysterious capacities called "insight" and "intuition," but by obliterating the questions themselves.[14]

Again, speaking of communism (the twentieth-century variety that secured power in Russia) and fascism, Berlin acknowledges communism to be the "treacherous heir of the liberal internationalism of the previous century" and fascism to be the "culmination and bankruptcy of the mystical patriotism which animated the political movements of the time." But he goes on to say:

> Yet it is a fallacy to regard Fascism and Communism as being in the main only more uncompromising and violent manifestations of an earlier crisis, the culmination of a struggle fully discernible long before. The differences between the political movements of the twentieth century and the nineteenth are very sharp, and they spring from factors whose full force was not properly realized until our century was well under way. For there is a barrier which divides what is unmistakably past and done with from that which most characteristically belongs to our day. The familiarity of this barrier must not blind us to its relative novelty. One of the elements of the new outlook is the notion of unconscious and irrational influences which outweigh the forces of reason; another the notion that answers to problems exist not in rational solutions, but in the removal of the problems themselves by means other than thought and argument.[15]

My only addition to these observations would be to relate the two principal pitfalls to each other by recognizing that the role of the study of ideas, even the treacherous kind of study suggested by Sir Isaiah Berlin, dwindles steadily as a dissident movement such as fascism passes through its three stages. As an ideology is adapted to the needs of a party or movement seeking power, and still more so if it succeeds in this aim, the weight of analysis shifts sharply from the realm of ideas to the realm of sociopolitical circumstances and forces. Thus, the studies in this volume strike me, in their relatively greater concentration on circumstance than on ideologies as such, as pertinently conceived analyses, for they are concerned mainly with the machinations of fascist movements seeking power.

For the sake of additional perspective it may now be appropriate to mention two samples of sociopolitical analysis that attempt to delineate fascism as one of the overweening political phenomena of the twentieth century. One such attempt, by Seymour Martin Lipset,[16] focuses chiefly on the social base of political movements and results in a modification of the right-center-left spectrum of conventional political analysis. Instead of grouping fascism with other authoritarian movements of the far right, Lipset argues that the social base of fascism differentiates it fundamentally from traditional conservatism. He offers as his classificatory addition the recognition that in the twentieth century each political orientation—left, right and center—has acquired two distinct versions, the one moderate and parliamentary, the other extremist and extra-parliamentary. In such a scheme one notes that left, right, and center all retain their anchorages in working, upper, and middle classes, but each at the same time develops an extremist variant. Lipset's analysis of the mass base of fascism in its classic manifestations purports to establish that it is rooted in the same social stratum that has traditionally sustained liberalism. Fascism thus becomes the extremist variant of the center or middle class. It follows that Peronism, often regarded as a kind of fascism, is ruled out, because however many "fascistoid" characteristics it manifested, it was based on working-class support and thus falls, along with communism, within the extremist left. Similarly, the traditional authoritarianism of Franco's regime is distinguished from the fascism of its supporting Falangist movement because their respective social bases are different. Needless to say, Lipset's classification, if accepted, has great consequences for the way in which allegedly fascist movements of Eastern Europe are to be viewed.

Another sociologist, Barrington Moore, Jr., provides a different perspective by focusing on alternative routes toward modernization. He sees three distinguishable routes that agrarian societies have taken to reach modern industrialism: "bourgeois revolutions culminating in the Western form of democracy, conservative revolutions from above ending in fascism, and peasant revolutions leading to communism,"[17] the three displaying themselves either as alternatives or as successive historical stages. Moore recognizes substantial differences among the national versions of fascism, but since for his analysis the path leading to modernization is the crucial element, he has no difficulty in labeling as fascist the Japanese regime of the period just before World War II. After the differences have been spelled out,

> ... the underlying similarities between German and Japanese fascism still remain as the fundamental features. Both Germany and Japan entered the industrial world at a late stage. In both countries, regimes emerged whose main policies were repression at home and expansion abroad. In both cases, the main social basis for this program was a coalition between the commercial-industrial elites (who started from a weak position) and the traditional ruling classes in the countryside, directed against the peasants and the industrial workers. Finally, in both cases, a form of rightist radicalism emerged out of the plight of the petty bourgeoisie and peasants under advancing capitalism. This right-wing radicalism provided some of the slogans for repressive regimes in both countries but was sacrificed in practice to the requirements of profit and "efficiency."[18]

In this view, though the mass characteristic of fascism is acknowledged ("fascism is inconceivable without democracy or what is sometimes more turgidly called the entrance of the masses onto the historical stage"), the phenomenon occurs not so much as a feature of the twentieth-century climate of political opinion, and still less as a peculiarly European aberration responding to a loss of efficacy on the part of democratic ideals and practices, but rather as a universal possibility wherever modernization is brought to pass by a conservative elite anxious to preserve its traditional privileges while adding the possibilities of industrial development.

Once again, this scheme of analysis, like Lipset's, has clear implications for the assessment of the East European cases presented in this book. The sociological samples both have the advantage of universal applicability, in theory at least, and thus stand partly at variance with historical studies confined to one region, even one as variegated as Europe. The final vantage point to be summarized here comes precisely from two such historical studies.

Francis L. Carsten[19] concerns himself with the most important fascist movements (not the regimes that ensued) and their significance throughout Europe. Like all serious students of fascism, Carsten recognizes the marked differences among national versions of fascism; but he also finds enough similarities to justify the term used in the singular for a set of movements distinct from traditional authoritarian or reactionary movements of the right wing. These fascist movements were sufficiently alike that they could borrow readily from each other's ideologies and they shared the goal of obliterating, not just vanquishing, all competing parties and thus creating single-party monopolies of political influence and activity. All of them emphasized paramilitary organization and correspondingly aggressive action against opponents, combining mass appeal with elitist postulates that placed political participation in a strictly hierarchical arrangement under dictatorial leadership. The elements of love and hate were combined in the fascist movements in different ways (e.g., the differential role of anti-Semitism) but the movements were at one in their celebration of a glorious past and a correspondingly glorified future for the particular nation; also in their reliance on the dynamism of violence and action. Carsten further suggests that the rise of fascist movements depended less on any given relationship between working class and bourgeoisie than on the existence in various social groups, but notably among the lower middle class, of a profound dissatisfaction with prevailing socioeconomic and political circumstances.

Nolte's weighty inquiry into three manifestations of fascism does not contradict Carsten's conclusions. It is, however, a more ambitious effort—the most ambitious I have yet seen—to grasp the quintessential nature of fascism, while acknowledging its many variations, as the trademark of an epoch in European history. As the basis for his study of Action Française, Italian Fascism, and National Socialism, Nolte proposes this working definition:

> Fascism is anti-marxism which seeks to destroy the enemy by the evolvement of a radically opposed and yet related ideology and by the use of almost identical and yet typically modified methods, always, however, within the unyielding framework of national self-assertion and autonomy.[20]

I find this preliminary definition less persuasive than a good many of Nolte's insights into the intimate relationship between the appearance of fascism in Europe and the characteristic intellectual and spiritual crises that followed each other in rapid succession after World War I. As Nolte observes, to label an era by its dominant characteristic, the Counter Reformation for example, is not to deny the inherent variety of the era in question.

> In order to describe a period marked by powerful religious elements, [the historian] simply uses the religious phenomenon which, being central to this trend, represented its most novel and thus most typical manifestation. In the same way, if we are to name an era marked by political conflicts after the most novel phenomenon in the center of events, we cannot do otherwise than call the era of the world wars an era of fascism.[21]

The historical sections of his book illustrate the appropriateness of this assertion, but also lead the author to a more philosophical effort to grasp the essence of fascism as a metapolitical phenomenon with implications reaching far beyond its specific manifestations in the political arena.[22] Nolte thus returns on a much profounder level to fascism as a feature of intellectual history, more specifically as the spiritual crisis of the bourgeoisie, thereby linking the aforementioned observations of Sir Isaiah Berlin with such sociological analyses as have been mentioned here by way of illustration.

This is not the place for an evaluation of any of the attempts to synthesize the study of fascism in a theoretical construct. Nor do the essays in this volume touch directly on these theoretical considerations. But I would suggest that the fullest value of these studies can only be extracted by relating them to the as yet only incipient effort to refine the concept of fascism.

*   *   *   *   *

The editors of the Twentieth Century Series believe that this collection of studies of fascism in Eastern and Central Europe provides a notable addition to the literature that attempts to make sense of the political phenomena of our era. It is in the nature of symposia that synthesis or all-embracing theory is not to be expected. All of the studies gathered here pertain chiefly to the second stage of social movements—the stage in which a movement is striving to secure power. The editor has drawn some relevant conclusions from these investigations, generalizations that apply to fascist movements of the second stage in the particular region under consideration. It is anything but lamentable that the symposium halts at this modest goal; more ambitious attacks on the theoretical problem are made possible only by the kind of sifting of varied evidence that this set of studies represents. It may be anticipated that many more efforts will be made to synthesize evidence and conflicting opinion about the very special twentieth-century phenomenon known as fascism. Its manifestations in Eastern and Central Europe will have to be taken into account, along with the more "classical" instances, if the pervasive quality of fascism is to receive its due. Wherever conceptual boundaries are drawn, whether or not the phenomenon of fascism is held to include the East European examples presented here, there is at least a kinship of both style and idea that requires attention.

Apart from their contribution to an understanding of fascism, the essays that comprise this volume are valuable in at least two other contexts: they illuminate some common problems of the post-Habsburg successor states, problems that are certainly suggestive in any attempt to fathom the processes involved in the dismantling of empires; and they add to an understanding of the interwar period in Eastern Europe, a period that was so crucial for that region which is only now beginning to receive its due measure of scholarly attention. These dimensions of the symposium may even outweigh in importance its addition to the literature of fascism.

It is precisely in this sense that the structure of the symposium is especially fitting. The juxtaposition of European and North American interpretations of more or less identical historical episodes should have particular appeal to the reader wishing to understand the national differences that have been stirring and, increasingly, finding expression in contemporary Eastern Europe. Scholarly interaction between native and foreign students of a given area or set of problems is vitally important to balanced historical judgment. It is exactly where concepts and interpretations vary—about fascism or any other political phenomenon—that studies such as these can be most illuminating, not only about the area or problem studied but also about the processes of international scholarly cooperation.

FOOTNOTES

1   Walter Laqueur and George L. Mosse, eds., *International Fascism, 1920-1945* (New York: Harper Torchbook, 1966), reprinted from *Journal of Contemporary History*, 1, no. 1.

2   Hans Rogger and Eugen Weber, *The European Right* (Berkeley and Los Angeles: University of California Press, 1965)

3   S. J. Woolf, ed., *European Fascism* (London: Weidenfeld & Nicolson, 1968). See also the second volume in the series also edited by S. J. Woolf, *The Nature of Fascism* (London: Weidenfeld & Nicolson, 1968).

4   Francis L. Carsten, *The Rise of Fascism* (Berkeley and Los Angeles: University of California Press, 1967), and three works by Ernst Nolte, *Three Faces of Fascism* (New York: Holt, Rinehart & Winston, 1966), *Faschistische Bewegungen* (Munich: Deutscher Taschenbuch Verlag, 1966), *Theorien über den Faschismus* (Cologne-Berlin: Kiepenheuer und Witsch, 1967).

5   Convenient surveys of the literature on Nazi Germany and Fascist Italy are contained in Robert G. L. Waite, ed., *Hitler and Nazi Germany* (New York: Holt, Rinehart & Winston, 1965), pp. 116-22 and in Alan Cassels, *Fascist Italy* (New York: Thomas Y. Crowell Co., 1968), pp. 117-27. Special mention must be made of such outstanding works as Franz Neumann, *Behemoth* (New York: Oxford University Press, 1942); Hans Buchheim, *Das Dritte Reich* (Munich: Kösel, 1958); Friedrich Glum, *Der Nationalsozialismus* (Munich: Beck, 1962); Karl Dietrich Bracher, Wolfgang Sauer, und Gerhard Schulz, *Die nationalsozialistische Machter-greifung* (Cologne: Westdeutscher Verlag, 1962); Alan Bullock, *Hitler* (New York: Harper & Row, 1962); and the first volume in the Twentieth Century Series: Martin Broszat, *German National Socialism, 1919-1945* (Santa Barbara, Calif.: Clio Press, 1966). Among the outstanding works on Italian fascism are: Luigi Salvatorelli and Giovanni Mira, *Storia d'Italia nel periodo fascista* (Turin: Einaudi, 1956); Ivone Kirkpatrick, *Mussolini; A Study in Power* (New York: Avon Book, 1968); Serge Hughes, *The Fall and Rise of Modern Italy* (New York: Minerva Press, 1968); and Christopher Seton-Watson, *Italy from Liberalism to Fascism, 1870-1925* (London: Methuen, 1967).

6   In addition to works already listed, see particularly Eugen Weber, *Varieties of Fascism* (Princeton, N.J.: D. Van Nostrand Co., 1964), and John Weiss, *The Fascist Tradition* (New York: Harper & Row, 1967). Special studies, illustrative of interest in hitherto neglected instances of fascism, include: Walter Wolf, *Faschismus in der Schweiz* (Zürich: Flamberg Verlag, 1969); Nicholas M. Nagy-Talavera, *The Green Shirts and Others; A History of Fascism in Hungary and Rumania* (Stanford: The Hoover Institution, 1970); Marvin Rintala, *Three Generations: The Extreme Right Wing in Finnish Politics* (Bloomington: Indiana University Press, 1962); Colin Cross, *The Fascists in Britain* (London: Barrie & Rockliff, 1961); and Eugen Weber, *Action Française* (Palo Alto, Calif.: Stanford University Press, 1962). The difficulties that beset Soviet attempts to fit fascism into an accepted ideological framework have recently been reviewed and summarized by Theodore Draper, "The Ghost of Social Fascism," *Commentary* 47, no. 2: 29-42.

7   See especially Hannah Arendt, *The Origins of Totalitarianism* (New York: Harcourt, Brace & Co., 1958); Carl J. Friedrich and Zbigniew K. Brzezinski, *Totalitarian Dictatorship and Autocracy* (Cambridge: Harvard University Press, 1956); J. L. Talmon, *The Origins of Totalitarian Democracy* (New York: Frederick A. Praeger, 1960); Hans Buchheim, *Totalitarian Rule* (Middletown, Conn.: Wesleyan University Press, 1968); and Sigmund Neumann, *Permanent Revolution* (New York: Harper & Bros., 1942).

8   Good examples are: Ernest Frankel, *The Dual State* (New York: Oxford University Press, 1941); Alfred Cobban, *Dictatorship, Its History and Theory* (New York: Charles Scribner's Sons, 1939); and Zevedei Barbu, *Democracy and Dictatorship* (New York: Grove Press, 1956).

9   The most noteworthy is T. W. Adorno et al., *The Authoritarian Personality* (New York: W. W. Norton & Co., 1969), but see also Erich Fromm, *Escape from Freedom* (New York: Farrar & Rinehart, 1941); Harold Lasswell, *Psychopathology and Politics* (Chicago: University of Chicago Press, 1930); and E. K. Bramstedt, *Dictatorship and Political Police; The Technique of Control by Fear* (London: Kegan Paul, 1945).

10   The most successful direct approach to this issue is George L. Mosse, *The Crisis of*

German Ideology; Intellectual Origins of the Third Reich (New York: Grosset & Dunlap, 1964). Examples of successful illumination by indirection include Eric Bentley, *A Century of Hero-Worship* (Boston: Beacon Press: 1957); Fritz Stern, *The Politics of Cultural Despair* (Berkeley: University of California Press, 1961); and Peter Gey, *Weimar Culture* (New York: Harper & Row, 1968).

11 See n. 10 above.

12 George H. Sabine, *A History of Political Theory* (New York: Holt, Rinehart & Winston, 1960), p. 855.

13 Arthur Koestler, *The Yogi and the Commissar* (New York: Collier Books, 1961), p. 116.

14 Sir Isaiah Berlin, "Political Ideas in the Twentieth Century," in his *Four Essays on Liberty* (New York: Oxford University Press, 1969), p. 23.

15 Ibid., p. 7.

16 Seymour Martin Lipset, *Political Man* (Garden City, N.Y.: Doubleday & Co., 1960), pp. 127 ff. See also Talcott Parsons, "Some Sociological Aspects of the Fascist Movement," in his *Essays in Sociological Theory*, rev. ed. (Glencoe, Ill.: The Free Press, 1954); and David J. Saposs, "The Role of the Middle Class in Social Development," *Economic Essays in Honor of Wesley Clair Mitchell* (New York: Columbia University Press, 1935).

17 Barrington Moore, Jr., *Social Origins of Dictatorship and Democracy* (Boston: Beacon Press, 1967), pp. 413-14.

18 Ibid., p. 305.

19 The last chapter of Carsten's *The Rise of Fascism* spells out the conclusions summarized here.

20 Nolte, *Three Faces of Fascism*, pp. 20-21.

21 Ibid., p. 6.

22 Ibid., pp. 429 ff.

II
Austria

Fritz Fellner

R. John Rath

A

The Background of Austrian Fascism*

Fritz Fellner

This paper is not intended as an elaborate analysis of Austrian fascism. Rather, it will single out in a loose form some aspects of the ideological and psychological background of fascism and national socialism in Austria, while Professor Rath will concentrate on the constitutional aspect and the details of the character of Austro-fascism.

Since 1945 many monographs have been published dealing with numerous facets of national socialism in Germany, but apart from extensive research in the Anschluss controversy, little examination has been made of Austrian fascism.[1] Immediately after the collapse of the Third Reich, research concentrated on diplomatic affairs and the governmental aspects of national socialism. In the 1960s the treatment of the phenomenon of fascism underwent a decisive change: in lieu of the meticulous factual research accounts, a new approach was preferred. Fascism was now dealt with in a comparative way; Italian, German, Romanian, and Hungarian fascism were considered the offspring of a common European ancestor reaching back to the turn of the century and developing into a common totalitarian experience in the interwar period.

Totalitarianism was dealt with in great detail in the 1950s. But even the totalitarianism studies of those days suffered from shortcomings similar to the research on national socialism. Most of the studies on the subject, like the books by Carl Friedrich or Brzezinski,[2] concentrated on the governmental aspect of totalitarian rule, neglecting the social and spiritual background of totalitarianism as an ideology. Only in the excellent books by Ernst Nolte and Eugen Weber do we get new insight into the problem of fascism as an ideology and explanations of its background.[3]

On the same scholarly level as Nolte's and Weber's studies, though little known outside Germany, is the book published by Hans Buchheim, *Totalitäre Herrschaft.*[4] Buchheim is an enlightened Catholic writer of the younger generation of German historians who explains national socialism as one offspring of a general European development. He stresses the view that national socialism and fascism were so successful because of their declared opposition to liberalism and their counterrevolutionary appeal to a generation that was brought up in an elitist educational system. In this view we find also, in my opinion, the key to the understanding of the rise of Austro-fascism (called clerico-fascism by its political opponents, not without justification), as well as to the success of national socialism in Austria. To understand the history of these two movements in Austria, to grasp their temporary success and their lasting influence,

15

fascism and national socialism must be seen against the general background of the antidemocratic approach that dominated political thought in many European countries, including Austria, in the 1920s and 1930s. After 1945, Germans tended to describe fascism and national socialism as their national error and guilt. This is what they had been told by the victorious Allies. They saw it as their main task to *Ihre eigene Vergangenheit zu bewältigen* (there is no proper English term for this German phrase, meaning roughly: "to cope with one's past"). In Germany, however, as well as in Austria soon after the collapse of the Third Reich, a fateful decision was made by the historians. Pretending that the task of *die Vergangenheit bewältigen* had a special nature and too many immediate political and personal implications, they claimed that the historical interpretation of the most recent past was too complicated in method and scope to be included in regular historical research. The history of national socialism and the history of the interwar period were separated from general modern history and made into a special category: *Zeitgeschichte*. This decision turned out to be a very convenient way of escaping political and scholarly responsibility. By making *Zeitgeschichte* a special field of research, historians had a formal excuse for cutting national socialism from its historical roots. This gave them the chance to claim that national socialism was foreign to German historical and national tradition rather than the logical result of it. By leaving research of national socialism to *Zeitgeschichte*, German historians evaded the responsibility for the rise of national socialism in their own research. Up to the present day the older members of the German *historische Zunft* are rather reluctant to include national socialism in the natural evolution of German history.

Austrian historians knew this *Zeitgeschichte* approach too. Being generally more conservative than historians usually are, the Austrians had a long time ago decided to stop doing research on anything that occurred after 1918, and for a long time they left the period after the dissolution of the Habsburg monarchy to foreign historians and to journalists. There was another reason, too, for this action to be deliberately played down in Austria. Accepting the thesis forwarded in the Moscow Declaration of 1943 that Austria was the first victim of Nazi aggression, Austrians could easily shed responsibility for fascist thinking, blaming the disaster of 1938 on foreign aggression. Turning back to the pre-1938 days, and to pre-1938 personnel, Austrians avoided analyses of their way of thinking and their way of life in those critical days.

In addition to these psychological (and political) handicaps, research in *Zeitgeschichte* got off on the wrong track. German and Austrian historical scholarship had concentrated on diplomatic history since the controversy over the war guilt problem. Since national socialism had led the world into a new war the foremost task seemed to be to investigate once again the origins of the war rather than the roots of the ideology. Copious volumes were published on the origin of World War II. The source material of the Nuremberg trials directed research to the history of the concentration camps, and some historians concentrated on constitutional questions, such as Hitler's seizure of power, trying to prove that he came to power in an illegal way or at least by misusing the parliamentary rights. In a similar manner Austrian *Zeitgeschichtler* investigated the way in which Arthur Seyss-Inquart was appointed chancellor, checking whether Wilhelm Miklas, the Federal President, actually signed Seyss-Inquart's appointment in order to find out if the Anschluss can be regarded as a constitutional act. In doing this they are forgetting that the Constitution of 1934 itself had been the result of an unconstitutional maneuver. Austrian historians devoted most of their research time to collecting documents on the Nazi rising of 1934 and other detailed questions of this type. This approach was not only by-passing the real issue, but was actually hiding and weakening it, since the historical problem of fascism was pushed into the background and soon seemed to be forgotten. It is time to restore the proper perspective. National socialism and fascism in Europe, especially in Austria, should be dealt with not as a result of constitutional or diplomatic events but in their real character as ideological and spiritual as well as social problems.

In order to be able *unsere Vergangenheit zu bewältigen,* we will have to turn to a sociological analysis of the interwar period, looking first into the educational system and then to the way in which public opinion was formed. In this field of investigation of schools, newspapers, films, and radio many more of the roots of fascism can be found than in the economic situation of the late 1920s, which is far too often mentioned as the final cause of the victory of fascism and national socialism.

In my opinion the economic explanation of the rise of national socialism is just another attempt to shift the responsibility in the minds of Germans and Austrians to external and material factors beyond their control. Historians and politicians, who like to point to the parallel development of the rise of national socialism and the economic crises, have so far failed to explain why the United States of American was not plagued by the danger of totalitarianism (Louisiana excepted) when the number of unemployed there was higher than in Germany. The economic depression might have helped in pushing certain social groups toward radicalism, but when a social analysis of the Nazi following is finally undertaken, the results, I suppose, will show that the greater bulk of the unemployed did not join the Nazi ranks.

In regard to Austria the question should be put this way: what were the reasons that drove such a large part of Austrian conservatives to destroying the democratic order? What made more than 500,000 Austrians, almost 10 percent of the population, turn to national socialism as an alternative to clerico-fascism instead of fighting for a return of parliamentary rights? Something must have made them believe in that totalitarian ideology, and what this was can be understood only by fitting the entire development of the interwar period into the social-educational setup of the years before the collapse of the Central Powers in 1918.

In this short essay the history of the origins of totalitarian thinking cannot be presented, nor even sketched. I must restrict myself to emphasizing, even overemphasizing, a few elements that I believe are the most important factors in this historical process.

First I wish to present one argument in which I believe strongly, although many will object to it: There is, in my opinion, a clear spiritual connection between a traditional religious attitude and the rise of totalitarianism. A look at the map of Europe makes it apparent that secular totalitarian movements and authoritarian governments had been successful in countries with an uninterrupted Catholic tradition. It is a fact that national socialism had its origin in Bavaria, where, by the way, the *National Demokratische Partei* has shown amazing strength in the recent elections. It is well known that Hitler was greatly impressed by the political leadership of the Christian Socialist mayor of Vienna, Karl Lueger. By pointing to this coincidence I do not want to imply that Catholicism is by definition fascistic. I only want to show that people who had gone through an unbroken Catholic tradition developed a certain habit of thinking, a certain pattern of concepts of human affairs, which made it possible, once the contents of the religious tradition were lost, to replace them with concepts equally unquestionable. The belief in an absolute truth, the belief in the infallibility of a leader, the belief in authority and a preestablished order, the belief that social and political activity has to be based on orders from above and not on requests from below, the hierarchical organization, the demand that the revealed truth be accepted without question or doubt —these are some of those basic concepts that were part of the Austrian educational system. They made possible the organization, once the belief in the transcendental religion was lost, of a new secular religion along similar lines.

In *Mein Kampf* Hitler stressed that one can learn from the Catholic church and, using its methods, win over the people for an entirely opposite, substitute religion. Here, in my opinion, is the key to an understanding of the success of fascism in Central Europe. Fascism, like other totalitarian systems, is a secularized religion that requires that society be organized according to the principles of an unchallengeable religion. Seen from this point of view societies as such have a tendency, in the course of history, to be totalitarian, and in this respect the totalitarianism of the twentieth century is nothing new. Carl Friedrich is mistaken when he claims that totalitarianism is an entirely new concept, one unknown to former generations. On the contrary, totalitarianism has existed ever since we have had human activities in the world. The medieval societies were totalitarian, only it was possible then for the individual to move away without being followed and persecuted in the next place. The early American colonies had been quite totalitarian in their strict regulation of society, though at that time it was possible to move from Massachusetts to Rhode Island and establish a new totalitarian society. In the twentieth century this possibility of escape is lost because modern, civilized, technological society knows more perfect means to enforce conformity on its citizens. That is why twentieth-century totalitarianism appears so cruel and so dangerous, and looks new to the political scientist.

It is against this general historical background that we must examine the rise of fascism in Austria. The Austrians had never completely relinquished their totalitarian thinking habits. Throughout the nineteenth century attempts to liberalize politics and social order were made but opposed and hindered by the educational system. Education in Austria was not directed towards the recognition of pluralistic values, people were not readied for compromise but rather they were taught to obey and to believe, not to challenge or to show initiative in searching for progress. Another aspect of education has to be mentioned as being a very important root of fascism in Austria and in Germany: in both countries education was used to prepare the young for war. Worship of heroes, worship of war, worship of sacrifice were the main themes of teaching in history and literature. The young men were told that there was no higher achievement than to sacrifice one's life in battle, and young women were made to believe that their duty was to bear soldiers to be sacrificed on the *Altar des Vaterlandes*. Violence and war were presented in education as constituting factors in history.

I further think it quite significant that the political language in German-speaking countries is made up of words taken from war and fighting, using terms of strategy, tactics, and military planning. Political parties quite often were called "fronts" (like the *Vaterländische Front* in Austria). Behind this attitude there seems to be a kind of primitive social Darwinism. The creed of the survival of the fittest is one of the ideological elements conditioning the rise of fascism.

Closely connected with this interpretation of life as an incessant struggle for survival is the concept that politics is a confrontation of enemies, not a competition of partners. In Austria the political opponent was never seen as a partner with whom one might exchange the command post for a certain time, a partner one could trust not to change the basic rules of the game. Here the political opponent was always the enemy to be destroyed. Political victory was a victory only when the opponent was annihilated —not only as a political force, but physically. From this mentality the road leads straight to the concentration camps of Auschwitz or Buchenwald or Mauthausen, to the *Endlösung* carried out by the SS.

Another quite important factor in fascist mentality is the over-all fear of social revolution and the fear of mass rule. Again we can trace this attitude to education. The mistaken interpretation of national socialism and fascism as vulgar criminal perversions of human behavior, the "monster" interpretation given to national socialism by American war propaganda, has blocked the insight into this elitarian root of fascism. German youth, especially the academically trained, believed in individuality but only as the activity of a great individual functioning as a driving force in history. Educated classes in Austria and in Germany worship Jakob Burckhardt, whose individualism had made him suspicious of the rise of the masses, which he could observe in the nineteenth century. Burckhardt's elitist individualism was carried further in the rather unscholarly form in which Nietzsche's philosophy was vulgarized by many second-rate writers who were convinced that democracy and the pluralistic system would block the individual's efforts to improve humanity and reduce it to its lowest common denominator. Fritz Stern has dealt in a very enlightening way with the influence of writers like Langbehn and Moeller van den Bruck.[5] Sociologists like Vilfedo Pareto and Gaetano Mosca might be added to the list of thinkers paving the road for fascism. They considered democracy as the defeat of quality by quantity. The antidemocratic character of fascism and its emphasis on heroism made it attractive to those who thought of themselves as the elite. Fascism became an elitist movement with the party representing the elite of the nation, while for those who could not make it into the higher party ranks there remained the consoling fact that they belonged at least to a superior race, the Aryan, the Nordic race, the German *Volk*.

Against this background drawn from the nineteenth century we have to see the interwar period. Shortly after the collapse of the Central Powers and the dissolution of the Habsburg monarchy in 1918, this event was referred to as a revolution, a revolution from within, a socialist, Marxist revolution, a "stab in the back," as the Germans called it. Rarely was it mentioned that the famous "German revolution" had occurred only after the military defeat and that there was no social revolution at all. It was a change of constitutions, an overthrow of dynasties, but the social, political, and economic structures remained untouched. The bureaucracy remained in the offices, the teachers—university professors above all—stayed on their jobs. The entire social stratification remained the same; the only difference was that the nobility was not allowed to use its titles, at least not legally. The only change of significance was the selection of cabinet ministers from a different social group, a group considered inferior, uncultured as the word then went, by the propertied and academically educated people. The new leaders of the Austrian republic, whether they were Christian Socialists or Social Democrats, represented the democratic mass parties. They came from social ranks that until then had rarely participated in executive governmental functions and never had done so in their own right and on their own responsibility. (As a matter of fact in Austria, whenever a member of a lower class achieved a certain higher position in civil service, politics, or the military, he was ennobled and in this way severed from his social origin.) Before 1918 the parliamentary reforms had been accepted by the ruling classes only reluctantly. Now, in the fall of 1918, full parliamentary government was enforced, and the cabinet ministers were chosen from the ranks of the mass parties. Otherwise the government structure remained the same: the *Sektionschef*, who before 1918 had complained about the lack of factual knowledge of his minister, the Baron, after 1918 did naturally not value either the factual expert opinion of his new minister of agriculture, a simple farmer before 1918, or that of the former trade-union functionary who was now minister of social affairs. The in-group of upperclass people and of all those who had academic training formed an antidemocratic element in Austria from the very beginning of the republic, although they occupied key administrative positions and the top positions in education. In 1918 Austria and Germany were not democratized, they only accepted a republican constitution. Since this change coincided with their defeat in war, it was regarded as being forced upon them by a victorious enemy. It was opposed as a foreign import that did not fit the tradition of the nation. Out of this feeling grew a resentment against the Austrian Republic and the democratic order at the very moment of their birth. The situation was aggravated by the fact that Austrian politicians were unaccustomed to the basic rules of parliamentary politics. The main idea of democracy, that differences can and should be overcome in compromise, that only by a readiness to give and to take could general agreement of all concerned be reached, was resented and rejected. Political bargaining was not accepted as a practical, useful, and positive attitude in politics, but was discredited as a betrayal of principles, called *Kuhhandel*. Austrians lacked respect for the rights of the minority and instead of political deals they asked for clear-cut, spectacular decisions. Democracy never has been able to make ruthless decisions: compromise by its nature is less spectacular than forceful violent decisions. It was, therefore, easy for a malign propaganda to blame compromising democratic governments for all the shortcomings and failures of the 1920s.

Actually, historical research has shown in many instances that most of these so-called failures were not the result of democratic rule, but the consequences of the obstructionist activities of the antidemocratic forces. In Austria, democracy was sabotaged by people who, due to their training and social positions, should have been its leaders. Their destructive attitude, the defaming of democracy in schools and newspapers, in political campaigns, and in the bureaucratic process produced the downfall of democracy in the 1930s. The generation that received its education in these years was told in Austrian schools not only that democracy was forced on the country as a consequence of a lost war and that it was un-Austrian (the term used in those days was "un-German"), but they were also taught to believe that only a strong man, a so-called "man of principles," could lead the country out of its difficulties. By attributing all hardships to the pluralistic value system of parliamentary rule, by demanding that society be shaped according to the main ideas of an absolute monistic value system, by asking for a restoration of lost values, the educational leaders in Austria undermined democracy. The generation born shortly before World War I and entering political maturity in the early 1930s in a modern, technological civilization could not return to the value system of a transcendental religion praised by their elders and it turned to a substitute, a secular religion, it became the victim of fascism. Another aspect should also be taken into account: the special social situation of the 1920s. The collapse of the Habsburg monarchy had brought two important social problems, the first being the problem of social readjustment of war veterans, especially the social adjustment of professional soldiers. The officer deprived of his social position, of his income, seeing himself as a professional leader and finding himself just a common man now, was unable to adjust to civilian life. He found shelter and new command positions in the veterans' organizations and the semi-fascist organizations like the early Heimwehr. Here the officers soon were joined by the disillusioned noncommissioned officers and war heroes who had exchanged their habitual social surroundings for command positions during the war and were not able to return to their low position at home. This socially dissatisfied group with its fighting spirit and its primitive battle mentality became the nucleus of fascist party armies.

The other important social problem was the insecurity felt by the white-collar workers, who, thinking themselves better than the blue-collar workers, were afraid of a socialist revolution and its leveling consequences. They were joined by the high school and university graduates, who, being a relatively small, select group, always thought of themselves as superior to the masses and were afraid that a leftist revolution might destroy their claim to leadership. From these groups, students, white-collar workers, dispossessed officers, professional adventurers, fascism and national socialism recruited their followers in the 1920s and the early 1930s.

An atmosphere of conflict, of hatred and suspicion characterized political life in Austria since the early days of the republic. Adam Wandruszka has written an excellent study of Austrian political parties in the *Geschichte der österreichischen Republik*,[6] in which he presented a valuable interpretation of Austrian politics and in which he gave a quite convincing explanation of Austrian political strife. Wandruszka sees Austria split into three political camps, in each of which an antidemocratic wing opposed a democratic wing. The ruling camp of the first Austrian republic, from 1920 to 1938, was the Catholic camp, which changed from its originally democratic and moderate character to the fascist program of the Dollfuss regime. The second camp was the Pan-German camp, the party of the academic youth and the civil service, which finally was taken in by the Nazis. The third camp was the Social Democrats. Here there had been revolutionary extreme leftist tendencies in the beginning, but the party managed to keep its democratic character until it was brutally beaten in the civil war by Dollfuss and the Heimwehr in 1934. But even the socialists in Austria in the 1920s talked of democracy only as a road leading to socialism, not as an end in itself. But the socialists, who did not take advantage of their numerical strength in 1918 and 1919 when they abstained from revolution and chose the evolutionary road to social reform to reach their goal, were promptly defeated in the first elections in 1920. They then remained in opposition, never getting another chance to introduce social reforms in Austria. Being in opposition, their propaganda language turned increasingly radical, frightening the middle classes who could not believe that the Social Democrats actually had never attempted or planned a revolutionary overthrow of the parliamentary government. The socialists felt themselves on the defensive, and they were indeed on the defensive, because conservative and even moderate bourgeois groups decided to destroy socialism out of fear of a revolution.

There was a rather strange situation in almost all European countries in the interwar period. To the same degree to which the danger of a revolution from the left diminished, the pretended threat of revolution was used more and more as a propaganda slogan by the rightists. Real or imaginary leftist terror receded and the socialists became more and more defensive in their attitudes, even refraining from strikes as a weapon to settle social claims, while rightist propaganda tried and managed to sell its own aggressive terror to the public as the only means to save the country, the only protection against Bolshevist terror. This danger of Bolshevism, as the historian now knows, did not exist in Italy in 1922, it did not exist in Germany in 1919 and 1933, and it did not exist in Austria in 1934. Still it was the pretext used by the fascists to overthrow the parliamentary governments. Though there was no factual basis for this fear of leftist revolution, the middle classes of the interwar period believed in it. The moderate middle class, ademocratic but not necessarily antidemocratic, joined the fascists out of a fear of communism or socialism, not realizing that they put themselves into the hands of defenders who were worse than the enemy they were trying to escape. The rise of fascism and national socialism in Austria cannot be understood unless the country's social and educational aspects are studied in detail. Both of these aspects have been neglected by Austrian scholars who did research on the interwar period.

In the interwar period, Austria's historians studied the question of war guilt. In their belief in the value of documents of the "great" political problems, they gave preference to diplomatic history over and above all other historical topics. In their research as well as in their over-all outlook on life, they neglected the social and ideological questions of their time. In their scientific methodology as well as in their political commitments they opposed progress and the pluralistic interpretation of the past and the present. By taking this position they not only made fascism and national socialism possible, they did more than that, they helped to prepare the way for these movements. It should be the duty of the historians "to cope with this past of their own." If they would do this, we would come much closer to an explanation of the historical phenomenon known as fascism.

FOOTNOTES

* Replacing a colleague who could not attend the Seattle conference, Professor Fellner prepared these remarks in three days without benefit of a library. He was very reluctant to permit the publication of these impromptu remarks, but finally gave permission after the editor assured him that his contribution contains much valuable material. For his participation at the conference and for his consent to publish his remarks, all those involved in the preparation of this volume thank Professor Fellner.

1 Since the 1966 conference in Seattle two important works have been published on Austrian fascism. K. R. Stadler, "Austria," in *European Fascism*, ed. Stuart J. Woolf (London: Weidenfeld & Nicolson, 1968) and Grete Klingenstein, "Bemerkungen zum Problem des Faschismus in Österreich," in *Österreich in Geschichte und Literatur*, Vol. 14 (Graz, 1970).

2 Carl J. Friedrich unter Mitarbeitung von Zbigniew K. Brzezinski, *Totalitäre Diktatur* (Stuttgart: Kohlhammer, 1957).

3 Ernst Nolte, *Der Faschismus in seiner Epoche* (München: R. Piper, 1963)
Die faschistischen Bewegungen (München: Deutscher Taschenbuch Verlag, 1966)
Die Krise des liberalen Systems und die faschistische Bewegung (München: R. Piper, 1968).
Eugen Weber, *Varieties of Fascism* (Princeton, N.J.: D. Van Nostrand Co., 1964).

4 Hans Buchheim, *Totalitäre Herrschaft. Wesen und Merkmale* (München: Kösel Verlag, 1962).

5   Fritz Stern, *The Politics of Cultural Despair.* A Study in the Rise of the Germanic Ideology (Berkeley: University of California Press, 1961).

6   Adam Wandruszka, "Österreichs politische Struktur. Die Entwicklung der Parteien und politischen Bewegungern," *Geschichte der Republik Österreich*, ed. Heinrich Benedikt (München: Oldenbourg, 1954).

B

Authoritarian Austria

R. John Rath

On the evening of February 24, 1938, in a ringing speech delivered to eighteen hundred legislators, government officials, diplomats, and other lucky ticket holders jammed together in the federal diet building in Vienna and to countless thousands of other deeply worried Austrians assembled in coffeehouses and public squares all over Austria, Chancellor Kurt von Schuschnigg summarized the fundamental principles that underlay his government. The Austrian constitution, he emphasized, "recognizes no parties and no party state." It was based on the concept of the "corporative (*berufständische*) articulation of the populace," with "an authoritarian political leadership" as "the controlling element." For this reason, there could be "no coalitions, either in political life or in the government." The regime was based on the principle of "the concentration of all the positive forces of our people."

> What we want in Austria can not and must not be described in terms of the political concepts of the Right and the Left or the political colors of Red and Black, Brown and Green. It is not a popular front connected with parties but the united solid front of all our people, no matter to what rank or class they may belong. To serve, realize, and preserve this common front of the Austrian people is the essence of the government's aim and program.[1]

The constitution to which the chancellor referred in his speech had been drawn up by the Vorarlberg Christian Socialist politician and jurist, Dr. Otto Ender, and subjected to thirteen major redrafts. It was enacted on April 24, 1934, on the basis of a 1917 wartime law that gave the government the right to rule by emergency decree. Then, by a vote of 74 to 2 by a "rump parliament" of only 76 members, from which the Social Democrats had been carefully excluded, the constitution, along with 471 other decrees promulgated since March, 1933, was accepted in a session on April 30 that lasted only twenty minutes. The constitution was officially proclaimed the next day, May 1.[2]

The opening statement of the document, which was actually a mishmash of various, often conflicting, ideological concepts held by the variegated factions gathered around Chancellor Engelbert Dollfuss, makes it clear that those who drafted it drew their inspiration from Catholic rather than from the popular sovereignty doctrines that prevailed in Austria during the interwar period. Whereas the opening sentence of the democratic constitution adopted in 1920 announced that "Austria is a democratic republic" whose "power emanates from the people,"[3] the preamble of the 1934 document read: "In the name of God, the Almighty, from Whom all justice derives, the Austrian people receive this constitution for their Christian, German federal state on a corporative basis."[4] Thus, the 1934 constitution provided for a Christian, German, federal, and corporative state. Although the provision was never spelled out in the constitution, the leaders of the "new Austria" also made it clear that, at least for an interim period, their country was to be under strong authoritarian leadership.[5]

The basic concept of the constitution was the idea that Austria was a "Christian state." The emblem adopted for the state, the *Kruckenkreuz,*[6] symbolized the fact that the country was thenceforth to be governed "in a Christian spirit and according to religious principles."[7] Even though complete freedom was given to all non-Catholic religious groups to worship God according to their own beliefs,[8] "the ethical and moral principles of Christianity" were to be stressed.[9] Under genuine Christian leadership,[10] the Christian spirit of the Austrian people was to be renewed[11] and Austrian Germanism was to be brought "into an indissoluble union ... with religion and faith"[12] in order "to make possible the moral and spiritual uplifting of our whole populace."[13] The Austrian Christian state would be "an ethical state in a Christian sense, a state in which respect for moral and religious life" was "the guideline for all private and public life."[14]

For Dollfuss and his supporters, governing in accord with Christian principles meant creating a corporative state based on the fundamental reforms advocated in the papal encyclical *Quadragesimo anno* (1931).[15] For Dollfuss this encyclical was, in fact, "the Magna Charta of the Austrian constitution."[16]

In the eyes of the proponents of the "new order," a Christian corporative state was to serve as a powerful bulwark to protect the Austrian people against the many evils of godless and materialistic Marxian socialism, with its destructive class struggle ideas,[17] and liberal democracy, which, they asseverated, resulted in perpetual conflict and rule by those party bosses who could momentarily win a majority vote in parliament.[18] By organizing all economic and cultural activities into corporations, faintly resembling the medieval guilds and possessing a considerable amount of self-rule, the makers of the new state hoped to create a new social and political order in which the fundamental moral and social precepts of *Quadragesimo anno* would be put into practice and in which the evils prevalent in socialistic, liberal, and capitalistic states would be remedied.

The corporative bodies were intended to become a responsible substitute for popular representation and the abolished parliamentary system.[19] The members of small vocational and cultural groups, which were eventually to become autonomous, were to select men of their personal acquaintance to look after their interests. They were to be accorded the right to regulate their own professional affairs as soon as they were in a position to handle them. Under the mayor's direction representatives of both groups were to deliberate on the cultural and economic affairs of the municipalities, and, after a transitional period, they were also to have a voice in the handling of provincial affairs.[20]

On the federal level, two of the four advisory bodies in the complicated legislative system established by the May 1, 1934, constitution, were corporative in nature: the cultural council, which was composed of between thirty and forty members chosen by various cultural organizations (schools and educational authorities, religious communities, scientific and cultural associations, and so on); and the economic council, which was made up of between seventy and eighty delegates from the seven occupational and professional groups that were named in the constitution: agriculture and forestry; industry and mining; arts and crafts; trade and transportation; banking, credit, and insurance; the free professions; and civil servants.[21] After the makers of the new Austria finished the reorganization of the cultural, social, and economic life of the country on a corporative basis, the members of these two councils were to be chosen by the cultural and occupational and professional groups themselves. During the interim period before the new corporative structure was completed they were to be named by the federal president, acting upon the advice of the chancellor, who was to consult the various existing cultural communities and vocational and professional organizations before making his choice. The president also had the right to dissolve these two councils.[22]

The other two national advisory bodies were the council of state, a kind of upper house consisting of no fewer than forty and not more than fifty persons, selected and appointed by the president for a term of ten years from among "worthy citizens of good character whose previous conduct and achievements justify the expectation that they have complete understanding of the needs and tasks of the state."[23] The fourth of the advisory bodies, the provincial council, was composed of the Landeshauptmann and chief financial official of each province and of Vienna and the mayor of the capital city.[24]

These four councils had no initiative in legislation, and their sessions were not open to the public. Their only function was to give advice to the government on such legislative proposals as it chose to submit to each of them. The government, however, was supposed to take their counsel into account in preparing bills for submission to the federal diet, which alone had the power to enact its legislative proposals into laws. The diet was composed of fifty-nine members, twenty of whom were chosen by the council of state, ten by the cultural council, twenty by the economic council, and nine by the provincial council. In contrast to those of the advisory bodies, its sessions were open to the public and the protocols of its proceedings could be published; however, it had no initiative in legislation.

In addition to the four councils and the diet, there was a sixth body, the federal assembly, whose membership included all the members of the four advisory councils. It met to authorize declarations of war, to nominate three persons from whom the mayors of all the Austrian communes could choose in electing the federal president, and to administer the oath of office to the president.[25]

Thus, the much heralded corporative principle was reflected only in a very minor way in the complicated legislative processes set up by the May 1, 1934, constitution. This was also true of the much touted federal concept on the "authoritarian" state. Although the very first article of the constitution explicitly stated that "Austria is a federal state,"[26] and although much lip service was paid in the official propaganda to the necessity of preserving the historic individuality and the political autonomy of the provinces,[27] the chief provincial official, the Landeshauptmann, who, in turn, selected the other principal administrators, was appointed by the federal president, with the approval of the chancellor, from a list of three persons submitted to him by the provincial diet.[28] Furthermore, most legislation of real importance—criminal and civil law; the administration of justice; the preservation of public peace; the regulation of commerce, industry, communications, and transportation; social and welfare legislation; general matters pertaining to religion, education, and culture, and so on—was carefully reserved for the federal government. Then, too, the federal chancellor could veto all provincial and local laws and ordinances and could remove all officials on these levels.[29] In short, although the provinces still retained their separate personality, they had to relinquish many of their cherished freedoms of former days to the federal government.[30]

This was true because the authoritarian pillar of the Dollfuss-Schuschnigg state overshadowed all the others. At the apex of the whole complicated structure there was an authoritarian leadership that was intended to be strong enough to protect the interests of the community but which supposedly had numerous constitutional safeguards providing for a "democratic" expression of popular will in the corporations and guaranteeing that "the clear dividing line between authoritarian government and forcible dictatorship shall not be overstepped."[31]

The president was chosen for a seven-year term from the three nominees of the federal assembly (the majority of the members of which were his own appointees) by the more than four thousand mayors in Austria. The vote of the mayor of a conservative little Alpine community of three hundred inhabitants counted as much as that of the mayor of "red" Vienna. The president named and dismissed the chancellor and the other members of the federal government, but only upon the recommendation of the chancellor. All his other actions required the countersignature of the chancellor. As a consequence, the president was little more than a figurehead. Nearly all real power in the state lay in the hands of the chancellor, who was referred to, not as the chairman, but as the "leader" of the federal government.[32]

To make it clear that Austria was no longer dominated by political parties, to provide a rallying point for all who supported an independent, Christian, German, corporative, and "authoritarian" Austria, and to serve as a vehicle to rekindle the flame of Austrian patriotism were the tasks of the Fatherland Front, which Dollfuss organized in 1933 to consolidate the various groups that supported his government. Everyone who believed in Austrian independence and who supported the principles of the new state was invited to join.[33]

The Fatherland Front and all patriotic organizations and vehicles of communications were to be utilized to instill a feeling of Austrian nationalism and patriotism in the Austrian people.[34] This facet of the Dollfuss-Schuschnigg regime—the first systematic countrywide effort to proselytize a spirit of *Austrian* nationalism since the war of liberation more than a century before—has been too much overlooked by historians. The leaders of "authoritarian" Austria strove to formulate an idea of an Austrian nation and to awaken in the populace a strong feeling for their Fatherland.[35]

The essence of this new national idea was "the preservation of Austria's historical mission in the German" and "Central European realm."[36] According to the creators and prophets of the "new Austria," this historical mission was mainly a cultural one. Austria had for centuries, they asserted, not only produced the greatest culture in the whole German realm, but, in addition, had functioned as "the carrier, go-between, and bridge" for German and Slav cultures.[37] Now the Austrian people had to take over this "immensely precious spiritual and cultural heritage of the old Fatherland."[38] Only by doing so could they justify their national existence.

Just as important to the formulation of a national idea as the resumption of Austria's historical cultural mission, the advocates of Austrian nationalism argued, were the preserving and strengthening of the two most essential props upon which this culture had rested: Catholicism and Germanism. It was impossible to think of an Austrian culture, they asserted, without taking into account both its Catholic and German elements. Catholicism had for over a thousand years been "decisive in shaping the whole cultural scene" in Austria[39] and had "always been one of the foundation-pillars of genuine patriotism";[40] hence it was almost impossible to establish a strong national state in Austria "without emphasizing its Christian design."[41]

The leaders who came to the foreground in 1933 also insisted that it would always be necessary to preserve the "universal German spirit"[42] and to stand in the front line trenches in its behalf.[43] Ever since Austria "existed in European history," they contended, it had "had an eminent German significance."[44] Its history had always been a German one, but one quite different in many particulars from that of other German states. Throughout its history Austria "has always had its own tasks within the common German realm"[45] and its own literature, art, music, and other forms of cultural accomplishments. In short, the formulators of the new national idea argued, Austro-German culture had developed according to "specific Austrian forms."[46] Austrian tradition and culture could be fostered only through carrying out the idea of the old "German" Holy Roman Empire, with its theory of local self-government, its federalism, its tolerance of other peoples, its internationalism and universality, and its skillfulness in bringing together the inhabitants of Central Europe into peaceful and harmonious relationship with each other.[47]

The hastily patched together "authoritarian" regime, based upon the May, 1934, constitution and a number of statutes that were frequently prompted by nothing more than spur of the moment decisions made to plug up a hole in the existing framework or to take care of an emergency, was destined to endure barely four years. Yet the fact that it was devised raises a number of interesting questions. In the first place, did it come into existence merely as a consequence of the machinations of a willful group of men bent upon assuming dictatorial powers, or was it formed because the previous democratic parliamentary system proved inadequate to cope with the urgent needs of the day? What were the basic concepts upon which the new constitution was based? Did the responsibility for the establishment of the "authoritarian" system fall upon the shoulders of just one man or group? Did it come into existence as a result of powerful forces beyond the control of any men or organizations operating on the Austrian scene? Was the regime truly "authoritarian" or something else? Were the real principles of the "authoritarian" constitution ever put into practice or did that constitution merely serve as a cover for an out-and-out fascist dictatorship? To attempt to answer these other questions—and many of them are unanswerable—we need to turn briefly to the history of Austria both before and after the enactment of the 1934 constitution.

Before 1934 the Austrian Republic was faced with a number of problems that at the outset appeared to the overwhelming majority of the populace to be insuperable. The Austrians were utterly exhausted at the end of the war, and many of them were on the verge of starvation. With the breakup of the empire, the economy was completely disrupted. The new republic suddenly found itself cut off from all normal sources of supply and faced with a serious inflation.[48] Believing that their economy was totally lacking in viability, and feeling that they belonged to the Greater German realm, the Austrians clamorously agitated for union with the democratic German Republic when the dynasty—the traditional edifice binding the various peoples in the monarchy together—collapsed in 1918. The very fact that the victorious Allied Powers forced independence upon them incited the Austrians to deny their own individuality and traditions and to stress their Germanism all the more. As a result, the Austrian Republic was hardly more than an empty, artificial structure, unwanted by the people, and what little Austrian patriotism existed was limited largely to the small monarchist circles hovering behind the coulisses.[49]

The almost desperate economic crisis and lack of confidence in the republic's future during its early days naturally sharpened the suspicions, fears, antagonisms, and hatreds between the various social groups that had led to the destruction of the monarchy.[50] Unfortunately, the contradictory interests of the various economic and social classes and groups were all too frequently exploited by the leaders of the extremist factions of the various political parties existing in Austria during the 1920s. To the left, the Social Democrats, who were divided into a radical wing led by Otto Bauer and a moderate group under Karl Renner, championed the interests of the proletariat and working classes of the capital and other industrial areas in the little republic. To their right were the Christian Socialists, made up of peasants, Catholics, petty bourgeois traders and shopkeepers, miserably paid provincial teachers, clerks, and professional people, large landowners, and wealthy businessmen and industrialists. There was even a Christian Social workers' movement. In general, the Christian Socialists advocated the interests of the villagers and provincials over and against those of "red Vienna" and other manufacturing areas. They were also split into several camps: a liberal element under the influence of men like Leopold Kunshak, the leader of the Viennese workers' union; a pro-Catholic, conservative wing led by Monsignor Ignaz Seipel, which exerted the predominant influence over the party; and an extreme rightist faction of big industrialists and landlords. The relatively minor Greater German People's Party and the Peasants' League completed the political spectrum. The first of these two groups was founded in 1920 out of no fewer than seventeen Pan-German provincial and national groups. It was an amorphous organization held together mainly to champion the idea of a German folk community. The Peasants' League was a small anticlerical democratic party that championed the interests of the peasants.[51]

Although the more liberal Christian Socialists and the moderate socialists under Renner and Theodor Körner steadfastly exerted themselves to find a modus vivendi between the conflicting interests of Austria's two principal parties, there was such a profound divergence between the political ideologies of the extreme Austro-Marxists gathered around Otto Bauer and Julius Deutsch and the violent antisocialist conservative wing of the Christian Socialists that it proved to be impossible to find a compromise between them. Unfortunately, a large number of frightened members of the Austrian middle and upper classes associated the whole Social Democratic Party with the class struggle and proletarian dictatorship concepts of the left-wing after Bauer mesmerized the majority of the party leaders into inserting a statement in the party program adopted at Linz in 1926 announcing that if the counterrevolutionary forces would seek to prevent the socialization of the means of production after the Social Democrats came to power by democratic processes the socialists would use "the methods of dictatorship" to break the resistance of the bourgeoisie.[52] Among them was Ignaz Seipel, Austrian chancellor between 1922-24 and 1926-29, the savior of Austria's financial system, and the country's leading Christian Social politician, who became increasingly skeptical of democracy after the issuance of the Linz program and the socialist-led riots before the ministry of justice building on July 15, 1927.[53] As the 1920s drew to a close the Austrian political scene was increasingly dominated by an acrimonious personal feud between Seipel and his conservative Christian Social following and Bauer and the more radical Austro-Marxists.

Unfortunately, as Seipel became more worried about the growing turbulence in Austrian political life and the extremism of left-wing Social Democrats he turned increasingly for support to the Heimwehr,[54] a reactionary fascist private army that had developed from the voluntary armed troops that had taken up arms during the time of the collapse of the monarchy to protect the country against marauding bands, communists, and Yugoslav soldiers invading Carinthia[55] and which had by 1930 adopted an out-and-out fascist platform.[56] More ominous for the future, by 1928 the conservative Hungarian and fascist Italian governments had come to the conclusion that, for foreign policy reasons of their own, they should assist the Heimwehr in coming to power in Austria by providing it with liberal gifts of money, arms, and ammunition.[57]

The Social Democrats also had a private army of their own, the paramilitary Republican Schutzbund, headed by Julius Deutsch, to protect themselves and the "democratic republic" against attack from the Right. It also grew out of the voluntary military formations that had sprung into existence during the turbulent months of 1918 and 1919.[58]

The existence of two private armies, one of them subsidized from abroad, to protect the interests of political parties with widely divergent ideologies became an ever growing danger to the Austrian democratic state as the 1930s succeeded the 1920s. It was the ominous emergence of a third force that did not shrink from any kind of violence to bring about the destruction of the Austrian government—the National Socialists—which, however, posed the greatest threat to Austrian democracy. Various National Socialist party groups were to be found in Austria throughout the 1920s,[59] but they did not become an actual source of danger before their spectacular success in the second presidential elections in Germany in April, 1932, when Hitler polled 36.7 percent of the total vote and the Austrian Nazis polled 16 percent of the vote in the Vienna city council and made significant inroads in municipal elections in other provinces, which were held almost simultaneously.[60] Then, when the Nazis seized power in Germany and almost immediately began their attacks to undermine the regime in Austria the government felt itself forced to take drastic actions to preserve the state.[61]

Meanwhile, long before Hitler assumed power in Germany a large number of Austrians had lost all faith in democratic institutions. In 1920 they had adopted one of the most democratic constitutions in Europe—one that vested control of both the legislative and executive branches of government in a parliament in which the upper house, the federal council, amounted to little more than mere window dressing. There precisely lay the trouble. The Austrian people were simply not ready for that much democracy. Whatever political techniques their parliamentarians had acquired had been gained entirely too much through participation in obstructionist tactics in the parliaments of the old monarchy. Now that the restraining hand of the Habsburgs was gone, all too many of them, whether they belonged to the Left or to the Right, found it impossible to differentiate between liberty and license. As a consequence, political fanatics and demagogues of all stripes had a field day. Important issues were usually decided strictly on the basis of the advantages that would accrue to the various parties, and the radicals rather than the moderates within each party all too frequently had the dominant voice. After 1920 no single party proved to be strong enough to run the government without making some kind of a deal to bring one or two of the minority parties into the cabinet.[62] When Dollfuss took over the chancellorship in May, 1932, he could muster a majority of just a single vote in parliament and then only by making an agreement with the eight Heimwehr representatives whereby they obtained three important cabinet posts. After an embarrassing constitutional crisis on March 4, 1933, created by the resignation of the president and both vice presidents of parliament during the course of a debate over whether disciplinary action should be taken against striking railway workers, Dollfuss declared that parliament had abolished itself through its own actions.[63] Except for the Social Democrats and National Socialists, few Austrians were in a mood to shed tears over its demise. The parliamentary system had already proved itself woefully inadequate to cope with the urgent dangers that confronted the Austrian republic.[64]

Genuinely democratic as he was by nature, Dollfuss certainly had no desire to establish anything resembling an all-out dictatorship when he took advantage of the March 4, 1933, constitutional crisis to inaugurate an era of rule by decree.[65] Nevertheless, although he was fully aware that a dictatorship was unnatural, the threat to the republic seemed so ominous that he believed that the time was at hand to use exceptional methods[66] and to embark on an entirely new course that would restore peace and tranquillity and would promote the well-being of the whole population rather than just that of parliamentary politicians.[67]

Contradictory ideas about the direction such a course should take, which bore more than a faint resemblance to similar antiliberal and anticapitalistic concepts voiced in the 1920s in Spain, Italy, and Portugal, as well as in Germany and France,[68] had been discussed in antidemocratic circles in Austria for some time before 1933. Many of them went back to the romanticist ideas about the reestablishment of the medieval corporative social and political order of Karl Vogelsang and his pupil, Anton Orel. In the 1920s Austrian intellectuals like Karl Lugmayer, Johannes Messner, and Seipel himself wrote on the same theme. By far the most influential among the champions of a corporative social reform, however, was Othmar Spann. It was Spann who converted the Heimwehr to the corporative idea and convinced its members that this concept was a panacea for the future and a strong intellectual weapon in their contest with Marxian socialists. When the papal encyclical *Quadragesimo anno* (1931) seemed to confirm the corporative concepts of Spann and his circle, a whole new generation of Austrian Catholics, whose faith in parliamentarianism had already been badly shaken, came to look on the establishment of a corporative society as the answer to their country's economic, social, and political problems.[69] For a time Seipel remained true to his earlier position that it was necessary to operate within the framework of parliament. By 1929, however, he changed his mind, and from then until his death in 1932 he advocated the reconstruction of society on a corporative basis and began to defend the Heimwehr openly as the only hope for "true democracy" in Austria.[70]

Dollfuss was, of course, familiar with the antiliberal corporative ideas that were circulating in Vienna and was also strongly influenced by the ideas in *Quadragesimo anno*. Furthermore, he regarded Seipel as his political mentor and looked upon himself as a continuator of his policies. Nonetheless, had he been left to his own devices,

Dollfuss might conceivably have ended up by inaugurating a Catholic social reform through which democratically chosen representatives of corporative organizations would have supplanted parliament.[71] Certainly, with his democratic peasant background, he originally had no intention of becoming a dictator. In fact, he had so many friends among the Social Democrats that he issued an open invitation for them to join him. However, events all too frequently force men to embark upon a course of action diametrically opposed to their natural proclivities. This was the case with Dollfuss. When the National Socialists came to power in Germany he became convinced that Hitler's victory gave proof "that the democratic era was at an end" and that "the hour for totalitarianism had also come to Austria."[72] Faced with a Nazi terror campaign against his own country, he either had to yield to Nazi pressure or else find allies wherever he could, without too many scruples about whether their aims were above reproach. Having already agreed to appoint three Heimwehr men to his cabinet when he assumed the chancellorship in May, 1932, he now turned to them more than ever before for support, only to find out within the next few months that, entirely against his will, he had become their prisoner.[73]

However, this was not all. Feeling himself forsaken by the western democracies, he grasped the outstretched hand of Mussolini in his struggle against a resurgent Germany. This involved him in carrying out an internal policy based on an even closer relationship with the Heimwehr than before, for by 1933 the Heimwehr had unquestionably become an important instrument of Italian foreign policy. Heimwehr leaders were in constant touch with Mussolini's officials,[74] and in April, 1933, Dollfuss himself paid the first of several visits to the Italian dictator. As a consequence, he procured badly needed economic aid, full diplomatic support, and even a pledge of military assistance from the new Caesar at Rome.[75] But the price was high. It amounted to constant interference in Austrian internal affairs by the Italian dictator.[76] It put Mussolini in an excellent position to bring strong pressure to bear (although it was not really needed) on the ruthless and ambitious Heimwehr leader and then Minister of Defense, Emil Fey, to take those provocative actions that goaded the Republican Schutzbund into a catastrophic civil war on February 12, 1934.[77]

Mussolini was thus not only responsible for provoking "a decisive calamity for Austria"[78] which ended in turning the workers "away in resignation from their own state,"[79] but it is also apparent that he was able to influence Dollfuss to incorporate various fascist features in the May 1, 1934, constitution that the chancellor had originally not wished to include.[80] There is evidence that Mussolini played at least some part in helping to create the Fatherland Front in May, 1933, on the pattern of a fascist phalanx[81] and that he put pressure on Dollfuss "to carry through a programme of effective internal reforms in the decisive Fascist sense."[82] He urged him to take a "determined stand against the Social-Democratic Party," to "press hard against all the disruptive tendencies which are in opposition to the authoritarian principle of the State,"[83] to give his government a pronounced "dictatorial character," and to put through extensive "political, economic, and social" reforms "along fascist lines."[84] Above all, he admonished him to rely heavily on the Heimwehr.[85]

The fact that strong pressure was exerted upon Dollfuss by Mussolini to put through constitutional reforms in the Italian fascist image in return for his support against the ominous threats from National Socialist Germany is by itself evidence that the specific form which the "authoritarian" state actually assumed must be ascribed, at least in part, to powerful external forces beyond the control of any single man or group operating on the Austrian scene. No doubt, whether directly or indirectly through the Heimwehr, Mussolini either compelled or cajoled Dollfuss to give the "new authoritarian regime" a much stronger fascist tone than the chancellor or many of his non-Heimwehr supporters wanted it to have. This fact should be kept in mind by anyone who ventures to decide just exactly what type of government was given to the Austrian people by the May 1, 1934, constitution.

Although the supporters of the "authoritarian" regime were adamant in insisting that the "new Austrian constitution" did "not in any way deny or seek to root out the healthy democratic ideal"[86] and merely sought to make democracy more effective through "new, modern ways, ways that were in conformity with our needs and our times,"[87] it is obvious that very little room was left for "a genuine democratic way of life" in the "new Austria." It is true that the May 1, 1934, constitution contained a bill of rights that guaranteed many of the personal freedoms of advanced democratic states; however, freedom of speech was carefully circumscribed, freedom of assembly was permitted only "within legal limits," and no mention whatever was made about suffrage rights or the right to bear arms.[88]

In his analysis of the fundamental principles of the new constitution that he wrote in 1936, Schuschnigg stated that "the healthy democratic element" in Austria was conserved in the "authoritarian" state "through the preservation of the autonomy of the communes, the sending of representatives chosen by the corporative associations which are to be established," and "the adherence of the topmost organs of the state to the principle of political responsibility."[89] As we have already seen,[90] in actual practice little real autonomy was left to the communes. However, it was mainly through the corporative organization of society that the creators of the new Austria hoped to incorporate all genuine and healthy democratic elements into the framework of the government.[91] As we have seen, not only was an important role eventually to be assigned on the local and provincial levels to delegates chosen by local corporative bodies and cultural organizations, but also representatives of these bodies were to take a significant part in the federal legislative process. The trouble, as far as democracy is concerned, was that until the corporative reorganization was completed all these "representatives" were to be selected either by the federal president, on the advice of the chancellor, or by the Landeshauptmann, who was the president's appointee.[92] And this work was still far from completion when the "authoritarian" regime collapsed in March, 1938.[93]

As for Schuschnigg's assertion that genuine democratic elements were protected by the very fact that the chief authorities in the state would adhere to principles of political responsibility, it should not be difficult to convince an American audience of the speciousness of this argument. It cannot be denied that, insofar as they remained free agents and were able to resist Heimwehr pressure, both Dollfuss and Schuschnigg made a sincere effort always to act in accord with genuine Christian principles of responsibility, as they interpreted them. But what protective devices were at hand to insure that everyone who might conceivably become chancellor, let us say a man like Major Fey (and had the Heimwehr had its way early in 1934, he might have been), would likewise always adhere to such high-minded ideals?[94]

It is obvious that the regime that governed the country between 1934 and 1938 was "authoritarian" rather than "democratic" in nature. Whether it would ever have acquired anything resembling a genuine democratic character had it remained in existence longer than four years is a question that can probably never be answered.

But was it a fascist government? Certainly on the surface it appeared to have many of the characteristics of the usual fascist state: censorship of the press, restrictions on the right of public assembly, the proscription of opposition parties, the appointment of all key officials by the president upon the advice of the chancellor, a hierarchical chain of command from the top down to the local commune, the retention of effective control over legislation and of wide emergency powers by the chancellor, and even a few concentration camps. Nonetheless, the supporters of the regime still repeatedly and loudly proclaimed that Austria was not a fascist state.[95] If one looks at the actual political practices, he can easily conclude that it is just possible that they might have been at least partly right. It is obvious that neither Dollfuss nor Schuschnigg wished to make his state a mere copy of Mussolini's fascist state and that both of them resisted the efforts of the Austrian Heimwehr to force them to do so. The very fact that it was an open secret that the Federal President, Wilhelm Miklas, frequently loudly criticized the "authoritarian" regime among various circles of personal friends[96] is only one of many examples that there was much greater personal freedom in Austria than in Italy or Germany. If the "authoritarian" state was fascist, it was certainly modeled much more closely on the pattern of Portugal than on that of either Italy or Germany. However, it is much more likely that Dollfuss' and Schuschnigg's friend, Ernst Karl Winter, came closer to the actual truth when he wrote that the "authoritarian" regime was "a compromise between political Catholicism and Heimwehr fascism."[97] The promulgators of the "authoritarian state" were influenced by both the crossed keys of St. Peter and the emblems of the Black Shirts.

Largely on account of the fascist element in Austria's composition, the repeated efforts of both Dollfuss and Schuschnigg to come to terms with the workers and with left-wing intellectuals ended in failure.[98] Then, when Schuschnigg finally attempted to rid himself of Heimwehr influence in the cabinet by dismissing Prince Ernst Rüdiger Starhemberg as vice-chancellor[99] in May, 1936,[100] and dissolved the Heimwehr the following October, he embittered a large number of the members of the organization that most ardently championed the "authoritarian" idea.[101] The Fatherland Front, into which the Heimwehr and all the other paramilitary formations were incorporated, never realized its intended objective of uniting "in a common front all who believed in an independent Austria" and never amounted to much more than "a cover under which the old party dissension continued."[102]

In spite of the strenuous efforts of the government to arouse a feeling of Austrian patriotism throughout the whole brief period of the "authoritarian regime," the Austrian people remained sharply divided and deeply distrustful of each other. On the left, the workers were highly suspicious of the regime, while many intellectuals were also estranged from it. In the center, the Catholic supporters of the "new Austria" were rent with personal dissensions, while the Heimwehr was angered over its ouster in 1936 from its favored position in the government. On the right a growing number of National Socialists, aided and abetted by the government and their party cohorts in Germany, were actively preparing to seize the reins of government from Schuschnigg and his supporters.

Meanwhile, handicapped by the same Pan-German tendencies that directly or indirectly affected the large majority of the Austrian populace,[103] and pressured by

Hungary and Italy,[104] Schuschnigg made concerted efforts to pacify both the Austrian Nazis and the German government. Fully aware of the ominous significance of the Rome-Berlin axis, cognizant of the fact that the Western Powers had rearmed too late to give Austria more than diplomatic support, and too short of time to make a firm agreement with the Little Entente, Schuschnigg could do little else than engage in delaying tactics. He continued his connections with Mussolini and appeased the Nazis as best he could in the hope that eventually the international situation would return to normal and the French, British, and Italians might again be able and disposed to render military aid to Austria if she were attacked by Germany.[105] That hope was never to be realized. When the National Socialist government in Germany moved to liquidate the "authoritarian" government exactly fifteen days after Chancellor Schuschnigg gave the ringing defense of Austria described at the beginning of this paper, the western democracies sat on the sidelines. The very man who forced Dollfuss and Schuschnigg to take over enough of the trappings of his own fascist system in their own authoritarian government seriously to cripple their efforts to reconcile the Austrian workers to the "new government" left Schuschnigg in the lurch. From his safe refuge in Switzerland, Mussolini's right-hand man in Austria, Prince Starhemberg, exerted himself to restore good relations between his old Heimwehr companions and the National Socialists.[106]

If the regime that suddenly disappeared on the evening of March 11, 1938, is to be judged solely by the criterion of whether or not it was successful, there is no doubt that it was a miserable failure. But is it fair to indict any government of any little country with barely seven million inhabitants that was the victim of a serious shift in the whole European balance of power merely because it was unable to resist the overwhelming might of an aggressive power? However, be that as it may, no matter how harshly one may censure the governors of "authoritarian" Austria, he has to admit that the Austrians of the Second Republic have at least learned something of value from the lessons of the first one. Through working together in a coalition government, the political parties have learned how to get along with each other in relative peace and harmony. They have found out how to survive in the face of a strong aggressor, in this case a Russian one. And, most important of all, Austria has finally become a "nation." One of the pillars of the "Austrian idea" formulated and proselytized by Austria's "authoritarian" leaders (the German pillar) in itself contributed toward weakening the will of the Austrian people to resist aggression in the 1930s. Nevertheless, the concerted efforts inaugurated by Dollfuss and continued by Schuschnigg to convince the Austrian people that they constitute a distinct nationality all their own have at last borne a rich and tasty fruit.

FOOTNOTES

[1] Text of Chancellor Schuschnigg's speech as published in the *Reichspost* (Vienna), February 25, 1938, pp. 1-6; and in *Correspondance Politique*, Edition C, Year VI, no. 8 (Vienna, March 5, 1938), pp. 1-8. Excerpts from the parts of the speech most germane to this discussion can be found in Ludwig Jedlicka, "Ernst Rüdiger Fürst Starhemberg und die politische Entwicklung in Österreich im Frühjahr 1938," in *Österreich und Europa. Festgabe für Hugo Hantsch zum 70. Geburtstag* (Graz: Styria Verlag, 1965), pp. 547-48.

[2] Alexander Novotny, "Die berufsständische Gedanke in der Bundesverfassung des Jahres 1934," *Österreich in Geschichte und Literatur*, 6, no. 5 (May, 1961), 216-17; Heinrich Benedikt, ed., *Geschichte der Republik Österreich* (Munich: Oldenbourg, 1954), p. 221; Walter Goldinger,

Geschichte der Republik Österreich (Vienna: Verlag für Geschichte und Politik, 1962), pp. 198-99; Charles A. Gulick, *Austria from Habsburg to Hitler*, 2 vols. (Berkeley: University of California Press, 1948), 2: 1404-17; Malcolm Bullock, *Austria 1918-1938. A Study in Failure* (London: Macmillan Co., 1939), pp. 227-28; Anton Rintelen, *Erinnerungen an Österreichs Weg. Versailles-Berchtesgaden-Grossdeutschland*, 2d ed. (Munich: F. Bruckmann, 1941), pp. 253-55.

[3]See article 1. For the text of the 1920 constitution, see *Das Bundes-Verfassungsgesetz samt Übergangsbestimmungen und den in Artikel 149 als Verfassungsgesetze erklärten Gesetzen, nach dem Stande vom 1. November 1931* (Vienna: C. W. Stern, 1932), p. 8.

[4]See *Die neue Bundesverfassung für Österreich samt Übergangsverfassung. Mit Erläuterungen von Dr. Kurt Schuschnigg* (Vienna: Steyrermühl-Verlag, 1936), p. 95. See also Schuschnigg's comments on the intrinsic meaning of the preamble in ibid., pp. 92-93.

[5]See, for instance, Dollfuss' speech in Vienna on September 11, 1933, Anton Tauscher, ed., *So sprach der Kanzler. Dollfuss' Vermächtnis. Aus seinen Reden* (Vienna: Ferdinand Baumgartner, 1935), p. 46; Kurt Schuschnigg, *Dreimal Österreich* (Vienna: Thomas-Verlag, 1937), pp. 294-95; and Vaterländische Front, Bundeswerbeleitung, *Richtlinien zur Führerausbildung. Zum Eigenbrauch*, 2d ed. (1936), pp. 123-25, 173.

[6]For an "official" interpretation of the meaning of the *Kruckenkreuz*, see Vaterländische Front, Bundeswerbeleitung, *Richtlinien zur Führerausbildung*, pp. vii-ix.

[7]See Dollfuss' speech at Graz on April 15, 1934, Tautscher, *So sprach der Kanzler*, p. 11.

[8]See articles 27-30 of the May 1, 1934, constitution, in *Die neue Bundesverfassung für Österreich. Mit Erläuterungen von Dr. Kurt Schuschnigg*, pp. 99-101.

[9]See Schuschnigg's speech at Vienna on June 13, 1937, *Österreichs Erneuerung. Die Reden des Bundeskanzlers Dr. Kurt Schuschnigg*, 3 vols. (Vol. 1 published in Klagenfurt by "Carinthia" Verlag; vol. 2, in Vienna by Alfred Raftl; and vol. 3 in Vienna by the Österreichische Staatsdruckerei. Vol. 2 was published in 1936; no publication date is given for vols. 1 and 3.), 3, 128; and Guido Zernatto, *Die Wahrheit über Oesterreich* (New York: Longmans, Green & Co., 1938), p. 80.

[10]For an interpretation of what was meant by Christian leadership by one of the devotees of the "new order" in Austria, see Dietrich von Hildebrand, "Autorität and Führertum," *Der Christliche Ständestaat* 1, no. 2 (December 10, 1933): 7.

[11]Dollfuss' speech at Neusiedl on May 21, 1934, Tautscher, *So sprach der Kanzler*, p. 13.

[12]Dollfuss' speech at Sonntagsberg on July 1, 1934, ibid., p. 12.

[13]Dollfuss' speech at Salzburg on May 6, 1933, ibid., p. 47.

[14]Franz Rehrl, "Praktisches und theoretisches zum Staatlichen Neuaufbau," *Der Christliche Ständestaat*, 1, no. 9 (February 4, 1934): 3. Rehrl was Landenshauptmann of the Province of Salzburg.

[15]Among the numerous works describing the views of Dollfuss' ideological supporters in regard to what was involved in putting the principles of *Quadragesimo anno* into effect in Austria, see especially Alfred Diamant, *Austrian Catholics and the First Republic: Democracy, Capitalism, and the Social Order, 1918-1934* (Princeton, N.J.: Princeton University Press, 1960), pp. 153-285; Vaterländische Front, Bundeswerbeleitung, *Richtlinien zur Führerausbildung*, pp. 99-107 and 112-16; Ernst Karl Winter, *Monarchie und Arbeiterschaft* (Vienna: Gsur & Co., 1936), pp. 76-77; Johannes Messner, "Auf dem Wege zur Volksgemeinschaft," *Österreichische Rundschau. Land, Volk, Kultur* 1, no. 3 (n. d.): 103-5; Johannes Hollnsteiner, "Mutterboden der Kultur," *Monatsschrift für Kultur und Politik*, January, 1937, pp. 1-7; Karl Gustav Bittner, "Gedanken zur österreichischen Staatsidee," *Der Christliche Ständestaat*, 3, no. 15 (April 12, 1936): 350-52; and Rudolf Hausleithner, *Der Geist der neuen Ordnung. Einblicke in das päpstliche Gesellschaftsrundschreiben "Quadragesimo Anno"* (Vienna: Typographische Anstalt, 1937), pp. 12-96.

[16]Dollfuss' speech at Geneva on September 27, 1933, Tautscher, *So sprach der Kanzler*, p. 15. Although late in 1937 Schuschnigg wrote that *Quadragesimo anno* was "never intended to be a record of a state constitution," (see his *Dreimal Österreich*, p. 292) he admitted that "the guidelines of this papal encyclical were acknowledged in Austria as fundamental and correct." (ibid.) Furthermore, as late as in 1936 he acknowledged that "before the new constitution was proclaimed the basic ideas of the papal encyclical 'Quadragesimo anno' were repeatedly referred

to" and that, "in accord with its leading ideas, the carrying out of the corporative arrangement is the first and indispensable prerequisite for the reconstruction of the state." See *Die neue Bundesverfassung für Österreich. Mit Erläuterungen von Dr. Kurt Schuschnigg*, p. 28.

[17]Schuschnigg's speech to the Fatherland Front, Vienna, February 14, 1937, *Österreichs Erneuerung* 3: 122-23; Messner, "Auf dem Wege zur Volksgemeinschaft," p. 103.

[18]For typical views of "authoritarian" Austrians on liberalism and democracy, see Leopold Andrian, *Oesterreich im Prisma der Idee. Katechismus der Fuehrenden* (Graz: Schmidt-Dengler, 1937), pp. 232-40, 277-304; Othmar Langer, *Einst und Jetzt. Ein Beitrag zur Geschichte des Parlamentarismus* (Vienna: Alfred Raftl, 1935), pp. 5-6, 8-22; Zernatto, *Wahrheit über Oesterreich*, pp. 109-15; Schuschnigg's speech at the League of Nations, Geneva, September 12, 1934, *Österreichs Erneuerung* 1: 26-28; Schuschnigg's speeches to the Fatherland Front on June 9 and October 17, 1936, ibid. 2: 34-35, and 3: 7-8; and Schuschnigg, *Dreimal Österreich*, pp. 104-16.

[19]Aurel Kolnai, "Austria and the Danubian Nations," *Journal of Central European Affairs* 3, no. 2 (July, 1943): 168.

[20]See articles 32, 108, 109, and 127 of the May 1, 1934, constitution, *Die neue Bundesverfassung für Österreich. Mit Erläuterungen von Dr. Kurt Schuschnigg*, pp. 101, 124-26, 133 (see also Schuschnigg's explanation of these articles on pp. 66-69 and 73-75); Odo Neustädter-Stürmer, *Die berufständische Gesetzgebung in Österreich* (Vienna: Österreichischer Bundesverlag, 1936), pp. 5-6, 9, 10-12; paragraphs 29-31 and 39 of the *Übergangsgesetz* of June 19, 1934, Otto Ender, ed., *Die Übergangsbestimmungen zur neuen österreichischen Verfassung* (Vienna: Österreichischer Bundesverlag für Unterricht, Wissenschaft und Kunst, 1934), pp. 27-29, 32-33 (see also Ender's explanations of these paragraphs on pp. 11-13, 14-15); Zernatto, *Wahrheit über Oesterreich*, pp. 122-24; Schuschnigg, *Dreimal Österreich*, pp. 292-93; Messner, "Auf dem Wege zur Volksgemeinschaft," pp. 104-5; and Erich Voegelin, *Der autoritäre Staat. Ein Versuch über das österreichische Staatsproblem* (Vienna: Julius Springer, 1936), pp. 206-14, 236-37.

[21]See articles 47 and 48 of the May 1, 1934, constitution, *Die neue Bundesverfassung für Österreich. Mit Erläuterungen von Dr. Kurt Schuschnigg*, pp. 110-11. See also Schuschnigg's explanation of these articles in ibid., pp. 48-50.

[22]Ibid., pp. 57-58, 90-91; par. 4, sec. 4 of the *Übergangsgesetz* of June 19, 1934, Ender, *Die Übergangsbestimmungen zur neuen österreichischer Verfassung*, pp. 25-26 (see also Ender's explanation of this section in ibid., p. 9); Voegelin, *Der autoritäre Staat*, pp. 238-39.

[23]Articles 46 (1) of the May 1, 1934, constitution, *Die neue Bundesverfassung für Österreich. Mit Erläuterungen von Dr. Kurt Schuschnigg*, pp. 109-10.

[24]Articles 46 and 49 of the May, 1934, constitution, ibid., pp. 109, 111.

[25]See articles 50-72 of the May 1, 1934, constitution, ibid., pp. 111-18; Schuschnigg's explanation of the meaning of the above articles, ibid., pp. 51-58; Novotny, "Die berufsständische Gedanke in der Bundesverfassung des Jahres 1934," p. 217; P. T. Lux, *La leçon de l'Autriche* (Neuchâtel: Victor Attinger, [1937]), pp. 83-85; Zernatto, *Wahrheit über Oesterreich*, pp. 121-22; Voegelin, *Der autoritäre Staat*, pp. 233-35, 237-51- and Gulick, *Austria from Habsburg to Hitler*, 2: 1441-47.

[26]See *Die neue Bundesverfassung für Österreich. Mit Erläuterungen von Dr. Kurt Schuschnigg*, p. 95.

[27]See, for example, Minister of Education Hans Perntner's speech at Budapest on November 13, 1935, *Reichspost* (Vienna), November 14, 1935, p. 8; Schuschnigg's speech at Milan on April 21, 1936, *Österreichs Erneuerung* 2: 25-27; Zernatto, *Wahrheit über Oesterreich*, pp. 53, 120-21; Vaterländische Front, Bundesbewerbeleitung, *Richtlinien zur Führerausbildung*, pp. 115, 147; and Hans Karl Zessner-Spitzenberg, "Österreichertum und Föderalismus," *Der Christliche Ständestaat* 1, no. 15 (March 18, 1934): 6-8.

[28]Article 114 of the May 1, 1934, constitution, *Die neue Bundesverfassung für Österreich. Mit Erläuterungen von Dr. Kurt Schuschnigg*, pp. 126-27.

[29]See articles 34-43 of the May 1, 1934, constitution, ibid., pp. 102-9.

[30]See also Gordon Brook-Shepherd, *Dollfuss* (London: Macmillan, 1961), pp. 165, 167; and Diamant, *Austrian Catholics and the First Republic*, pp. 275-76.

[31]Schuschnigg, *Dreimal Österreich*, p. 292. See also Schuschnigg's speech to the League of Nations, Geneva, September 12, 1934, *Österreichs Erneuerung* 1: 28; Schuschnigg's speech to the Fatherland Front on January 19, 1936, ibid. 2: 88; Schuschnigg's speech in Vienna, April 17, 1936, ibid. 2: 17-18; Schuschnigg's speech at Baden on April 24, 1936, ibid. 2: 27-29; Schusch-

nigg's speech in Vienna on June 13, 1937, ibid. 3: 127-28; Schuschnigg's speech to the Fatherland Front in Vienna on February 14, 1937, ibid. 29; and Vaterländische Front, Bundesbewerbeleitung, *Richtlinien zur Führerausbildung*, pp. 123-25, 147, 173.

[32]See article 81 (1) of the May 1, 1934, constitution, *Die neue Bundesverfassung für Österreich. Mit erläuterungen von Dr. Kurt Schuschnigg*, p. 120. See also articles 10 and 73-94 of the constitution in ibid., pp. 30-32, 58-62, 76-78; Voegelin, *Der autoritäre Staat*, pp. 189-99; Diamant, *Austrian Catholics and the First Republic*, p. 270; and Gulick, *Austria from Habsburg to Hitler*, 2: 1447-56.

[33]Law of May 1, 1934, concerning the Fatherland Front, *Bundesgesetzblatt für den Bundesstaat Österreich*, Jahrgang 1934, no. 4, pp. 53-54; *Between Hitler and Mussolini. The Memoirs of Ernst Rudiger Prince Starhemberg* (New York: Harper & Bros., 1942) (hereafter cited as "Starhemberg, *Memoirs*"), pp. 169-70; Zernatto, *Wahrheit über Oesterreich*, p. 79; Schuschnigg, *Dreimal Österreich*, pp. 221-24; Robert Ingrim, *Der Griff nach Österreich* (Zürich: Europa Verlag, 1938), pp. 78-80; Brook-Shepherd, *Dollfuss*, pp. 103-6.

[34]For a discussion of how the Austrian schools were used for this purpose, see my "Training for Citizenship, 'Authoritarian' Austrian Style," *Journal of Central European Affairs* 3, no. 2 (July, 1943): 121-46.

[35]Among the rather extensive writings on this subject, see especially Schuschnigg, *Dreimal Österreich*, pp. 214-15, 286; Lux, *La leçon de l'Autriche*, pp. 29-30, 34; Brook-Shepherd, *Dollfuss*, pp.104-5; D. Graham Hutton,"Germany and Austria," *The Nineteenth Century and After*, September, 1934, p. 274; and W. Walter Crotch, "Whither Austria?," ibid., April, 1935, p. 410.

[36]Dollfuss' speech at Vienna on December 31, 1933, Tautscher, *So sprach der Kanzler*, p. 90.

[37]Schuschnigg's speech at Paris on February 23, 1935, *Österreichs Erneuerung* 1: 132.

[38]Schuschnigg's speech at Klagenfurt on March 1, 1936, ibid. 2: 45.

[39]Schuschnigg, *Dreimal Österreich*, p. 230.

[40]Schuschnigg's speech at Vienna on May 26, 1936, *Österreichs Erneuerung* 2: 81.

[41]Schuschnigg's speech at Linz on February 10, 1935, ibid. p. 157.

[42]Dollfuss' speech at Vienna on December 24, 1933, Tautscher, *So sprach der Kanzler*, p. 80.

[43]Schuschnigg's speech at Salzburg on January 20, 1935, *Österreichs Erneuerung* 1: 136.

[44]Schuschnigg's speech at Vienna on December 1, 1934, ibid. p. 108.

[45]Dollfuss' speech at Vienna on January 22, 1934, Tautscher, *So sprach der Kanzler*, p. 82.

[46]"Mussolini über Österreichs historische Mission," *Der Christliche Ständestaat* 2, no. 8 (February 24, 1935): 180.

[47]For samples of the typical Austrian viewpoint on this, see Karl Bittner, "Gedanken zur österreichischen Staatsidee," *Der Christliche Ständestaat* 3, no. 15 (April 12, 1936): 350-52; "Die Bedeutung der vaterländischen Traditionspflege für das neue Österreich," ibid. 4, no. 47 (November 28, 1937): 1117-18; Viktor Buchgraber, "Die Sendung Österreichs," ibid. 1, no. 51 (November 25, 1934): 3-6; and Zernatto, *Die Wahrheit über Oesterreich*, pp. 41-43; 120-21.

[48]For the best brief study of the Austrian economy during the interwar period, see K. W. Rothschild, *Austria's Economic Development between the Two Wars* (London: Frederick Muller, 1947).

[49]For good impartial histories of Austria before 1933, see Mary MacDonald, *The Republic of Austria 1918-1934. A Study in the Failure of Democratic Government* (London: Oxford University Press, 1934); Benedikt, *Geschichte der Republik Österreich*, pp. 17-199; Goldinger, *Geschichte der Republik Österreich*, pp. 9-177; and Erich Zöllner, *Geschichte Österreichs. Von den Anfängen bis zur Gegenwart* (Munich: R. Oldenbourg, 1961), pp. 492-512. Useful information can also be found in Hanns Leo Mikoletzky, *Österreichische Zeitgeschichte. Vom Ende der Monarchie bis zum Abschluss des Staatsvertrages 1955* (Vienna: Österreichischer Bundesverlag, 1962), pp. 47-236. An interesting earlier volume by a Christian Social labor leader is Leopold Kunschak, *Österreich 1918-1934* (Vienna: Typographische Anstalt, 1934). Good accounts written from a pro-socialist point of view are in Gulick, *Austria from Habsburg to Hitler*, 1, and 2: 775-971; and Julius Braumthal, *The Tragedy of Austria* (London: Victor Gollancz, 1948), pp. 13-94. Interesting information and insights can also be gained from reading Jacques Hannah, *Karl Renner und seine Zeit. Versuch einer Biographie* (Vienna: Europa Verlag, 1965), pp. 303-50.

[50]For an interesting analysis of the effects of this "class struggle" upon Austrian democratic institutions by a left-wing Austrian socialist, see Otto Bauer, *Der Aufstand der österreichischen Arbeiter. Seine Ursachen und seine Wirkungen*, 2d ed. (Prague: Verlag der Deutschen sozialdemokratischen Arbeiterpartei in der Tschechoslowakischen Republik, 1934), pp. 27-28. For a more moderate interpretation of the effects of economic conditions on Austrian political life, see Frederick F. Reitlinger, "Die Wirtschaft in der Ersten Republik," *Österreich in Geschichte und Literatur* 7, no. 2 (February, 1963): 60.

[51]The best discussion of political parties in Austria since 1918 can be found in the section on "Österreichs politische Struktur. Die Entwicklung der Parteien und politischen Bewegungen," written by Adam Wandruszka, in Benedikt, *Geschichte der Republik Österreich*, pp. 289-485.

[52]Charles Gulick insists that this statement was not a profession of the "dictatorship of the proletarian ideas" of radical Marxian socialism but rather amounted to "an abandonment of Marxist tenets." It was inserted into the program in order "to draw a clear and distinct line between democracy and dictatorship." See his *Austria from Habsburg to Hitler*, 2: 1388-93. Jacques Hannak tends to agree with Gulick's evaluation of the real meaning of the Linz program, but he goes on to state that Renner was unhappy with it because it served to intensify existing political divisions at a moment when an amelioration of party tensions was badly needed. See his *Karl Renner und seine Zeit*, pp. 474-78. The commander of the socialist Schutzbund, Julius Deutsch, claimed in his memoirs that he objected to the insertion of the above phraseology in the party program. Later events proved, he wrote, that the Linz program only gave the enemies of the Social Democrats all the more reason to ascribe proletarian dictatorship ideas to them. See Julius Deutsch, *Ein weiter Weg. Lebenserinnerungen* (Vienna: Amalthea-Verlag, 1960), pp. 163-64. The Christian Social editor of the *Reichspost*, Friedrich Funder, maintains that the Linz program was the revolutionary program of the radical Bauer wing and the "fighting group" in the party under Deutsch. See his *Als Österreich den Sturm bestand. Aus der Erste in der Zweite Republik*, 3d ed. (Vienna: Herold Verlag, 1957), p. 27.

[53]For excellent discussions of Seipel's increasing conservatism, see especially Klemens von Klemperer, "Chancellor Seipel and the Crisis of Democracy in Austria," *Journal of Central European Affairs*, 22, no. 4 (January, 1963): 468-78; and Josef A. Tzöbl's brief article on Ignaz Seipel in *Gestalter der Geschicke Österreichs*, ed. Hugo Hantsch (Innsbruck: Tyrolia-Verlag, 1962), pp. 596-609.

[54]For Seipel's increasing reliance on the Heimwehr, see Brook-Shepherd, *Dollfuss*, p. 67; Deutsch, *Ein weiter Weg*, pp. 162-63; Klemperer, "Chancellor Seipel and the Crisis of Democracy in Austria," p. 477; and Ludwig Jedlicka, "The Austrian Heimwehr," *Journal of Contemporary History* 1, no. 1 (1966): 133-34.

[55]For the origins and early development of the Heimwehr, see especially Starhemberg, *Memoirs*, pp. 5-12; Jedlicka, "The Austrian Heimwehr," pp. 129-32; Rintelen, *Erinnerungen an Österreichs Weg*, pp. 124-46; Andrew Whiteside, "Austria," in *The European Right. A Historical Profile*, eds., Hans Rogger and Eugene Weber (Los Angeles: University of California Press, 1965), pp. 330-31, 334-35; and *Heimatsschutz in Österreich*, herausgegeben unter Aufsicht des österreichischen Heimatschutzes Amt des Bundesführers—Propagandastelle (Vienna: Zoller Verlag, 1934), *passim*.

[56]See the Korneuburg oath of May 18, 1930, as given in English translation in Jedlicka, "The Austrian Heimwehr," pp. 138-39. The background of this oath is discussed in detail in Ludwig Jedlicka, "Zur Vorgeschichte des Korneuburger Eides," *Österreich in Geschichte und Literatur* 7, no. 4 (April, 1963): 146-53.

[57]See Lajos Kerekes' interesting articles, based on recent discoveries in the Hungarian foreign ministry archives, entitled "Akten des Ungarischen Ministeriums des Äusseren zur Vorgeschichte der Annexion Österreichs," *Acta Historica* (Budapest) 7, no. 3-4 (1960): 355-90; "Akten zu den geheimen Verbindungen zwischen der Bethlen-Regierung und der österreichischen Heimwehrbewegung," ibid. 11, no. 1-4 (1956): 299-339; and "Italien, Ungarn und die Österreichische Heimwehrbewegung 1928-1931," *Österreich in Geschichte und Literatur* 9, no. 1 (January, 1965): 1-13. See also Starhemberg, *Memoirs*, pp. 21-35.

[58]See especially Deutsch, *Ein weiter Weg*, pp. 151-55. Whether or not the only reason for the founding of the Schutzbund was that of protecting the Social Democrats against provocative attacks by the Heimwehr is still being disputed by historians. For the socialist viewpoint, see ibid., pp. 154-55; and Gulick, *Austria from Habsburg to Hitler*, 1: 132-33. For the conservative view,

see Schuschnigg, *Dreimal Österreich*, pp. 142-43. In passing, it should be noted that Renner was quite unhappy because both the Heimwehr and the Schutzbund had ever been established and that he saw the inherent dangers in the existence of private military formations long before February, 1934. See Hannak, *Karl Renner und seine Zeit*, 469-70.

[59]Whiteside, "Austria," pp. 333-34; Benedikt, *Geschichte der Republik Österreich*, pp. 406-11.

[60]Whiteside, "Austria," p. 340; Brook-Shepherd, *Dollfuss*, p. 87; Heinrich Drimmel, "Das österreichische Staatsbewusstsein in der Zeit von 1918-1938," *Österreich in Geschichte und Literatur* 9, no. 6 (June, 1965): 313; Otto Reich von Rohrwig, *Der Freiheitskampf der Ostmark-Deutschen. Von St. Germain bis Adolf Hitler* (Graz: Leopold Stocker Verlag, 1942), p. 82.

[61]See also Wilhelm Böhm, "Februar 1934," *Österreich in Geschichte und Literatur* 2, no. 2 (1958): 74. For a Marxist interpretation, see Bauer, *Der Aufstand der österreichischen Arbeiter*, pp. 7-8.

[62]Lux, *La leçon d'Autriche*, pp. 18, 106-9; Bullock, *Austria 1918-1938*, pp. 223-25; Ingrim, *Der Griff nach Österreich*, pp. 11-14; Böhm, "Februar 1934," pp. 660-74; Funder, *Als Österreich den Sturm bestand*, p. 54. It should be noted that the Austrian parliamentary system also has strong defenders. See especially Gulick, *Austria from Habsburg to Hitler, passim*; and, more recently, Robert Endres, "Die politischen und sozialen Wurzeln des 12. Februar 1934," *Österreich in Geschichte und Literatur* 2, no. 2 (1958): 77-82.

[63]Kunshak, *Österreich 1918-1934*, pp. 172-74; Ernst Karl Winter, "Die Staatskrise in Österreich," *Wiener Politische Blätter* 1, no. 1 (April 16, 1933): 28-32; Goldinger, *Geschichte der Republik Österreich*, 178-79.

[64]Dollfuss and other conservatives, as well as a large number of moderates, for instance, were quite disturbed about the viability of parliament on account of the obstacles that confronted the government in obtaining parliamentary approval in 1932 for a loan from the Western Powers that was desperately needed to restore Austria's faltering financial stability. Arguing that the agreement that had been made to extend the ban on the Anschluss for another twenty years in order to procure the loan was unacceptable, the Social Democrats and Greater Germans combined to forestall passage of the bill. Dollfuss managed to gain acceptance by a majority of just one vote in the first of three separate polls only because a substitute for Seipel, who had died the previous day, was rushed to Vienna posthaste. The second favorable vote of 82-80 was acquired through the providential absence of an opposition deputy, and third, again of 82-80, through the Greater German leader John Schober's unexpected timely assistance. Brook-Shepherd, *Dollfuss*, pp. 94-95; Goldinger, *Geschichte der Republik Österreich*, pp. 173-74; Kunschak, *Österreich 1918-1934*, pp. 155-63.

[65]Hugo Hantsch, "Engelbert Dollfuss (1892-1934)," in Hantsch, *Gestalter der Geschicke Österreichs*, p. 619; Brook-Shepherd, *Dollfuss*, p. 100. Julius Deutsch himself states that during the first few months of his chancellorship, Dollfuss "had no fixed program, but sought to find his way between parliamentary democracy and the corporate state." See his *Ein weiter Weg*, p. 188.

[66]Willi Frischauer, *Twilight in Vienna. The Capital without a Country* (Boston: Houghton Mifflin, 1938), p. 255.

[67]Funder, *Als Österreich den Sturm bestand*, pp. 65-66; Louis Rambaud, *Dollfuss 1892-1934* (Paris: Emmanuel Vitte, 1948), pp. 113-14; 119-20.

[68]Vaterländische Front, Bundeswerbeleitung, *Richtlinien zur Führerausbildung*, p. 121.

[69]Novotny, "Die berufsständische Gedanke in der Bundesverfassung des Jahres 1934," pp. 210-13; Zernatto, *Wahrheit über Oesterreich*, pp. 116-17; Hantsch, "Dollfuss," pp. 619-20; Benedikt, *Geschichte der Republik Österreich*, pp. 324-25, 334-38; Diamant, *Austrian Catholics and the First Republic*, pp. 70-207.

[70]Diamant, *Austrian Catholics and the First Republic*, pp. 91, 112, 189-93; Jedlicka, "The Austrian Heimwehr," pp. 133-34; Tzöbl, "Ignaz Seipel," p. 608; Benedikt, *Geschichte der Republik Österreich*, pp. 324-25.

[71]Böhm, "Februar 1934," pp. 74-75; Funder, *Alas Österreich den Sturm bestand*, pp. 67-68, 181; Hantsch, "Dollfuss," p. 620.

[72]Deutsch, *Ein weiter Weg*, p. 189.

[73]Ibid., p. 186. See also Hantsch, "Dollfuss," p. 618; Elizabeth Wiskemann, "The Problem of Austria," *The Nineteenth Century and After* 114 (September, 1933): 296-98; William L.

Smyser, "Dollfuss, Chancellor of Austria," *Contemporary Review* 144 (November, 1933): 535-39; Funder, *Als Österreich den Sturm bestand*, p. 78; and Brook-Shepherd, *Dollfuss*, pp. 99-107.

[74]Note, for instance, Starhemberg, *Memoirs*, pp. 89-94, 103-7.

[75]See Kerekes, "Akten des Ungarischen Ministeriums des Äusseren zur Vorgeschichte der Annexion Österreichs," pp. 357-58; and Paul R. Sweet, "Mussolini and Dollfuss. An Episode in Fascist Diplomacy," in Braunthal, *The Tragedy of Austria*, pp. 160-83, especially the documents published in full on pp. 184-213. See also W. Walter Crotch, "Whither Austria?" *The Nineteenth Century and After* 117 (April, 1935): 410-11; and Julius Deutsch, "Central European Problem," *Free World* 3, no. 1 (June, 1942): 74.

[76]See, for example, Mussolini to Dollfuss, Rome, July 1 and September 9, 1933, Sweet, "Mussolini and Dollfuss," pp. 184-87 and 195-96; note to Federal Chancellor Dr. Dollfuss, n. d., ibid., pp. 192-93; notes made for the foreign office file of Dollfuss' discussions with Mussolini at Riccione, August 19 and 20, 1933, ibid., p. 194; and Suvich to Dollfuss, n. d., ibid., pp. 199-201.

[77]That Mussolini bore a heavy guilt in provoking the February, 1934, civil war is apparent to anyone who reads the Mussolini-Dollfuss correspondence and the reports of the British, German, and French ambassadors discovered since World War II that were published in Ludwig Jedlicka, "Neue Forschungsergebnisse zum 12. Februar 1934," *Österreich in Geschichte und Literatur* 8, no. 2 (February, 1964): 69-87; and Ludwig Jedlicka, "Die Österreichische Innenpolitik 1934-1955," ibid. 6, no. 6 (June, 1962): 247-58. See also Ingrid Adam, "Zum 12. Februar 1934," ibid. 8, no. 1 (January, 1964): 1-8. That the Austrian socialists strongly suspected in 1934 that this was the case can be seen by reading Bauer, *Der Aufstand der österreichischen Arbeiter*, pp. 15-16.

[78]The words are those of Kurt von Schuschnigg in his *Austrian Requiem* (New York: G. P. Putnam's Sons, 1946), p. 187.

[79]Karl Renner, *Denkschrift über die Geschichte der Unabhängigkeitserklärung Österreichs und Bericht über drei Monate Aufbauarbeit* (Zürich: Europa Verlag, 1946), p. 23.

[80]See, for instance, Funder, *Als Österreich den Sturm bestand*, pp. 70, 74, 76-78; note of President Miklas, Vienna, November 25, 1933, Jedlicka, "Neue Forschungsergebnisse zum 12. Februar 1934," pp. 72-73; Miklas to Dollfuss, Vienna, January 6, 1934, ibid., p. 73; and Sir W. Selby to Sir J. Simon, Vienna, February 17, 1934, ibid., p. 79.

[81]Brook-Shepherd, *Dollfuss*, p. 103; Sweet, "Mussolini and Dollfuss," p. 165.

[82]Mussolini to Dollfuss, Rome, July 1, 1933, Sweet, "Mussolini and Dollfuss," p. 185.

[83]Ibid., pp. 185-86.

[84]"Note to Federal Chancellor Dr. Dollfuss for his Consideration," n.d., ibid., p. 193.

[85]Suvich to Dollfuss, n.d., ibid., pp. 199-200.

[86]Schuschnigg, *Dreimal Österreich*, p. 293.

[87]Schuschnigg, *Austrian Requiem*, p. 163. See also Schuschnigg's speeches at the opening of the Austrian federal council on December 1, 1934, and at Mariazell on August 5, 1934, *Österreichs Erneuerung* 1: 29, 90-91; and Langer, *Einst und Jetzt*, p. 23.

[88]See articles 15-33, in *Die neue Bundesverfassung für Österreich. Mit Erläuterungen von Dr. Kurt Schuschnigg*, pp. 97-101. For a sharp critique of these articles, see Gulick, *Austria from Habsburg to Hitler*, 2, 1428-41. For a defense, see Zernatto, *Wahreheit über Oesterreich*, pp. 118-20.

[89]Die neue Bundesverfassung für Österreich. Mit Erläuterungen von Dr. Kurt Schuschnigg, p. 7.

[90]See *ante*, pp. 6, 7.

[91]See especially Schuschnigg, *Dreimal Österreich*, pp. 293-94; and Schuschnigg, *Austrian Requiem*, p. 163.

[92]See par. 21, sect. 2, and par. 29, sect. 1 of the *Übergangsgesetz* of June 19, 1934, Ender, *Übergangsbestimmungen zur neuen österreichischen Verfassung*, pp. 25, 28.

[93]Zernatto, *Wahrheit über Oesterreich*, p. 124. The whole process of setting up the corporative state became so complicated and so enmeshed in bureaucratic red tape that it proceeded at a snail's pace. Furthermore, the Christian Socials and Heimwehr were deeply divided over the form which the corporative state should take. Many Christian Socials sincerely wanted to establish a new society in which a genuine effort would be made to carry out the principles of *Quadragesimo anno*. The Heimwehr, on the other hand, wished to install a mere copy of the Italian corporative system in Austria. In the end, Schuschnigg himself became skeptical about the corporative idea.

See George N. Shuster, "The End of Austria," *Catholic World* 147 (June, 1938): 298; Ernst Benedikt, "Austria and Czechoslovakia," *The Contemporary Review* 151 (May, 1937): 544; Friedrich Weiss, "Die Vollendung des berufsständische Ständestaat," *Der Christliche Ständestaat,* May 23, 1937, pp. 471-72; George N. Shuster, "Deep in Austria," *The Commonweal* 27 (March 11, 1938): 541; Martin Fuchs, *Showdown in Vienna. The Death of Austria* (New York: G. P. Putnam's Sons, 1939), pp. 21, 166; Lux, *La leçon d'Autriche,* p. 45; Ingrim, *Der Griff nach Österreich*, pp. 81-83; and Schuschnigg's speech to the Foreign Press Association, July 12, 1937, *Österreichs Erneuerung* 3: 68.

[94]See also Béla Menczer, "Thoughts on Austria," *The Contemporary Review* 150 (September, 1936): 328.

[95]See, for example, Rehrl, "Praktisches und Theoretisches zum Staatlichen Neuaufbau," pp. 3-6; Hausleithner, *Der Geist der neuen Ordnung*, pp. 97-98; Wilhelm Böhm, "Staatsform und Regierungsform," *Der Christliche Ständestaat* 4, no. 17 (May 2, 1937): 397; Zernatto, *Wahrheit über Oesterreich*, pp. 37-38; Schuschnigg's speeches at Baden on April 26, 1936, and in Vienna on May 9, 1937, *Österreichs Erneuerung* 2: 30-31; 3: 123-24; and Schuschnigg, *Dreimal Österreich*, pp. 291-92.

[96]See, for instance, the entries of October 15, 1937, and January 10, 1938, in Emmerich Czermak's diary, Ludwig Jedlicka, "Aus dem politischen Tagebuch des Unterrichtsministers a. D. Dr. Emmerich Czermak 1937-1938," *Österreich in Geschichte und Literatur* 8, no. 8 (October, 1964): 333, 362-63.

[97]See his "Das Ende der Aktion," *Wiener Politische Blätter* 3, no. 3 (July 21, 1935): 147.

[98]See, for instance, Brook-Shepherd, *Dollfuss*, pp. 109-21; P. K. Sheridon, *Kurt von Schuschnigg. A Tribute* (London: The English Universities Press Ltd., 1942), p. 122; Schuschnigg, *Dreimal Österreich*, p. 212; Clemens Wildner, *Von Wien nach Wien. Erinnerungen eines Diplomaten* (Vienna: Herold Verlag, 1961), p. 188; Funder, *Als Österreich den Sturm bestand*, pp. 122-28, 131-34; Ernst Karl Winter, *Arbeiterschaft und Staat* (Vienna: Reinhold-Verlag, 1934); Ernst Karl Winter, *Monarchie und Arbeiterschaft*; Elizabeth Wiskemann, "Austria and the Vatican: A Check to National Socialism?", *The Nineteenth Century and After* 115 (February, 1934): 180-81; Ingrim, *Der Griff nach Österreich,* pp. 60-65, 74, 157-58; and Fuchs, *Showdown in Vienna*, pp. 37-38, 165.

[99]Apparently this was done with Mussolini's approval—at least he wrote Schuschnigg: "If there are unbridgeable differences between the head of the government and his lieutenant I can fully understand that the lieutenant has to yield. But in view of my personal friendship with Starhemberg I would be very glad if the latter would be, politically speaking, treated decently, i. e., that he will not be held to account." Schuschnigg, *Austrian Requiem*, p. 121.

[100]For Starhemberg's account of why and how he was dismissed, see his *Memoirs*, pp. 223-31.

[101]For Starhemberg's views on the consequences of the dissolution of the Heimwehr, see ibid., pp. 256-58.

[102]Ibid., p. 195. See also entries of February 13, and November 22, 1937, in Czermak's diary, Jedlicka, "Aus dem politischen Tagebuch Dr. Emmerich Czermak," in *Österreich in Geschichte und Literatur* 8, no. 6 (June, 1964): 271; and no. 8 (October, 1964): 359; and Ernst Karl Winter, "Grossdeutsch-Kleindeutsch," *Wiener Politische Blätter* 4, no. 7-8 (July 5, 1936): 255.

[103]Among other sources, see Starhemberg, *Memoirs*, p. 172; Schuschnigg, *Dreimal Österreich*, pp. 154, 178; Ingrim, *Der Griff nach Österreich*, pp. 102-6, 159; Fuchs, *Showdown in Vienna*, pp. 22-23, 232-36; Ernst Karl Winter, "Dollfuss," *Wiener Politische Blätter* 2, no. 2 (December 23, 1934): 114-15; and Ernst Karl Winter, "Österreichische Sozialpolitik," ibid., 3, no. 3 (July 21, 1935): 109.

[104]See especially Funder, *Als Österreich den Sturm bestand*, p. 246; Kerekes, "Akten des ungarischen Ministeriums des Äusseren zur Annexion Österreichs," pp. 360-66; daily report on the conference between Kánya and Hassel, Rome, March 24, 1936, ibid., pp. 372-73; and Wettstein to Hungarian foreign ministry, Prague, April 28, 1937, ibid., p. 376.

[105]See especially Schuschnigg, *Austrian Requiem*, pp. 193-94; entries of March 1 and 19, April 28, and May 12, 1937, and January 13, 1938, Czermak's diary, Jedlicka, "Aus dem politischen Tagebuch Dr. Emmerich Czermak," in *Österreich in Geschichte und Literatur* 8, no. 6 (June, 1964): 272; no. 7 (September, 1964): 323, 326; no. 8 (October, 1964): 363; Wildner, *Von Wien nach*

Wien, pp. 192-93, 219-22; and Starhemberg, *Memoirs*, pp. 205-16.
[106]Jedlicka, "Ernst Rüdiger Fürst Starhemberg und die politische Entwicklung in Österreich im Frühjahr 1938," pp. 550-60.

III
Czechoslovakia

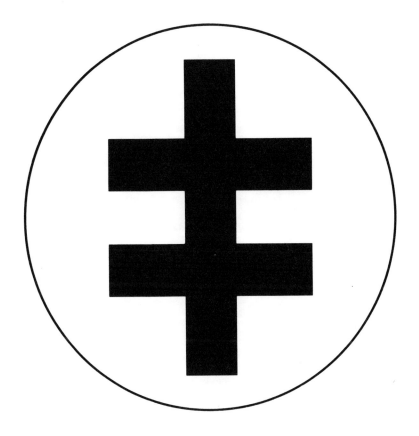

Jan Havránek

Joseph F. Zacek

A

Fascism in Czechoslovakia

Jan Havránek

When I told my colleagues in Prague that I would lecture in the United States on Czechoslovak fascism their first reaction was that I had accepted an impossible assignment. They agreed that there was German and Slovak fascism in interwar Czechoslovakia, but denied the existence of either Czech or Czechoslovak fascism. Yet I shall include Czech fascism, too, in my remarks. This seeming contradiction can be explained by the fact that fascism today is an expression that carries strong emotional connotations. The emphasis is always negative. This is even true in West Germany where those who have recently established a new political party with certain connections with the Nazi tradition avoided all possible negative identification and called their organization *Nationaldemokratische Partei*. In doing this, these Germans utilized a word that represents the other side of the emotional coin, and carries only a positive meaning—democracy.

The problem we all face is that it has become almost impossible to define fascism, because in the attempt one automatically passes moral judgment and condemns those who, according to the definition, are classified as fascists. As far as our investigation is concerned, the task is further complicated because we are interested in native fascist movements, and it is very difficult to isolate them from the international implications with which they were always connected. It is this separation of the local phenomenon from the broader context that is the main difficulty faced by a student of Czech fascism. Although it was relatively unimportant and weak, I will discuss Czech fascism at some length because it developed in relative isolation from other similar manifestations and its social, cultural, political, and economic roots can be traced with surprising accuracy.

To anyone familiar with fascist movements in Eastern Europe, it is quite obvious that there are few, if any, connections between its developments in the various Eastern European countries. It would be very hard, for example, to find a link between the Iron Guard and the Arrow Cross. This is certainly true of Czech fascism, which had practically no connection with similar movements elsewhere. Developing indigenously, these Eastern European fascisms, unlike their counterparts in the great fascist states, especially Germany, developed no international policies except those involved in the irredentist movements.

In spite of the fact that such right-wing radical parties as the *Deutsche Arbeiter-partei* in the Czech lands existed prior to World War I, fascism originated in the 1920s. The statement of the Czech historian, Jiři S. Hájek, that the fascist movement was an expression of the "anticapitalist radicalism of the petty bourgeoisie" shocked by the results of the war, points to the main reason that made the development of fascism possible. Defeated or dissatisfied nations were especially vulnerable to the teachings of this new radicalism. In these countries the "average" citizen, bewildered by the world around him, looked for scapegoats—either focusing on such individuals as Matthias Erzberger or Walther Rathenau or on entire social groups. Whereas the hatred of individuals could and did lead to murder, only to lose its justification with the death of the victim, hostility towards social groups developed into the ideological bases justifying the existence of movements and parties. Groups that were usually singled out as responsible for the nation's problems included minorities, especially those—like the Jews—dispersed throughout a country, professional organizations like trade unions, or ideologies like democracy or socialism. The fascists became the self-proclaimed protectors of the nation against foreign influence or any social or socialist revolution.

While industry was the predominant economic activity in Western Europe, agriculture played that role in Eastern and Southeastern Europe, and the corresponding social structures, economic changes, and political mass activities differed sharply. As a consequence, different types of fascism developed in Western and Eastern Europe. In the industrial countries fascism looked to the masses for support, attempted to appear simply as one form of the national-social revolutionary movements (of which there were several), even if it did not intend to overthrow the established social order, and called its activities "our revolution." These were the groups whose organization included their own shock troops and who followed a leader, typically a good demagogue who addressed his main arguments to the man in the street. In these movements, more than in the movements that grew out of agricultural countries, irrational arguments played a large part and much depended on the personal appeal—the charisma —of their leaders. Under these conditions even names became important. While the most typical of these leaders, the master of the most important "industrial" fascist movements, Adolf Hitler, had no difficulties, the leaders of two small Czech fascist parties whose names recalled the Habsburg monarchy had to change their names. Instead of his given name, Ferdinand, Stříbrný used Jiři, while Gajda turned Rudolf into Radola.

In the almost purely agrarian countries like Bulgaria, authoritarian governments, which are customarily called fascistic, relied mainly on the bureaucracy and the regular army, and de-emphasized uniformed party units. The ideology of these regimes was basically conservative and antirevolutionary, but they, nevertheless, built up extensive mass organizations in the fascist mode to support them. Most of the fascist movements in Central and Southeastern Europe represent various mixtures of these two basic types, but all of them were antidemocratic and tried to establish totalitarian or at least authoritarian regimes.

In the 1930s, German fascism was a dominant force on the European scene, and Czechoslovakia, as one of Germany's neighbors, had to reckon with this force. German fascism had gained a great domestic victory, was successful in solving many economic problems in a country that had been hit extremely hard by the Great Depression, and was, in fact, supported by a great percentage of the Germans, not only in Germany itself but also by those Germans living on the other side of the border in Austria, Czechoslovakia, and Poland. National socialism, as a movement, and Nazi Germany, as a state, were extremely well organized and much stronger than any other fascist party or state had been in the past, and, to some degree, they became the models for any reorganization of society along fascist lines.

Between the two world wars, Czechoslovakia was the most democratic state in Eastern and Central Europe. Here parliamentary rule, individual liberties, and the laws in general were really respected. Czechoslovakia was, nevertheless, in a very difficult position because its population consisted of 53 percent Czechs, 16 percent Slovaks and 25 percent Germans, and these three different peoples developed individual fascist movements. Fascist movements also developed among the other ethnic groups living in Czechoslovakia (for example, the Hungarians), but they were not important enough to warrant our attention.

Let us first look at Czech fascism. It was not very important, had relatively few followers, but is extremely interesting as a representation of a special kind of fascism. When historians are involved in typology, even negative examples or weak movements may shed valuable light. To give an illustration of this negative but fruitful approach, let us remember the historical attempt, centered at present at some German universities and in Czechoslovakia, which aims to discover why some nationalities—like the Bretons, Mazurians, and several others—did not succeed in developing into modern nations. Czech fascism has a similar interest. During World War I, the Czechs fought under the banner of democracy, and were victorious, and democracy became Czechoslovakia's dominant ideology. Fascism was weak among the Czechs not only because of this ideological basis, but also because totalitarianism had a very small social basis prior to the 1930s. Prague was growing rapidly, and most of the city's inhabitants were relatively successful economically. Czech fascism was started by former politicians, all of whom gained recognition during the war but who had been dismissed from state service and excluded from political life for personal reasons. Gajda, one of the leaders of Czech fascism, was a general who had been dismissed from the Czech army for lack of discipline and for contacts with a foreign power. Stříbrný, who rose to the dignity of cabinet minister, was finally dismissed after he twice embezzled money. He was a talented politician and leader of the National Socialist Party, the party that Edvard Beneš joined when he returned from abroad. Stříbrný was also a national hero. He had distinguished himself as one of the men who engineered the coup in Prague on the 28th of October. On this critical day he felt that it was less important to decide whether the future state was to become a monarchy or republic than it was to work up enthusiasm by organizing street dances and creating an atmosphere of optimism and satisfaction. Among the small people of Prague, Stříbrný enjoyed a certain degree of popularity. He shared the only common sentiment that the various fascists in Czechoslovakia had, the hatred for the *Hrad* (the castle), for the Masaryk-Beneš group, and for the socialists.

This fascist credo was paired with Czech nationalism, but this nationalism was less pro-Czech than it was anti-German. This fact alone made any connection between the Czech and German fascists impossible. The historian, Wolfgang Wolfram von Wolmar, a National Socialist who participated in the Nazi movement in the Sudetenland, wrote a thick book, *Prague und das Reich*. In this book he expressed the opinion that it was tragic that Czech and German National Socialists could not find a common basis for action as they shared so many goals, including anti-Semitism. However, I think that this lack of cooperation was unavoidable because, to use only one example, the anti-Semitism of both movements was basically nothing but metamorphosed nationalism. Czech anti-Semitism was not directed so much against Jews per se, as against Jews as

Germans, because nearly half of the Jews in Prague, for example, were German. This connection between nationalism and anti-Semitism limited the appeal of anti-Semitism among the Czechs because it was directed almost exclusively (some Czech-Jewish intellectuals were included) against German Jews.

More important were the "Three Musketeers," the three politicians, Gajda, Stříbrný, and Karel Pergler, the last a former Czech diplomat who formed a political party in 1929 and gained three seats in the National Assembly. This corresponds to 1 percent of the seats. While this low percentage does not seem to be important, one must remember that of the votes cast in the capital city it represented 5 percent in 1929, and in 1931 11 percent, an important consideration because Prague was the center of Czech life. This party, which published some papers, attacked movie houses that showed German films, and committed some violent acts of a terrorist nature, had relatively weak support from the politically important student groups. Some support came from small tradesmen and from some segments of the working class, but the main support of the Three Musketeers was the *Stehkragenproletariat*, people who were disappointed and dissatisfied with their social positions. Small tradesmen and shop-keepers did not provide support because another party, one with an ideology similar to that of the Poujadist movement in France, represented their interests. With no clear-cut ideology, the Czech Poujadists simply defended the interests of the small tradesmen and craftsmen, yet they managed to win more votes than the fascists of the Three Musketeers. Apart from Prague, the fascists received only 20,000 votes in the country at large. Obviously, fascism did not represent a serious force among the Czechs during the years of the great economic crisis that followed the world-wide depression.

Radical reaction to the crisis of the depression turned Czechs toward the left, not toward the right, and the social policy of the Czech government paralleled the New Deal of Franklin Delano Roosevelt to a certain degree. This policy was not the result of any action by the Prime Minister, Antonín Švehla, whose Agrarian Party could not oppose it. Indirectly therefore, Švehla favored the program that enabled the government to master the difficulties faced by the state when one million of its fourteen million inhabitants were unemployed. Half of the unemployed lived in the German districts, and the reasons for the high incidence of unemployment among the Germans and its consequences will be discussed in connection with German fascism.

Czech fascism, aiming to enlist the support of the students, had one more partial success in 1934, when it backed the nationalist demands of the students of Charles University. The insignia of the university had been in the hands of the German University since the days when Prague University was divided into Czech and German institutions. It had great symbolic value because Prague had the oldest, as well as the leading university in the country, and it seemed right that the insignia should be kept in the much larger and more important Czech university. A law, transferring the insignia, was passed in 1920 but was not enforced. There were nationalistic student demonstrations demanding that the law be enforced and these the right wing tried to exploit and to transform into demonstrations against Masaryk and the left wing in general. But after only two or three days of riots it became obvious that the student support of the rightists was minimal. Even when they tried to establish common cause with the National Democrats and to form the National Unity Party of Rightists (*Národní Sjednocení*) on the Polish model, hoping to obtain 30 percent of the Czech votes, they were greatly disappointed, and the new party was defeated in the 1935 elections. The broom, which was their most important emblem, signifying something akin to "We shall sweep out all the leftists," only worked to sweep the Unity Party off the political scene. The Unity Party's leader, František Hodáč, who had resigned as secretary of the Industrialists' Association to enter politics and who had spent a lot of money on the party, departed from the scene with it. He did not even win a seat in parliament; and the Unity Party obtained only 15 percent of the votes cast in Prague, no more than the rightists had gained in previous elections. The defeat of Czech fascism is understandable in the light of the concurrent rise to power of German fascism, which represented a greater danger to the Czech nation and state than did the local left.

There was another group led by General Radola Gajda, whose right-wing policies were based not on nationalism but on Italian fascism. He received some financial support from Italy, tried to establish his party on a countrywide basis, and managed to win six mandates (2 percent) in the 1935 election. His party received as much as 8 percent of the votes in some parts of Bohemia, the districts in which agrarian radicalism was rising, and the vote for Gajda represented discontent with the policies of a government made up mainly of agrarian and clerical parties. Even this 8 percent was not sufficient, as no fascist movement supported by a segment of the peasantry alone has any chance of success. During the critical years of 1938-39, all Czech fascist parties disappeared, for the danger of German fascism forced not only the supporters but even the leaders of the native fascist parties to join the national movement in defense of the nation. It is no accident that, for example, Ladislaw Rašín, the son of former Minister Alois Rašín, who represented the extreme right wing within the National Unity Party, became one of the most vocal advocates of a national front and cooperation with the left. Another man who made the switch was Minister Ježek, who became a member of the government.

The development of Slovak fascism was centered in the Slovak People's Party, which was formed by Father Andrej Hlinka, and arose from a defensive reaction to principal areas of concern in their relationship with their conationals, the Czechs. The creation of the Czechoslovakian state offered the Slovaks, who were fewer in number than the Czechs, the possibility of a broad cultural, economic, and social liberation and subsequent development. Yet they represented the economically less-developed half of the country; the industry of the new state was concentrated in western Czechoslovakia, and Slovak industry was often unable to compete with the more developed Czech companies. Because of their oppression under Hungarian rule, few Slovaks were trained to serve in the administration or in the professions, and Czechs were sent to Slovakia to fill government offices and teach in the elementary and high schools. Most of these people did not understand that they were to serve in Slovakia for a limited time, only until the Slovaks were able to take over. Compounding the affront to the Slovaks, the Czechs came from completely different cultural surroundings and failed to meet the Slovak standards of behavior. Among the Slovaks there is quite a sharp differentiation between the social status of an elementary school teacher and a high school professor, and a man's behavior was expected to reflect his position. If a person failed to meet this expectation—in dress, in behavior, in style of living—he was unacceptable to the Slovaks in the position he filled. This combination of circumstances: economic and administrative subordination and a culturally inspired lack of understanding—provided one major reason for anti-Czech feeling.

The other source of hostility was in attitudes toward religion: the Czechs were much less Protestant or Hussitic in spirit and outlook than is generally believed, and many of them leaned toward atheism. In strongly Catholic Slovakia, much of the basic anti-Czech feeling was that of a deeply religious people facing atheism.

With this background, it is difficult to appraise the Hlinka party as fascistic at its inception. It certainly had some fascistic elements, and served as the broad basis for fascist developments up to 1939, but it was not truly fascistic until after that year.

Support for the Hlinka party was not uniform throughout Slovakia, but it always won more than 50 percent of the vote in the poor rural districts, where the parish priest was the local leader and naturally sought support for the Catholic party. The party lost much of its popularity when it agreed, in the twenties, to join the government, but regained it during the thirties. In that decade it steadily won about half a million votes —from 30 to 40 percent of the Slovak vote.

The leaders of the party, Monsignor Jozef Tiso and Hlinka himself, were fairly tolerant towards the right-wing members of their party, led by Béla Tuka. In the thirties Tuka was joined by a younger, clearly fascistic generation, among them Fedor Ďurčansky, and it was this younger generation that made its views clear by disrupting the official celebration of *Pribina Nitra* in 1933. They forced the official speakers from the platform and replaced them with their own leaders. These Slovak autonomists (perhaps the best description of the Hlinka party) wavered uncertainly in their policies during the thirties. For example, in 1935 they cooperated with Konrad Henlein, yet decided the presidential election in favor of Beneš by voting against the right-wing candidate, Bohumil Němec. After 1935, influenced by developments on the international scene, Hlinka and Tiso inclined more and more toward fascism and strengthened their connections with Henlein's German fascists, the most disruptive element in Czechoslovakia. The party clarified its direction and purpose finally in January, 1938, when Hlinka declared, "If we do not achieve our autonomy we will secede from the republic." The Hlinka party differed quite sharply from other fascist organizations, in that despite its considerable national following and the harboring of many fascistic elements, its organization and program were not that of a fascist party until 1938.

To identify the Catholic church with Hlinka's party would be erroneous. Some priests, including Karol Kmetko, Bishop of Nitra and the most important Slovak clergyman, were not members of the party and even opposed it. But it cannot be denied that the party's most important members, its best agitators, and leaders of local party groups, were priests. Tiso himself, although a priest, became the head of a fascist state.

The third fascist group in Czechoslovakia were the German fascists. There were three million Germans in Czechoslovakia, spread through northern and western Bohemia, northern Moravia, and in narrow strips around the southern fringes of Bohemia. There were small German groups in various parts of Slovakia, and some 400,000 Germans in Prague, or 41 percent of its population. It was among the Bohemian Germans that, even before World War I, National Socialism had its origin. In the 1890s the *Deutschnationaler Arbeiterbund* (National German Workers' Organization) was established with the purpose of fighting the Czechs, and the leaders of the German Nazis in Czechoslovakia were fond of pointing out that it was not in Bavaria, Austria, or northern Germany that Nazism was born, but in the Sudetenland. In the 1890s, the original organization was chiefly interested in protecting the jobs and social position of Germans from usurpation by the Czechs, who were beginning to move into northern Bohemia. Despite its name, it was not just a workers' organization, but recruited members from among the tradesmen, too. It had accepted the ideology of the Pan-German, Georg von Schönerer, but its leader, Hans Knirsch, also included some socialistic elements in his program to appeal to the already existing German nationalistic trade unions. The *Deutschnationaler Arbeiterbund*, a proto-Nazi party, won 5 percent of the German votes in Bohemia, and the same amount in Silesia, although it could not gain any support in Moravia in 1911. Their representatives sat in the Diet of Bohemia and in the Reichsrat in Vienna. These men, recognized by the Nazis themselves as their forerunners, had an ideology compounded of nationalism and social demagoguery, quite typical of both the pre-World War I and the interwar fascist movements. There was, however, one important difference between the early Sudeten German Nazis and those elsewhere. While in Vienna anti-Semitism was already one of the strongest motivating forces, it was relatively unimportant in northern Bohemia, where the enemies were the Czechs, not the Jews. In 1920 the party obtained 120,000 votes and seated five deputies in parliament, but ten years later they mustered 200,000 votes and seated eight deputies. It would seem that the development of German Nazism was easier in Czechoslovakia than in Germany in the 1920s and certainly the *Hakenkreuzflagge* was seen much more often in Czechoslovakia's German districts than in Germany itself. The party's greatest support was around the cities of Most and Liberec, where the working class was both German and Czech. In the purely German districts in western and northern Bohemia, where there was no competition from the Czechs, the workers preferred the Social Democrat and Communist parties.

The party maintained close connections with the German Nazi party, and its leaders participated in the *Parteitage* in Germany. In the 1920s, before Hitler came to power, the German Nazi movement looked like one party with three branches: German, Austrian, and Sudeten German, each with its own leader representing its respective group. For its further development in Czechoslovakia, the group of German students in Prague became very important. These students, who came to Prague from the northern and western Bohemian districts, were not only isolated linguistically from the majority of the people among whom they lived, but also from the rich Germans in Prague, both Jewish and non-Jewish, and were, consequently, strongly influenced by nationalistic ideals. I do not think that at any German university the *Burschenschaftenideologie* was so thoroughly influenced by extreme nationalism as in Prague. It produced its own historically interesting documents, novels, and several other testaments of its views.

The *Deutschnationaler Arbeiterbund* was, of course, not the only organization that provided a basis for fascist development among Czechoslovakia's Germans. The more conservative *Deutschnationale Partei*, which had very few socialist elements, also harbored irredentist claims against Czechoslovakia. Its leader, Lodgman von Auen, was involved in all intrigues against the state after 1918. In the early 1930s, responding to the depression and the rising power of the Nazis, this second party also established much closer connections with Germany. In 1930, Joseph Goebbels spoke at a political meeting in Prague to show the close connection existing between the *Deutsche Nationalsozialistische Partei* in Czechoslovakia and the German Nazi party. His appearance was permitted by the Prague police, but when Baldur von Schirach, the Nazi youth leader, came to Prague, the police, well aware of what was happening, did not allow him to speak. At this moment the Rector of the German Technical University (the Germans had a technical and a liberal arts university in Prague) stepped in and invited von Schirach to speak, thereby abusing the privileges of academic freedom. It was around this time that SA groups, calling themselves *Volkssport* movements, developed at the German universities. These groups planned several anti-Czech actions, were arrested and sentenced to three to four years in prison, and became martyrs of the Nazi movement.

To understand this political development fully, the social situation must also be understood. Unemployment was more prevalent in the German districts than in the Czech districts. Jaroslav César and Bohumil Černy, present-day Czech authors of two books dealing with German policy towards Czechoslovakia, state that in 1935, the last year of the Great Depression, unemployment in the German districts was double that of the Czech districts. The reason for this was not political but economic. The German industry of northern Bohemia, mainly in textiles, was old, established, and consequently technologically somewhat out of date. Also, its connections with the large prewar Austro-Hungarian market were closed. The Czech industry was chiefly iron and steel, and was less dependent on these markets and more up to date technologically. Furthermore, during the 1920s, the German industrialists based themselves financially on the German mark, which was completely wiped out during the big inflation, while the Czechs, whose financial basis was the French franc, lost much less. While the Germans were, in fact, full citizens and enjoyed equality in Czechoslovakia (for example, among the four universities, two were Czech, one Slovak and one German, and among the four technical schools two were German and two Czech), they did not have the number of state employees corresponding to their percentage in the population because they did not speak Czech well enough. These economic problems, coupled with some psychological mistakes, supported an anti-Czech feeling in the German regions.

This was the situation when the Nazis in Czechoslovakia began to mount their attacks on the republic after Hitler's victory in Germany. These attacks included the *Volkssport* activities and the intensification of anti-Semitic demonstrations at Prague's German university, which had been traditional since the early 1920s. The success of these activities became clear when the Nazis won nearly 50 percent of the vote in local elections in western Bohemia. Now they represented a real danger for Czechoslovakia, and declared quite openly that they were ready to fight the police and even the army with the help of their paramilitary formations. At this time the government decided to dissolve both the National Socialist Party and the German Nationalist Party, which had a similar approach. The Germans then established the *Sudetendeutsche Heimatfront* and the *Sudetendeutsche Partei*, neither of which was officially connected with the dissolved parties, but whose leadership was practically identical, and who represented an even broader right-wing, nationalistic front than the organizations they replaced. At first they selected as their leader the Rector of the German University at Prague, but then they switched to Konrad Henlein, the chief of the *Deutsche Turnverband*, an organization of sportsmen. Henlein accepted the leadership.

In the party itself the group that originally backed Henlein, the *Kameradschaftsbund*, which was influenced mainly by the ideas of Othmar Spann and Austrian fascism in general, was soon pushed into the background and Hitler's agents, led by Karl Herman Frank, a publisher from Karlovi Vary (Karlsbad) took over the leadership. It surprised the people of Czechoslovakia that this new party, clearly leaning towards fascism and rapidly developing into a fascist party, managed to win two-thirds of all German votes in 1935. This meant that two-thirds of the Germans voted, not only against the continued existence of Czechoslovakia, but also against democracy. After this election the party's dependence on Hitler's Germany became quite clear, and in 1938 the party's policy became openly irredentist. During this same year, in the last elections ever held in pre-World War II Czechoslovakia, this party gained 88 percent of the German vote. There was no doubt any longer that the *Sudetendeutsche Partei* was simply the branch organization of Hitler's German Nazi party in Czechoslovakia. Clearly it was no longer a native fascist movement. Prior to this date one could have argued either way, that it was a native movement or that it was taking orders from Germany, but there was no doubt as to the situation in 1938.

Although it is very difficult to separate a country's or a population's native fascism from universal fascism, and although the German fascist movement was quite strong in Czechoslovakia in 1938, the anti-fascist forces were still strong enough to protect the republic and democracy. For example, the Czech mobilization in 1938 clearly proved that determined action could stop the Nazi danger. Not internal factors, not even the strength of local fascist parties, led to the destruction of Czechoslovakia. External forces did. German aggression, which used the German minority in Czechoslovakia as a tool, and the policy of the Western democracies, especially that of Great Britain, led to the tragedy of Czechoslovakia at Munich and the subsequent years. It was this international development that opened the way for Nazi expansion in Europe, although one should not minimize the important help that the existence of German fascism in Czechoslovakia represented in bringing Czechoslovakia to its knees and opening the road to Hitler's conquests.

B

Czechoslovak Fascisms

Joseph F. Zacek

At first thought it seems inappropriate to include Czechoslovakia in any survey of "native fascism in interwar Eastern Europe." Unlike practically all of the other countries under discussion, Czechoslovakia does not provide an immediate and striking example when this phenomenon is mentioned. To be sure, the mass acceptance of national socialism by the Sudeten German population of the Republic is well known, but this example is vitiated by its close connection with and subordination to the more important Nazi movement in the German Reich. There can be no doubt that by 1918 the Sudeten Germans themselves were "natives" of Bohemia-Moravia (regardless of whether their ancestors had been the original and continuous inhabitants of this area or merely later "immigrants and colonists," an issue heatedly debated by interwar historians), but Sudeten fascism appears to have been little more than a replica and ultimately an agent of the Nazi movement across the frontier. The Slovak autonomists and separatists are often referred to as "clerico-fascists," but it is doubtful that they deserve this label until 1938, perhaps not until after March, 1939, when they achieved their full independence from the Czechs. As for the Czechs themselves, it is generally conceded that fascism made few inroads among them. This dominant nationality in the country generally is given credit for the fact that in the interwar period Czechoslovakia remained "an island of order in a sea of chaos," a salient example of viable democracy not only in Eastern Europe (where its status was approximated only by Finland) but in all of Europe. Until Munich it remained a country where different political parties freely competed for office and where citizens could think and act, within very generous limits, as they pleased. It did not follow the pattern of political development common to the rest of East Central and Southeastern Europe between the wars. Although in 1923 and 1936 laws "for the defense of the Republic" were passed that provided for potential, severe limitation of the civil rights of extremist parties, the Czechoslovak constitution itself was not revised in the usual authoritarian manner (i. e., by increasing the powers of the executive to the detriment of those of the legislature). Nor did this parliamentary democracy make the standard transition to a dictatorship, either political, military, or royal.

This interpretation still prevails among western students of Czechoslovakia, although—largely as a result of the researches of Czechoslovak Marxist historians—it has been undergoing revision since the Second World War. Within communist Czechoslovakia, much has been and is being written about Sudeten fascism, especially in

56

connection with the regime-sponsored campaign of warning against the "revanchist" activities of Sudeten German exiles in West Germany. Nevertheless, our understanding of the Sudeten German case has changed less than that of Czech or Slovak fascism. The great mass of captured German evidence in the hands of "bourgeois" as well as Marxist historians has only corroborated what had been suspected by western observers before Munich and openly demonstrated and stated by the Nazis themselves after Munich. As for fascism among the Slovaks, Marxist historians working in Czechoslovakia are responsible for supplying practically all of the detailed studies we have of it. The few non-Marxists who have dealt with the subject are almost all exiles from Czechoslovakia and ex-officials of the Slovak Republic who defend the Hlinka-Tiso movement and deny its fascist character (notably Joseph A. Mikuš and Joseph M. Kirschbaum). However, while the Marxists (particularly Juraj Kramer̆) have filled in the factual picture considerably, they have partially obscured it again by superimposing upon it a class-conflict framework that is not entirely convincing. Finally, our understanding of Czech fascism has changed the most, although the changes have been subtle ones. Here, too, Marxist historians are chiefly responsible for our increase in knowledge. And here, too, new facts on currents and individuals have been coupled with distorted and exaggerated interpretations stemming from the Marxist predilection of inferring fascism from isolated symptoms and to label anything detrimental to communism "bourgeois-fascist." The few non-Marxist Czech historians working outside Czechoslovakia, as well as the equally few non-Czech historians who deal with Czechoslovak history in the West and are largely their disciples, have ignored or belittled the existence of Czech fascism. The revised picture is what logic would suggest: that in an interwar Europe generally on the move toward the right and peculiarly receptive to fascism, even the Czechs were not entirely immune to its appeal. But even Marxist researchers have arrived again at the old conclusions: Fascism was a very weak and foreign phenomenon among the Czechs; and fascism in interwar Czechoslovakia was almost exclusively a nationality phenomenon affecting the two largest "national minorities," the Sudeten Germans and the Slovaks, and stemming mainly from their frustration in this status. (I label the Slovaks a national minority even though they were officially part of the dominant "Czechoslovak nation" and one of the two "state peoples." Certainly they felt they were being treated like a minority group. Other national minorities within the republic—e. g., Magyars, Poles, Ruthenes—are not treated in this appraisal, though traces of fascism also appeared among them.)

I intend to devote the remainder of this account to separate treatments of these three leading nationalities. I shall briefly describe the origin and growth of fascist symptoms among the Sudeten Germans, then the Slovaks, and finally the Czechs, and suggest the causes—domestic and foreign, immediate and long-range—for each case. In the last case, it will also be appropriate to seek the reasons for the failure of fascism to have much drawing power among the Czechs.

Before about 1933, Sudeten German fascism was mainly an indigenous movement, embryonic, poorly coordinated, and viewed by the Czech government as a containable threat. After 1933, it increasingly came under the direction of Nazi Germany, absorbed wider and wider circles of the Sudeten population, and escalated its activities and demands until it succeeded in dissolving the "synthetic" Czechoslovak state.

After 1918, a network of nationalist organizations of a "defensive" nature (defensive against the Czechoslovak regime) arose out of the humiliation of some three-and-a-half million Sudeten Germans reduced from a dominant role in prewar Bohemia-Moravia to that of a "national minority" in the new Czechoslovakia. In such groups as the *Wandervögel*, the *Kameradschaftsbund*, and the *Turnverband*, the mass support, the ideology, and the leadership of Sudeten fascism developed. The most important of these was the Sudeten German National Socialist Workers' Party (DNSAP), a postwar reincarnation of the old Austrian *Deutsche Arbeiterpartei*. It grew rapidly and in 1929 formed the first of a series of paramilitary auxiliaries, the *Volkssportverband*. It dissolved itself in 1933, one jump ahead of being declared illegal as a subversive party, but was recreated almost immediately as the "nonpolitical" *Sudetendeutsche Heimatfront* under a new *führer*, Konrad Henlein. In this early period, Sudeten fascist ideology consisted chiefly of the old anti-Czech, anti-Jewish, and all-German slogans developed in Bohemia in the late nineteenth and early twentieth centuries by such men as Georg von Schönerer and Karl Hermann Wolf, and it appealed especially to the Sudeten German youth and a radically nationalist segment of the lower middle class. Significant for the future, however, was the emphasis upon a Sudeten German *Volks- und Kulturgemeinschaft*, a collective entity existing under an ethnic group law that would protect its members wherever they were found. Fascist tactics were simply obstructionist and were overshadowed by the constructive "activism" of other Sudeten parties such as the Agrarians, Christian Socialists, and Social Democrats.

After 1933, under the impetus of the Great Depression and the spectacular rise of Hitler, national socialism rapidly engulfed the Sudeten German mentality. The various "defensive" organizations, merged in 1934 in the *Bund der Deutschen*, soon fell under the control of the Henleinists, themselves increasingly supported and directed (covertly) by officials and institutions of Hitler's Germany. They even received financial support from elements of the Czech right wing, which hoped to use them tactically against the socialists. In the 1935 election, Henlein's new Sudeten German Party won a stunning victory, polling more than 60 percent of the German vote and receiving 44 of the 66 German seats in the Czechoslovak Parliament. Now controlling the Sudeten middle class and a majority of the working class, Henlein adopted a bolder stance, although he continued to deny that the Sudetens had become Hitler's agents and that their purpose was to dissolve the Czechoslovak state. The Austrian Anschluss was the signal for the first official pro-Hitler and pro-Nazi expressions, as codified in Henlein's eight Carlsbad demands. The Sudetens demanded complete self-government, recognition as a separate legal entity, and full freedom to profess German nationality and a "German world outlook," i. e., national socialism. The German population scrambled to climb on Henlein's bandwagon, and in the municipal elections of May, 1938, more than 85 percent of its votes went to the Sudeten German Party. The following few months witnessed open Hitler-Henlein consultations, Hitler's demand at Nürnberg for self-determination for the Sudeten Germans, Henlein's call for Sudeten secession, the forcible dissolution of the Sudeten German Party by the Czech government, Henlein's flight, and the provocative actions of the Sudeten German *Freikorps* in the border areas. After Munich, Sudeten fascism merged with its Great German relative and, in that guise, returned in triumph to the Protectorate of Bohemia-Moravia.

The bitter grievances that inclined the Sudeten Germans toward extreme solutions were political and economic: the sudden and radical reversion from being rulers to being ruled, and the particularly harsh effects of the depression on Sudeten German industry (chiefly light industry, heavily reliant on export). There were also German complaints of inequities connected with the land reform, the awarding of government contracts, the filling of state jobs, and the like, and these were not entirely without foundation. The specifically fascist nature of the Sudeten response was due, rather, to cultural-historical factors. A thousand years of Czech-German rivalry in Bohemia-Moravia had been codified in the late nineteenth century in a particularly rabid, "racial" form of Bohemian-German nationalism that had an overwhelming influence upon the Sudetens, particularly when it was reinforced by a new, similar current from across the frontier.

During most of the interwar period, Monsignor Andrej Hlinka's Slovak People's Catholic Party (*Slovenská ludová strana*), the chief vehicle of autonomist and, later, separatist sentiments in Slovakia, might better be labeled conservative-nationalist or reactionary-nationalist than "clerico-fascist." In the beginning, it simply rejected the concept of a single "Czechoslovak nation" and demanded full autonomy for Slovakia. In place of an ideology it coined slogans such as "Slovakia for the Slovaks" and "Introduce the Pittsburgh Agreement into the Czechoslovak Constitution." The party never represented a majority of the Slovaks, polling between 25 and 40 percent of their votes in elections. Led by clerics and its ranks filled with the rural petty bourgeoisie and the peasantry, it also became a catchall for disloyal and disoriented elements of all sorts. Indeed, some of the latter gradually gained control of the party and were responsible for reorienting it from autonomy to separatism and to outright fascism. This handful of young extremists, led by Béla Tuka and centered about the periodical *Nástup*, were open admirers of Hitler and German national socialism and aimed to set up an independent Slovak state under a dictatorship of the Slovak People's Party. Tuka himself tipped his hand early in the 1920s with his theory of a *vacuum juris*; he insisted that the Slovak acceptance of a joint Czechoslovak state in 1918 had included the stipulation that the agreement would automatically lapse in ten years' time and would have to be renegotiated, a fabrication that resulted in his imprisonment in 1929. These separatists established contacts with Hungarian irredentists and with Austrian and German Nazis, and in 1923 formed an armed auxiliary called the *Rodobrana*. In early 1938 they began systematically to coordinate their actions with Henlein's group. Following Munich, the Slovak People's Party successfully claimed the right to be the sole representative of the Slovaks and to exercise exclusive political power on their behalf. Under the pressure of the separatists, it established a dictatorship in Slovakia, liquidating all political opposition through outright suppression or by forcing it to merge in a new Party of Slovak National Unity. Its program was anti-Czech, anti-Semitic, anti-democratic, and anti-communist. Soon afterward, when—with Hitler's urging and support—a separate Slovak Republic was proclaimed and the separatists took full control of the party, this program was elaborated and incorporated into law and an official ideology. The party itself was closely remodeled on the German NSDAP, and all power was vested in a "leader."

After Hlinka, this leader was Monsignor Jozef Tiso, at once President of the Slovak State, Chief of the Slovak People's Party, and Supreme Commander of the elite paramilitary groups, the powerful Hlinka Guard, and the Hlinka Youth. A corporative state was established in which the position of the Catholic church was insured (the symbol on the armbands of the Hlinka Guard was the episcopal cross). Civil rights were severely restricted and secret police, special courts, prisons, and concentration camps were established to deal with opponents, including recalcitrant Slovaks. Finally, in a grand effort, Tuka himself tried to synthesize the papal encyclicals and German national socialism into a patchwork official ideology called "Slovak National Socialism." But his efforts and those of numerous eager assistants resulted in little more than a crude, unimaginative transfer of Nazi catchwords to the grossly unsuitable Slovak milieu. Slovak national socialism was declared to be "in complete harmony with Slovak national traditions," "an organic continuation of the Slovak national forces in the spirit of [Slovak] traditions," "the system best fitted to the needs of Slovak life because it facilitates a complete solution of all political, economic, social, and cultural problems," and (more realistically) "the best guarantee of Slovak statehood." The Slovaks were described as a racially pure nation led by one party and one leader—"One nation, one party, one Leader." Intermixture with Czechs and Jews was forbidden, and the Nürnberg solution recommended for the "problem" of the latter. The "foreign-imposed," "plutocratic," "liberalist-capitalist" system of interwar Slovakia was rejected for a "national socialist and Christian [i. e., corporative] economic structure." "Outdated" parliamentary-democratic forms were denounced and the whole executive and legislative process "simplified" by placing all power and responsibility in the hands of the Leader. Finally, the Slovaks were described as sharing a common destiny with the German Reich; fervent expressions of loyalty to Germany and adulation of Hitler became a constant public refrain.[1] The whole transformation was carefully (and, no doubt, cynically) watched by Nazi Germany through its local representative, Franz Karmasin, leader of the privileged German *Volksgruppe* remaining in Slovakia.

Though Hungarian irredentism doubtless stirred up Slovak grievances and German nazism was important in shaping them into fascism, the basic causes for the Slovaks' discontent and their susceptibility to radical solutions were certainly domestic —long-term historical differences (religious, cultural, and social) that set them sharply apart from the Czechs by 1918, and certain political and economic problems after 1918 that only exacerbated the former. The Slovaks were a staunchly Catholic people, distrustful of the "Hussite" and "free-thinking" Czechs. In the preceding century, Catholicism had been a major component in the growth of Slovak national consciousness, and the leadership and dominance of the Catholic priesthood was also a long tradition. Unlike the Czechs, the Slovaks were an overwhelmingly peasant and petty-bourgeois people, dismayingly illiterate and backward technologically. Nevertheless, they resented Czech tutelage (however well meant), and a fledgling Slovak intelligentsia clamored for positions of responsibility and power monopolized ("temporarily," until the Slovaks were equipped to fill them) by the Czechs. The Slovak peasant suffered considerable hardship from the regime's disruption of the prewar pattern of trade. Perhaps worst of all, Prague made no serious move to grant the Slovaks the autonomy "promised" them in the Pittsburgh Agreement. All of this was fuel for Slovak nationalism, long stifled by the Magyars and now free at last to assert itself vigorously. The most appropriate target were the Czechs, whose own nationalism, more than a century old, was now triumphant, mature, and relatively subdued.

Before Czech Marxist historians took the subject in hand, our knowledge of Czech fascism consisted of little more than disparaging and contemptuous references to the unimportant group gathered about General Rudolf Gajda. My account is almost entirely a brief summary of their researches (a good, though now dated summary of these is the official Marxist survey of Czechoslovak history).[2]

Immediately after 1918, no party with a clearly fascist program appeared among the Czechs, although several seemed to have such potential. For example, Karel Kramář's National Democrats, representing the wealthy bourgeoisie, were strongly nationalist and anti-socialist, but they steadily lost strength to the other parties. Eduard Beneš's own National Socialists, although stridently nationalistic, were a firmly democratic party. Outright fascist groups did not make their appearance until the early 1920s. In 1923, the *Ústřední výbor československých fašistů* (Central Committee of Czechoslovak Fascists) was formed, and pro-fascist individuals appeared also in the traditional parties. But it was only in the mid-1920s that the Czech bourgeoisie, fearful of a rising revolutionary labor movement, turned definitely toward a fascist solution. It vacillated between two alternatives—to cooperate with the bourgeoisie of the other nationalities to maintain control of the parliamentary government, or to set up an outright fascist dictatorship. There followed a series of covert attempts at the latter. For example, in 1925 Gajda established his *Národní obec fašistická* (National Fascist Community) and planned a coup for 1926. About the same time, a *levý blok* (left bloc), consisting of certain renegade National Socialists and veteran legionnaires, made plans for a presidential dictatorship a la Piłsudski. In 1929, a new fascist formation under the ex-National Socialist, Jiří Stříbrný, allied itself with Gajda. All of these plots were foiled, according to the Marxist account, by the democratic tradition deeply ingrained in the Czech people and the constant vigilance of the Czech Communist Party. A stalemate also resulted from the inability of the various national bourgeois-fascist elements to agree on a common program and the equal lack of success of the Communist Party in uniting all anti-fascist elements into a popular front.

With Hitler's coming to power, Czech fascists were encouraged to try openly for a dictatorship. In 1934 they formed a new coalition, the *Národní sjednocení* (National Union), and with the assistance of the *Živnostenská banka*, the largest credit institution in the country, prepared systematically for the 1935 elections. But they gained few parliamentary seats and later in the year failed to elect their candidate, Professor Bohumil Němec, to the presidential seat vacated by Thomas Masaryk. After these failures, the proponents of fascism turned to indirect means, working chiefly through the Czech Agrarian Party, the strongest party in the country between 1922 and 1938, to reorient Czechoslovak foreign policy toward Germany and to encourage cooperation with Henlein and Hlinka. But only the Munich capitulation gave them a free hand. They coalesced in a reactionary-conservative government headed by the Czech agrarian, Rudolf Beran, and set about fitting Czechoslovakia into Hitler's "New Order" and bringing authoritarian changes into the governmental structure. The Communist Party was dissolved, the ministerial parties merged into the Party of National Unity, and the socialists into the Party of Labor. In the Protectorate, the process of reactionary consolidation went even further; a collaborationist Czech government, the *Národní souručenství* (National Confederation), was set up, and even other fascist groups, such as *Vlajka* and Gajda's group, were disbanded.

How many of the movements and actions described in this account deserve the label *fascist* is difficult to determine, especially since the primary source materials are not readily available outside Czechoslovakia. At any rate, even the Marxists generally agree that fascism remained foreign to and unimportant among the Czechs. As one typical account puts it: "In contrast with neighboring Fascist or semi-Fascist countries, Czechoslovakia remained until Munich a state with definite bourgeois democratic rights and freedoms, despite the fact that these were artfully and systematically limited and despite the fact that a part of the bourgeoisie tried to abolish them completely."[3] Why was this so? Since the Czech population was exposed to essentially the same powerful, negative influences as the other nationalities of Eastern Europe—postwar dislocation, the depression, the rival pressures of neighboring nazism and communism—the answer must lie rather in the domestic sphere, in basic differences in the Czechs' historical make-up and in their postwar circumstances. As a victor in 1918, the Czechs had little incentive to revanchism or irredentism. Czechoslovakia had also been treated very generously in economic terms, possessing in Bohemia-Moravia a great proportion of the industrial and agricultural wealth of the Habsburg Empire. Scholars usually cite, as a deterrent to the appeal of fascism, the healthy balance of social classes among the Czechs, between a strong and capable bourgeoisie (itself recruited in the preceding century from the peasantry and proletariat), a trained proletariat, and an efficient peasantry. All of these received proportional representation in parliamentary life through a wide spectrum of political parties, including a legally existing Communist Party. Popular literacy and education were at a high level among the Czechs. An especially important stabilizing force was the Czech cultural tradition. Since the early nineteenth century, through the efforts of men such as František Palacký, Czech nationalism had been linked firmly with liberalism, specifically with the humanitarian and progressive tradition of the Hussites. In the interwar period, the greatest exponent of this tradition was the philosopher-president, T. G. Masaryk. Perhaps this revered man was, until his death in 1937, a sort of democratic *führer* for the Czechs, the greatest single bulwark against chauvinism and fascism among his people.

As I predicted, this review of interwar Czechoslovakia has not supplied us with classic examples of fascism. If we accept as a "fascist minimum" extreme "integral" nationalism, a system of state socialism, a one-party dictatorship, and totalitarian rule, then neither the Sudeten Germans nor the Slovaks were officially and openly espousing fascism before 1938 or actually practicing it before 1939. In both cases, there was heavy, unimaginative, and even (in the Slovak example) ludicrous imitation of the Reich model. And the Czechs supply us only with a good case study of a people's successful resistance to domestic fascism.

FOOTNOTES

 1 Jozef Lettrich, *History of Modern Slovakia* (New York: Frederick A. Praeger, 1955), pp. 151-56, 301-2.

 2 *Přehled československých dějin*, 3 vols. (Prague: Československá akademié věd, 1958-60), specifically vol. 3.

 Zdeněk Urban, *Příručka k dějinám Československa v letech 1918-1948* (Prague: Státní pedagogické nakl., 1959), p. 109.

IV
Hungary

György Ránki
George Barany

A

The Problem of Fascism in Hungary

György Ránki

In the 1920s the politicians and ideologists of the Hungarian political regime in power tried to stress the democratic features of Admiral Miklós Horthy's system, sometimes going so far as to deny that it contained anything that could be considered a legacy from the counterrevolution of 1919. But by the end of the 1930s and the beginning of the 1940s, leading Hungarian politicians frequently boasted that Hungary was the first country in Europe to introduce fascism, and they even insisted that Horthy's white terror and the subsequent system manifested the features of the ideology and practical system that conquered Germany and Italy.

The fact that the same state and political regime could be characterized in such a radically contradictory manner indicates, to a certain extent, the amorphous nature of the Hungarian social and political system between the two world wars in spite of several changes in the structure of the system in the 1930s.

Although the word *fascism* was not part of the vocabulary of the Hungarian counterrevolutionaries it is, in a historical sense, applicable to the Hungarian situation after 1919. The activities of the authorities during the counterrevolution and in the white terror of 1919-20 included several features that were also characteristic of the rising fascism in Germany and Italy. While democratic features and left-wing sympathies were developing in Europe, a political system that mercilessly persecuted both the labor movement and, in general, democratic ideas and their proponents arose in Hungary. Hungary initiated the idea of racial universalism that, in opposition to the West European sociological views and liberal theory, stressed the importance of the Hungarian "race" and the idea of a strong national state. It became the first official ideology of this sort in Europe.

The social stratum, or rather the strong political group, which became the propagator and the main supporter of these fascistic tendencies in Hungary during the two world wars, took the lead during the 1919-20 counterrevolution and the white terror. It was a rather peculiar agglomeration composed of the gentry, army officers, and civil servants. Representatives of a once powerful and important element in Hungarian public life, these people became poorer and poorer as capitalism matured in Hungary until they were reduced to the role of representatives of the political and administrative power of the large estates. Disdaining the typical occupations of capitalism—commerce and industry—as below their position and dignity, these people monopolized the various offices of the state and county government. Because a con-

65

siderable part of the Hungarian bourgeoisie was of Jewish or German origin, the reactionary, anticapitalistic conservatism of these officeholders led to extreme nationalism and anti-Semitism. During the development of capitalism, the gentry, army officers, and civil servants stratum, whose importance was diminishing, was joined by the rising petty-bourgeois elements whose outlook, as a result of conscious imitation, conformed to that of the leading gentry. This gentry, army officer, civil servant group became an integrated class, the lower stratum of the ruling classes. They carried out the policies reflecting the power of the large landowners and capitalists, but they were never satisfied with this position. Most of the leaders of the white terror that followed the Soviet regime in 1919 came from this group.

This newly integrated lower ruling class regarded the white terror and counterrevolution, which assigned a very important role to the executive, not only as a means of suppressing a revolutionary movement, but also as a system leading to their resumption of power by the seizure of control of the state apparatus. Therefore, they opposed the revolution as well as any liberal system that, in their opinion, could only have led to revolution. Similarly, they were against the leading politicians of the old monarchy, who might have tried to reclaim their leading position. Thus their theory, though never clearly formulated, was based on antisocialism and antiliberalism and incorporated many elements of fascist ideology. The most important points of their theory were: replacement of the parliamentary system by an unlimited military dictatorship; militarism; extreme chauvinism; anti-Semitism in accordance with the race theory; the total rejection of democratic institutions; the tyrannical persecution of the labor movement, and an attempt to eliminate it.

Undoubtedly the army officers, whose number was greatly increased during the war by the masses of reserve officers, gave full support to the political representatives of this trend. Some of these officers were active in the army detachments and other police groups of the counterrevolution. This trend was also supported by a significant part of the demobilized reserve officers who were not in the armed forces (which was officially limited to 35,000 after 1920). These officers, who during the war became adjusted to a carefree life, to the giving of orders, and to financial liberties, were unwilling to work for a living, unwilling to become nonentities after a return to civilian life or to their university studies.

The various fascistic slogans of the political leadership were echoed loudly by the gentry serving in the civil service, administration, courts, and police organizations. They hoped that the change would give them the opportunity to get better positions and to improve their financial status, which had degenerated because of the increasing inflation. Their number was increased by the tens of thousands of broken Hungarian civil servants and other groups of the nobility who, coming from the separated parts of the country, settled primarily in Budapest, where they formed the most extreme mass support for all sorts of social, chauvinistic, and irredentist demogogueries. They became the backbone of the openly fascistic organizations (the Association for National Defense, and the Association of Awakening Hungarians).

The gentry, which had declined in numbers during the monarchy, the petty bourgeoisie, who were waging an uneven battle against mainly Jewish big capital, the civil servants, whose existence was threatened during the inflation, all fought (with the approval of the ruling classes) first of all against communism. This fight also revived the romantic notion of agrarian anticapitalism. But an ideological change, distinguishing the anticapitalism of the nineteenth century petty bourgeoisie from that of the twentieth century, also became manifest in Hungary. Anticapitalists in the twentieth century, while encouraging criticism of capitalism, seek a way out of their difficulties in a revised form of capitalism. Criticism of capitalism in Hungary was narrowed down to the specific form it assumed during the Dual Monarchy. The positive and negative features of capitalism were distinguished, and the latter were presented as the vanishing, accidental manifestations of capitalism.

It is in this context that socialism is explained as a negative aspect of capitalism, as a trend hostile to culture and endangering the human personality, and which must be eliminated. Consequently, according to this new ideology, Jewish liberalism, which fostered socialism, and a new, controlled, Christian capitalism become antonyms, and the socialistic approach to anticapitalism is seen as incorrect. The basic social problem is: Who possesses the capital, and by what fundamental principles is capital directed and controlled? The situation, considered to be unsatisfactory, would automatically be reversed if Christians were the possessors of capital. Gottfried Feder's distinction between *exploitative* and *creative* capital (*raffendes und schaffendes Kapital*) is evident in this differentiation between Jewish and Christian capital that developed in Hungary, and thus forms one of the most important elements of fascist ideology during the post-1919 period in that country.

In this system of thought, "nation" was supreme, and the state, which unites the individuals and is superior to individual interest, expressed the interests of the unified nation. A national struggle had to replace the class struggle. The Peace Treaty of Trianon provided the opportunity for putting this theory into practice.

Thus arises the question of nationalism, one of the most decisive social factors leading to fascistic trends in Hungary. It was not difficult to fan the flames of chauvinism, to turn mass antagonism, which originated in nationalistic grievances, into a force supporting this particular system in a country that lost two thirds of its territory (in spite of the fact that those areas did not, for the most part, have Hungarian inhabitants) and which was faced with grave economic problems attributed by the official press solely to the changing of the boundaries. Revisionist propaganda incorporating the idea of Hungarian supremacy (akin to the fascist race theory) and the thought of leadership in the Danube Basin were able to win over to fascism the petty bourgeoisie who could trace, at least formally, the very poor economic conditions following the war to the loss of leadership in the Danube Basin as well as the civil servants who, streaming into Budapest from the lost minority territories, passionately desired a return to their former superior position. The injustices of the Trianon Peace Treaty became, more than anything else, the means of reviving aggressive Hungarian imperialism that, due to national bitterness, could win the intelligentsia, petty bourgeoisie, peasants, and a part of the workers to the support of the foreign and internal goals of the ruling classes.

The counterrevolution, however, did not result in a completely fascistic system in Hungary. Without attempting to cover the political and historical events involved, the pertinent causes for this development must be reviewed. The struggle that took place between the various groups within the ruling classes during the counterrevolution was decided in favor of those political groups that considered the stability of the new political organization best assured by a system embodying the traditional features of Hungarian conservatism.

The groups favoring the fascistic trend did not have a broad enough social basis to entertain even the hope of building up a considerable fascist mass movement or mass party because they did not succeed in gaining adherents among the working class and peasantry. Unlike Germany and Italy, it was not the impoverished middle class and the petty-bourgeois elements, but the army officers of gentry origin whose entire outlook on life was tied in with the old Hungarian ruling classes and a narrow political outlook, who supplied the bulk of these extreme right-wing movements in Hungary. They were not well versed in any essential social question, be it the land or labor issue, and the only thing they could do was substitute nationalistic slogans for knowledge.

Even the international situation was not favorable for the success of fascistic trends in Hungary. Its leaders, heading a country that faced total economic bankruptcy and was cut off from international affairs, could count on a certain amount of recognition by and support from the western powers only if they made their system somewhat similar to those of Western Europe.

In Hungarian politics the halt of the white terror was paralleled by the gradual suppression of the adherents of totalitarianism. The big landowning-capitalistic groups, headed by István Bethlen, got more and more control over politics and administration, while the political influence of the gentry and army officer groups headed by Gyula Gömbös decreased after great fights centered on internal politics.

In the autumn of 1922 fascistic forces, inspired by the international rise of fascism and especially by its victory in Italy, made another effort to regain their influence and to gain power. A contemporary report of the German Embassy noted: "After watching the success of their foreign counterparts, these elements believe that their time is approaching."

With the help of fascist groups and organizations, Gömbös, the leader of the purely fascist wing, prepared a coup in order to bring about the *Marcia su Budapest.* The countermeasures of the Bethlen government, the dissolution of the "Hungarian fascist camp," the dispersal of the picketing students, and finally the mobilization of the army against the battalions of the "Awakening Hungarians" succeeded in suppressing the Hungarian forces of fascism. The change in governmental leadership became quite obvious when Gömbös resigned from the governing party and established an open opposition, that of a racist party (*Fajvédök*) in the summer of 1923.

In summary, the most important features of the new system, consolidated under the leadership of Bethlen, contained elements of liberalism manifest in a restricted freedom of the press, certain limited political rights, parliamentarianism, and a multi-party system. But it maintained simultaneously several forms of political oppression that had been evident during the counterrevolution and were also characteristic of ruthless fascistic systems. Law III of 1921 made the Communist Party illegal. The labor movement in Hungary was subject to unlimited administrative and police tyranny, and the various rights associated with democracy were arbitrarily restricted. Rule was parliamentary, but its value was negated by the open voting system and the administrative tyranny that predecided elections. A contemporary fascist author stated: "Under these circumstances it is not necessary to suppress opposition parties because they do not endanger the right wing." Thus the party in power enjoyed an uncontested hegemony almost as total as that typical of one-party systems, and parliament was, for the most part, merely a tool of the government and the administration.

The government's domination of parliament was complemented by several institutions of the corporative type such as the Chamber of Agriculture, the Wage-fixing

Committee, and the Board of Arbitration, as well as various semi-fascist social organizations.

In 1927, Bethlen himself called this system a "democracy based on corporative correctives." It probably would have been more correct to speak about a corporative system with democratic trappings. If these fascist features are compared with the classical but nevertheless most extreme type of fascism found in Germany and Italy, then this system cannot be called fascist. A closer understanding of fascism in Eastern Europe can be gained, however, if the similarities of the monarchistic counterrevolutionary features of the predominant military dictatorship of Hungary and those of fascism are considered.

The views of G. D. H. Cole deserve attention even if they cannot be accepted fully. He distinguishes between German-Italian fascism (mass movements depending on the petty bourgeoisie and middle-class strata), and those forms found mainly in the underdeveloped countries of Southeastern Europe where fascism did not become a mass movement. In these countries it became primarily, or at least to a considerable extent, fused with the reactionary activities of the landed monarchistic elements and the clergy trying to preserve the social status quo. The analysis of the situation in Hungary necessarily involves the questions of the interconnections and interpenetrations of militarism and fascism in the twentieth century. In all countries militarism is closely related to fascism, and in certain countries it becomes its main support. This latter relationship is characteristic of Hungary, where the officers espoused fascist ideas for militaristic reasons and became the most ardent supporters of total fascism in Hungary. This statement brings us to the 1930s, when Gömbös, the main spokesman of total fascism, who went over to the opposition in the 1920s, once again rejoined the government party, and soon became appointed its leader and the Prime Minister of Hungary.

The trends toward total fascism are important primarily because of the economic problems and social antagonisms that became extremely sharp after the economic crisis of 1929–33. The consolidation of the state and social order once again emphasizes the role of the right-wing elements suppressed in the mid-1920s. The victory of nazism in Germany undoubtedly greatly increased the influence of the political leaders of the gentry, officer, and civil servant coalition. This rise in importance was made relatively easy because Hungarian foreign policy was designed to form close ties with Hitler from the moment he came to power. Most Hungarian politicians saw in him the potentially strongest supporter of their revisionist foreign policy, the attempt to reestablish a Greater Hungary.

Two trends can be discerned in this pro-German policy. The aristocracy and big capitalists, many of whom were Jewish, thought of an alliance with Germany in which Hungary would not be fully subordinated. They accepted several elements of the Nazi ideological and political machinery without intending to adopt them fully. The stratum of gentry and officers, on the other hand, saw in Nazi Germany not only the most modern form of counterrevolution and a support for its foreign political efforts, but also the force that might bring about a change in the internal politics of Hungary. Aggressive militarism, the absolute power of the state, control of the economy, anti-Semitism (together with the increased role of Christian national capital) could be harmonized with political goals to a greater extent by following the German example; the pseudorevolutionary character of the Nazi methods, with their social demagoguery, and so on, was not viewed as a threat by Hungarian fascists.

In the 1930s, therefore, when fascist tendencies became stronger in the government and in the party in power, a series of openly fascistic national socialistic groups and parties were formed. It must be emphasized that their leaders and social bases were not the petty bourgeoisie, but the gentry-army officers group that had been important during the counterrevolution of 1919. Their slogans and ideologies were mainly adaptations of those of 1919 and were only completed and modernized by partial adoption of the thoughts and goals of Hitler and Mussolini.

The programs of these new fascist parties were characterized by extreme revisionism, violent anti-Semitism on an increasingly racial basis (although its purely egotistic aspects of material gains were never disguised), the elimination of the liberal deviation from the 1919 counterrevolution, the suppression of the labor movement (both communistic and social democratic), and the national regulation of Jewish finance capital in harmony with "public" interests. Their agrarian program, if one existed, was extremely moderate. The fascists did not try to approach the working class, which was considered to be Marxistic and social democratic and treated accordingly.

Becoming stronger at the beginning of the 1930s, the fascist movement could not free itself from the ideology of the Hungarian gentry, and none of the small national socialistic parties could really get broad mass support. Moreover, during his term as prime minister, Gömbös divided the forces of fascism. The majority of the officer-civil servant stratum supported Gömbös who, they thought, would introduce a totally fascist transformation by introducing a one-party system, by outlawing the Socialist Party and the labor unions, and by building a corporative system. When it became clear that Hitler supported Gömbös unreservedly, and that in the governing party Gömbös was opposed by the large landowning-capitalist groups headed by Bethlen, who after the economic crisis did not attempt to deviate essentially from what had been established during the 1920s, Gömbös got even more support from the extreme right-wing groups.

The hopes of the fascistic elements ended with Gömbös' death. The extreme right recruited from the gentry-officer group, and from the 1930s on drew increasingly upon the help of new, rising elements of the bourgeoisie. It began to back the fully national-socialistic opposition parties more strongly, although it did not abandon hope of taking over power by conquering the governmental party.

Among the parties gaining in influence in 1935 was a new group led by Ferenc Szálasi, a retired staff officer. Originally, this group was not different from the other nationalistic-racist organizations of Hungary after 1919, but certain changes were observable after 1936, when Szálasi, after returning from his study trip to Germany, turned more and more toward the workers. After the autumn of 1937, more and more fascist groups were drawn to Szálasi's party, and the most infamous Hungarian Nazi party, the Arrow Cross Party, was formed with two clearly distinguishable wings. The first wing was composed of the traditional gentry-officer stratum, which was more sympathetic to the ruling classes and less radical, while the other wing, formed from the petty-bourgeois *Lumpenproletariat,* brought a new, extremely demagogic, and violent approach to the chauvinism and anti-Semitism of the first group.

In 1938 the international situation (Anschluss, etc.), the victory of Germany and her increasing influence in world affairs strengthened the Hungarian Arrow Cross movement's influence somewhat among the right wing of the ruling class, but especially among the petty bourgeoisie whose political outlook has, due to the peculiar development of Hungarian capitalism, always been more determined by the gentry than by democratic political trends. At the time of the counterrevolution of 1919 the petty bourgeoisie already formed a passive base within the extreme, right-wing, nationalist revival movements heralded by the popularity of anti-Semitic and anticapitalistic slogans. During the crisis of 1929–32, their economic situation deteriorated but the troubles were blamed, at least in part, on the failure to realize fully the goals of 1919. These people excoriated the state for not being entirely fascist and for still asserting a liberal bourgeois influence. Their oppositionary sentiment did not turn them toward the left, but toward the right, to total fascism, and they supported all of its movements and manifestations. The strengthening of the Hungarian Arrow Cross movement was facilitated by the fact that the government continued to view the left wing as its archenemy and, with the exception of a few minor police measures, did not oppose the Nazis. Moreover, the governmental party, interested in weakening the Arrow Cross movement by gaining the sympathies of its aristocratic members, decided to introduce some fascistic measures of its own and refused to make concessions even to its own left wing. In the autumn of 1938, when the Arrow Crosses were already contemplating the seizure of power, the Imrédy government was not only, after Germany, the first anywhere to introduce anti-Semitic legislation, but it also took the first steps to abolish parliament and to establish a moderate fascist mass movement. These attempts, although provoking some opposition by the conservative wing of the ruling classes, were inadequate to stop the spread of the Arrow Cross movement that had spread among the semi-proletarian element of the petty bourgeoisie and had even penetrated the industrial workers, gaining broad support from among the young unorganized laborers.

The influence of the Nazi movement reached its peak at the end of 1938 and the beginning of 1939, when it had 250,000 members and gained 25 percent of all votes when the secret ballot was used in Hungary for the first time. This success dealt a serious blow to the left-wing parties. The movement did not continue to grow, principally because the fascistic tendencies of the government (largely the anti-Semitic laws), divided the social support of the fascist factions. These laws gave the new bourgeois stratum of gentry and army officers significant economic positions and thus disarmed the moderate ruling gentry-officer wing of the Arrow Cross Party. Even a segment of the petty bourgeoisie received good positions at the expense of the Jewish intelligentsia. Furthermore, the wartime fascist development suddenly gave hopes for a total fascist transformation coming from above, from the government, making a change in party membership unnecessary for fascists.

The wartime economic boom, beginning in 1938, reduced the social tension and unemployment and improved wages. Between 1938 and 1941 German help in regaining some of the territories lost in 1919 increased the vehemence of chauvinistic demagoguery, but reduced antigovernment sentiment. It also became clear that it was safer for the Germans to depend on the pro-German attitude of the traditional ruling classes than to support a Nazi coup (see the events related to the Iron Guard in Romania). Thus the influence of the Arrow Cross Party was reduced sufficiently so that even after the occupation, the Germans had to use traditional right-wing help to effect the total *Gleichschaltung* of Hungary, and the Nazis were put into power only during the last months of the German occupation.

Finally it must be emphasized that the historical literature on fascism has not yet clarified the difference between the classical (German and Italian) and special (including the Hungarian) versions of fascism and the relationship of traditional militarism and fascism. The transition of the conservative reactionary forms (or that of the bourgeois-democratic system) into the modern forms of oppression have not yet been adequately clarified and no proper distinction has been made between periods of the fascist movement's growth and its seizure of power. Knowledge of all these factors will provide a clearer answer to the problems of the political systems of the Southeastern European countries between the two world wars without which the history of fascism in that part of the continent cannot be explained. We need this knowledge because considering fascism simply as a regressive mass movement or as the reactionary manifestation of big capital is a dangerous oversimplification.

B

The Dragon's Teeth:
The Roots of Hungarian Fascism

George Barany

The threefold impact of war, revolution, and counterrevolution has made a sizable portion of the Hungarian intelligentsia, and the underprivileged masses as well, susceptible to extremist political experiments. As a result of the Treaty of Trianon, Hungary lost more than two thirds of her prewar territory and almost the same proportion of her population. From a multinational kingdom, she was transformed into an almost homogeneous Magyar state, which included three to four hundred thousand refugees, of primarily middle-class background, who fled to Hungary from the areas ceded to Czechoslovakia, Romania, and Yugoslavia. Yet about one fourth to one fifth of the Magyars living in the Carpathian Basin remained in these successor states; to reclaim and "redeem" them became one of the main foreign political goals of all Hungarian governments between the two world wars.

Disillusionment with the *Entente*'s treatment of Count Mihály Károlyi's left-radical republican regime and a wave of resurgent Magyar nationalism were factors contributing to the establishment, on March 21, 1919, of a Hungarian Soviet Republic, the first communist government outside Russia to maintain itself for any length of time. Irresponsibility in both foreign and domestic affairs, including the abuse of the masses' sincere desire to find a solution to issues such as the long-overdue land reform, however, caused Béla Kun's fall by August of the same year. After a short period of caretaker administrations and a sad interlude of Romanian occupation of a great part of the country, Hungary succumbed to Admiral Miklós Horthy's "white" regime, the first to consolidate itself in post-World War I Europe, with an openly counterrevolutionary program. For a quarter of a century, the official policy of the Horthy era was based on the triple principle of irredentism, anti-Semitism and antibolshevism.

Irredentism had deep historical roots in the history of modern Magyar nationalism. It was based on the assumption that "thousand-year-old" Hungary was a "natural" historical–geographical unit, to be ruled by Magyar gentlemen, forming the Hungarian political nation; that it was a perverse idea to permit Slavs and Romanians to rule over Magyars; and that it was a moral duty of decent people to convince the leaders of the West of the historical need for making good, in the interest of Central Europe and the civilized world, the tragic error committed at the Paris Peace Conference. Thus, Hungarian irredentism reflected a peculiar mixture of arguments based on alleged historical rights, claims justified by presumed cultural supremacy, and a *sui generis* interpretation of national self-determination. Since the ideological subjects (history, geography, literature, and even religion) were taught in all Hungarian schools in accordance with this Magyar chauvinism and since the Treaty of Trianon, indeed, was not an example of fairness to Hungary from either the ethnic or the economic point of view, the slogan "Justice for Hungary" was to have a strong appeal to most politically articulate Hungarians and, in time, even to some influential circles in the West.

In a sense, the white counterrevolution was a reaction to the short-lived Bolshevik dictatorship. This dictatorship had "in the judgment of the great mass of people, who tend always to simplify and symbolize issues" as Oscar Jászi said, "the appearance of the domination of the town proletariat over the countryside, and of a foreign race, the Jews, over the Christian community."[1] Due to the anticapitalist and antiurban sentiments of an overwhelmingly agrarian society, whose business circles were mostly Jewish, and due to the disproportionately great participation of Jews in the leftist revolutionary movements after the collapse of the Dual Monarchy, the identification of "international" Jewry with both capitalistic exploitation and communist world conspiracy was widely accepted. It was further strengthened by such powerful critiques of Hungary's liberal period as Julius Szekfű's *Three Generations* (*Három nemzedék,* 1920) or Dezső Szabó's *The Village Swept Away* (*Az elsodort falu,* 1919). Populist-racist overtones, however, were only one aspect of that political anti-Semitism that, although not entirely absent from the pre-1914 Hungarian scene, came into its own only after the demise of the Hungarian Soviet Republic. Another form of it was the "white" terror of counterrevolutionary officer corps and military detachments. Hardly more charitable than its "red" predecessor, the "white" terror was ostensibly directed against former Bolsheviks and their sympathizers; in fact, its victims were chiefly Jews who were massacred without regard to age, sex, or active participation in the crimes of the communist misrule.

The white terror was also supposed to teach the workers and peasants: "mind your own business and stop thinking of political rights and social revolution." It lasted well over a year and was gradually abandoned only under foreign pressure, which demanded the restoration of law and order as a condition for granting recognition and economic aid to exhausted Hungary's new regime. In order to avoid relying exclusively on the openly terroristic methods of the Gömbös-led "Awakening Magyars" and other right-wing movements and paramilitary organizations, and also in order to control mistrusted popular passions, the government of Count István Bethlen reverted to the methods of the old, pre-World War I, Hungarian regime. This meant disfranchisement of the popular masses, abandonment of the idea of agrarian reform or any other meaningful social reform, and rescinding the worst excesses of radical racists and nationalists.

Bethlen's stabilization of the counterrevolutionary regime thus implied a more cautious and conservative version of the self-styled "Christian course" whereas Gyula Gömbös, who had excellent connections with the extreme right in both Germany and Italy, advocated a fascist-type concentration of all "truly" national forces against any potential revival of the "red" danger. While both Bethlen and Gömbös wanted to restore Greater Hungary, the former's more refined policies were preferred by Hungary's aristocratic policymakers: monarchists, great landowners, the high clergy, and financial circles. Gömbös, on the other hand, had many friends among army leaders, civil service bureaucrats, middle-class intellectuals, and even among the lower bourgeoisie who were desirous of dynamic leadership and resentful of the "reactionary" clique surrounding Bethlen. It is not without interest to add that in an article entitled "Quo Vadis Europe?" written in July, 1928, Mihály Károlyi has pointed out that Hungarian fascism, unlike its counterparts elsewhere, had its roots in the Magyar gentry and lesser nobility.[2]

In any case, Horthy, who had very close ties with Gömbös, nevertheless followed Bethlen's advice in the period from 1921 to 1931, and paid increasing attention to it again during the late thirties, after the prime ministership of Gömbös in 1932–36. This can perhaps be partly explained by his utter reluctance to rely on popular forces, which the demagogue Gömbös seemed to be quite willing to manipulate, following the example of Mussolini and Hitler.

Yet Horthy agreed with most Hungarian conservatives, who were afraid of playing with fire. Indeed, the regent's turn toward conservatism and his abhorrence of radical political experiments proved to be, in Professor István Deák's words, "a great asset in the stability of the counter-revolution." Not until the last phase of World War II could any domestic or external political force challenge his authority,[3] which, by the end of the thirties, was based on increasing popularity and became one of the few guarantees against a totalitarian coup in a Europe where dictatorships appeared to be in vogue.

In order to obtain respectability at home and abroad, the counterrevolutionary regime was "liberalized" by Bethlen. True, he restricted the franchise to the educated and propertied classes and restored the infamous open ballot everywhere except in the large cities. Thus the regime continued to have comfortable majorities in Parliament where, however, opposition was not altogether absent. This opposition came to a large extent from the Social Democratic Party which was permitted, on the basis of a secret agreement with the government, to organize in the urban areas provided it would not approach government employees. A political amnesty, the restoration of the freedom of the press, and the ignoring of Law XXV of 1920, which restricted the number of Jews in universities, were signs of a more relaxed attitude and of the regime's growing strength and confidence. This confidence was also bolstered by Hungary's admission to the League of Nations in the fall of 1922 and by a "reconstruction loan" received under the auspices of the League in the following year.

All this, of course, did not reflect the regime's sincere desire to introduce democracy in Hungary, or to relinquish its revanchist ideas. The *numerus clausus* law remained on the books and was applied, with increasing rigor, by Bethlen's successors in the thirties. More important, it was Bethlen who suppressed the long-overdue land reform and who, in 1927, concluded a treaty with fascist Italy. The latter, while marking the end of Hungary's diplomatic isolation, was to give Hungary much less maneuvering possibility in the late thirties than Bethlen hoped for at the time of signing the treaty. The "successful" frustration of any attempt at radical agricultural reform, on the other hand, resulted in an undue prolongation of feudal practices in the rural areas for the interwar period; this intended ossification of Hungary's social structure, in turn, deprived the country of the chances of economic modernization through democratic procedures.[4]

Indirectly, then, the social premises for the fascistization of Hungarian life were taking shape well before the full impact of fascism could be felt. Since radical change could not be initiated by the political left due to the experiences with Béla Kun's regime and yet change was bound to come in some form in the age of masses, those who were in favor of radical reform almost inevitably had to turn for guidance to the right. With the "overproduction" of college graduates demanding jobs at a time of world-wide economic depression, and with a sudden change in the international balance of power, many of Bethlen's former supporters began to look for new ideas and guidance, which they thought to have found first in the movement led by Gömbös and later in the one initiated by Béla Imrédy or in even more extreme trends.

Without trying to go into details that can be found in Professor C. A. Macartney's monumental work[5] or Professor Deák's excellent essay already mentioned, I should like to stress the built-in ambivalence characteristic of the Horthy regime. It endeavored to restrict social mobility by keeping people in their place, while walking the tightrope between an old-fashioned, aristocratic parliamentarianism and a fascistic authoritarianism advocated by a younger generation of counterrevolutionaries, who in turn seemed to be supported by the rising tide of totalitarianism all over Europe. The use of Law III of 1921 by the regime is a case in point.

This Law for the More Effective Protection of the Order of the State and Society, as Professor György Ránki has suggested, outlawed the Communist Party by enacting heavy penalties against those who "agitate or summon others to subvert violently or annihilate the legal order of the state and society, especially by demanding the forcible establishment of the exclusive domination of one particular social class."[6] Among the elastic clauses of the act, there were also provisions for "any person who makes or spreads a false statement calculated to reduce the respect for the Hungarian State and nation, or to detract from its good name."[7]

The last quotation reveals that the law could be, and was, indeed used to intimidate or silence all potential and real opponents of the regime, not just communists. True, it served as a legal weapon against communist organizations initially, but in the late thirties, the same law was also used in legal actions against representatives of the extreme right. Upon the publication of his *Sincere History of the Hungarian Nation* in 1937, Ödön Málnási, chief ideologist of the Arrow Cross movement, was convicted by the Budapest courts because "his book was an indictment of the system of large estates which sustained the Hungarian state over the centuries and an inadmissible criticism of the state sustaining capitalist system." Supporting the opinion of the lower courts, the Supreme Court of Hungary approved Málnási's conviction on the basis of Law III of 1921 because "the crime of insulting the nation can be committed not only by a Bolshevik but also by a well-known anti-Bolshevik and patriotic scholar."[8] It is a sad commentary on our times that the same outdated law was also used to "legalize" the mass deportations in Budapest in the summer of 1951.[9]

This example may remind us of the difficulties and ambiguities surrounding any streamlined interpretation of fascism as a twentieth-century phenomenon. If it is true that conservative circles in many European countries and the churches frequently encouraged fascist movements in their endeavor to resist the Bolshevik danger, it is also true, as Ernst Nolte said, that the traditionalist-conservative and the liberal interpretations of fascism tend to regard both fascism, and national socialism, as revolutionary trends dangerously close to bolshevism.[10]

Obviously, there is some oversimplification in this thesis. But it is noteworthy that in Hungary, many of the radical intellectuals called by the umbrella term *village explorers* became supporters of different fascist and national socialist organizations by the second half of the thirties, while others turned to the radical left. However diffuse and inconsistent the political program of the village explorers may have been (the term *program* is inadequate because of the lack of political uniformity among members of the group) one must not ignore the fact that the poet József Erdélyi, or the writer János Kodolányi, to mention but two of the most talented, became members of fascistic parties. Given the influence of populist writings among the new Hungarian intelligentsia, the impact of such "examples" on the fascist-oriented student and youth organizations was far from negligible.[10a]

Furthermore, according to Professor Deák, 41 percent of the membership of Ferenc Szálasi's Party of National Will were workers, 19 percent were professional people, 13 percent were peasants in 1940, and 17 percent were army officers in 1937, at a time when, among industrial workers, the Szálasi Party had to face the competition of Social Democrats and government-sponsored yellow unions and when the government itself tried to harass Szálasi and his supporters. If one adds that the membership of Szálasi's party was over one hundred thousand in 1940,[11] and that in the elections of May, 1939, held under the newly introduced secret ballot, different fascist and national socialist parties obtained 750,000 votes out of a total of approximately two million cast, one may conclude that the fascist disease must have penetrated all strata of Hungarian society fairly deeply by the time of the Second World War. The Arrow Cross Front, which included two deputies elected in Budapest's most industrialized suburb, "Red" Csepel, and at least one member of the Count Festetich, Pálffy, and Széchenyi families, became the strongest oppositional force in Parliament; more important, the government party itself, led by Count Pál Teleki at the time, experienced a shift to the right due to the influence of Imrédy and was thus increasingly forced to take the wind out of the sails of the extreme right.[12]

In looking for an explanation, one has to go beyond sloganlike answers such as the one implied in the indiscriminate identification of "the restored capitalist-feudal regime" with Horthy's "counter-revolutionary fascist dictatorship,"[13] or in the contention that "the conflict between the government circles of the big landowners and big capitalists and the groups of race-defenders" can be reduced to the struggle "between the total and less extreme versions of fascism."[14] Professor George Mosse is entirely right in pointing out that in Hungary (he also refers to Romania) fascism had a considerable appeal to the laboring classes because it tried to bring these segments of society into political participation by making them feel as organic parts of the national community.[15] In this context, he speaks of the relative weakness of the bourgeoisie as compared to the West but tends to identify the Jews with the middle class.[16] This assumption, however, requires critical examination, for, to cite Hugh Seton-Watson without necessarily going along with all his conclusions, "It is misleading to speak of 'the middle class'; there were three distinct middle classes, separated by vertical compartments—bureaucrats, business men, and intelligentsia."[17]

Seton-Watson's remarks show the difficulty inherent in the conceptualization of fascism as a phenomenon related to the appearance and behavior of a certain social class.

Our task, naturally, would be much easier if one could blame the sudden growth of fascist trends in Hungary between 1937 and 1939 on economic misery and ignorance, as was the case with Zoltán Böszörményi's Scythe Cross movement among the most destitute peasants in the early thirties. Although this consideration cannot be dismissed entirely, such an interpretation may reveal, at best, only part of the true picture. One has to keep in mind that some of the worst aspects of the depression had been overcome in Hungary by the latter half of the thirties. Due largely to an ambitious rearmament program enacted by Parliament in May, 1938, industrial output rose well over the production of the peak year 1929, and the number of workers employed in 1938 by the manufacturing industry was higher than in 1929 by more than 22 percent.[18] True, more than half of the country's work force was still employed in agriculture and the number of completely landless agricultural laborers and dwarf holders, families included, was still around three million;[19] industry was unable to absorb this rural overpopulation in the foreseeable future. However, the harvest of 1938 was extraordinarily good, and in good years Hungary had been able to feed her people. Also, by the second half of the thirties, Parliament began to pass moderate social legislation aimed at improving the living conditions and health of the working classes both in the urban and the rural areas.[20]

Furthermore, we know from the replies to a questionnaire sent out by the Social Democratic Party to its local organizations at the end of April, 1937, that Szálasi's as well as other national socialist and fascist parties found little support in the country. This was the year when circles close to Bethlen in the government party started to demand energetic action against right-wing extremists who wanted to transform Hungary into a totalitarian dictatorship; it was also the year when Málnási and Szálasi, the latter because of his antiparliamentary agitation and support of terroristic methods, were first convicted by the courts. Yet by the end of the same year, the different and frequently quarreling right-wing extremist factions and splinter groups agreed on a common platform represented by Szálasi's rather confused "Hungarist" ideology, and on the creation of a united Magyar National Socialist Party.[21]

Szálasi's and the Hungarian National Socialists' subsequent successes, achieved in spite of the attacks directed against them not only by liberals and leftists but also by moderate and conservative right-wing politicians supporting the government, had many causes. First, his arrest and trial gave him an aura of martyrdom in the eyes of those who were disappointed by Gömbös' performance as prime minister and who thought, especially after Gömbös' death, that the government party was not dynamic enough to renovate itself along totalitarian lines in accordance with the spirit of the times. Second, Szálasi and his followers were not afraid of calling the worker "a nation builder"; their social demogoguery and the ruthless methods advocated by them had an undeniable appeal to the masses. Third, Szálasi, due to his background, had excellent connections with the higher echelons of the army without whom no seizure of power could be accomplished. True, his loyalty to Horthy, which was unquestionable until the summer of 1944, may have deprived him of much-needed German help prior to the last phase of the war; on the other hand, the same stubborn insistence on the uniquely Magyar version of national socialism, to which he hoped to win over the Regent, made him less corrupt and more popular than were many of his competitors for leadership within the movement. Even so, his movement would have failed dismally, had it not been for three additional and closely interrelated reasons.

The first of these was the apparently overwhelming success of Nazi Germany in the international arena during the critical years of 1938 and 1939. These successes made it seem that the twentieth century, as Mussolini suggested, belonged to fascism and that the sooner Hungary made the appropriate adjustments, the better she might fare among lesser neighbors, who one after the other had decided to make a sharp turn to the right. This problem, naturally, brings up the issue of Hungary's long-awaited opportunity for territorial revision. After some initial hesitation, but certainly by the end of 1938, it looked as though this opportunity might disappear if Hungary failed to act in time and/or failed to obtain German-Italian support for her ambitions. However, the more dependent she became on this support, the less independent she turned out to be not only in foreign but also in domestic affairs. It proved to be very difficult, indeed, to rely on the help of the Axis powers in international relations and to try to stem the tide of fascism on the domestic scene, especially when the government, too, was prone to use restrictive police measures and refused, for example, passports to people who wanted to leave the country.[22] The privileges granted to the German *Volksgruppe* is a case in point, since the German minority's official representation, the *Volksbund,* soon became the Nazi organization *par excellence* that, for all practical purposes, enjoyed extraterritorial rights in Hungary. Another example is the revival of the infamous Ragged Guard (*Rongyos Gárda*) of Iván Héjjas, which obtained notoriety at the time of the Sopron (Ödenburg) plebiscite at the end of World War I. During the Czechoslovak and Ruthenian crises in late 1938 and early 1939, the government encouraged the formation of a new Ragged Guard out of hooligan and Arrow Cross elements, and connived at both the illegal raids by the Ragged Guard against Slovakia and Ruthenia[23] and at the excesses it committed against the Jewish population of the Northeastern countries.

In the endeavor to outdo, or at least neutralize, the most dangerous Hungarian Nazis, the government itself resorted to outright Nazi practices as shown by the series of increasingly inhuman anti-Jewish laws enacted in the years 1938–41. Without overstating the case, I should like to suggest that it was this vicious legislation that corrupted and undermined the moral resistance of the Hungarian people at large. It whetted the appetite of those whose greed was not satiated by legislative action alone, and confused those law-abiding citizens who otherwise would not have dared to take away the jobs, property, or lives of others. Few, very few, political or spiritual leaders ventured to raise their voices against the spread of the Nazi disease, and even smaller was the number of those who dared to do so in public. One of these few was Endre Bajcsy-Zsilinszky, Gömbös' former friend and himself a "race defender" in the early twenties. Yet most of those whose integrity and decency remained intact were left to themselves and isolated from one another; this loneliness amidst rampant inhumanity enforced by totalitarianism is one of the most horrible aspects of our age and Hungary, of course, is only one of the pertinent case studies.

The growth of fascism in Hungary could not be stopped when, after Miklós Kállay's appointment as Prime Minister in 1942, Hungary began to seek contacts with the Anglo-Saxon powers with the purpose of abandoning the Axis. This was the period when the rather weak Hungarian resistance movement, the origins of which could be traced back to the creation of the so-called March Front in 1937, began to organize with the government's tacit approval. It was also the time when Hungary, at least temporarily, became a real haven for Jewish refugees, former members of the Polish army, and Allied prisoners of war.

Yet the Kállay government's policy had very severe limitations. Its ambiguous attitude gave the Germans ample opportunity to exert increasing pressure on it by favoring their other satellites in Central Europe and by strengthening their connections with the extreme right both within and outside the administration and government party. Given the country's complete military and economic dependence on Germany, the situation was increasingly precarious, since even anti-German elements were determined to maintain Hungarian supremacy in the Carpathian Basin. This Magyar neoimperialism, which first relied on the ethnic principle in order to disrupt Czechoslovakia, Yugoslavia, and Romania, was quite willing to incorporate non-Magyar masses on the basis of the old theory concerning the unity of the lands belonging to the crown of St. Stephen. But the non-Magyars who lived in the areas returned to Hungary in 1938–41 were treated as second-class citizens, and frequently had to suffer, along with the Jews, from some of the most horrible excesses committed against a civilian population.

True, tradition-bound Magyar imperialism, despite its anti-Semitic racial overtones, was basically in conflict with *völkisch* thinking as shown by the Teleki government's angry and somewhat hypocritical reaction to the bill introduced by the Arrow Cross Party in Parliament in June, 1940. This bill would have recognized the ethnic-political entity of all non-Magyar "nation-sustaining" i.e., "Aryan" *Volksgruppen.* It was a sharp deviation from the concept of the unitary Hungarian political nation incorporated in the Compromise of 1867 and in the Hungarian Nationality Law of 1868, although the introductory part of the bill payed lip service to the Hungarian imperial idea. The latter, however, was formulated in accordance with the interests of national socialist Germany. To be sure, the Teleki government succeeded in frustrating the Arrow Cross Party's obvious bid for German support; but in the process, it had to resort to fascist methods, which ultimately helped the Germans to obtain the recognition of the *völkisch* principle with regard to the German minority.[24]

The emphasis on Magyardom's manifest destiny in the Danubian region, on spiritual–historical rather than ethnic–*völkisch* grounds, may have reflected in the given historical circumstances, at least theoretically, a confirmation of Hungarian goals not necessarily approved by Germany. Viewed from the Slovak, Ruthenian, Serb, or Romanian standpoint, however, it mattered little on what grounds the Magyar ruling castes claimed to be the master race, even in the shadow of Nazi power. What was important was the fact that the attitude of the Magyar government, aimed at keeping everything obtained with the help of the Axis, made it all but impossible to create a moral basis for anti-German national unity, let alone to reach agreement with other people's antifascist forces. All that was accomplished was a certain ambivalence about German-Hungarian relations in the minds of those who were not outright supporters or victims of the Nazis. Even in situations when anti-German popular indignation ran high, e.g., in the critical months when the fate of Ruthenia (Carpatho-Ukraine) was decided or when Ribbentrop was accused of having "stolen" Bratislava (Pozsony) from Hungary to which it "rightfully" belonged,[25] the government endeavored to use the chauvinistic mood of the masses only to impress the Germans and not to build up moral resistance against them.

The Germans, of course, were not much impressed. Hitler knew how to take advantage of the conflicting nationalisms in the East Central European power vacuum after Munich. But if the shift in the balance of power that favored Germany may serve as a background and even an explanation of the extreme right's victory in Hungary during the last year of World War II, it ought not to absolve those who held responsible positions in the administration, in the churches, or in the educational institutions. Their failure to live up to the expectations of humanity because the presumed interests of Magyardom seemed to be in conflict with elemental human rights must not be ignored, let alone justified by the historian. One need not necessarily share the view that the very establishment of the Horthy regime in 1919 made the Nazi alliance inevitable[26] in order to see that those guilty of silence when it was time to speak in order to avoid becoming "an accomplice among the guilty," as the great Catholic poet Mihály Babits put it in his last work, the *Book of Jonah* (1941),[27] also contributed to the sowing of dragon's teeth that was bound to bring some bitter fruits.

FOOTNOTES

1 Oscar Jászi, *Revolution and Counter-Revolution in Hungary* (London: P. S. King and Son, 1924), p. 156.

2 *Károlyi Mihály Válogatott Irásai*, 1920–1946, 2 vols. (Budapest: Gondolat, 1964), 1:218–41.

3 István Deák, "Hungary," in *The European Right*, Hans Rogger and Eugen Weber, eds. (Berkeley and Los Angeles: University of California Press, 1965), p. 373 f.

4 John Kosa, "Hungarian Society in the Time of the Regency (1920–1944)," *Journal of Central European Affairs* 16 (1956):254 f., 259–62.

5 C. A. Macartney, *October Fifteenth, A History of Modern Hungary*, 2 vols., 2d ed. (Edinburgh: 1961).

6 Erik Molnár, Ervin Pamlényi, and György Székely, eds., *Magyarország története*, 2 vols. (Budapest: Gondolat, 1964), 2:377.

7 As cited by Jászi, *Revolution and Counter-Revolution*, p. 184. For a detailed interpretation of the law, its amplifications, and its application in subsequent years by the courts, see Pál Angyal and Gyula Isaák, *Büntető törvénykönyv*, 4th ed., 2 vols. (Budapest: Grill, 1941), 2: 430–60. Paragraphs 1 and 2 and 5–8 of Act III of 1921 provided for "supplementary" punishments including deportation in the case of aliens and forcible designation of residence in the case of Hungarian citizens. Cf. ibid., p. 457.

8 Ödön Málnási, *A magyar nemzet öszinte története*, 2d enlarged ed. (Munich: 1959), p. 292 f.

9 Angyal-Isaák, *Büntető törvénykönyv*, 2:457 and William Solyom Fekete, "Draft of the New Hungarian Penal Code," *The Hungarian Quarterly* 1 (1961):48.

10 Ernst Nolte, *Three Faces of Fascism*, trans. Leila Vennewitz (New York: Holt, Rinehart & Winston, 1965), p. 18 f.

10ª George Gömöri, "Social Conflicts in Hungarian Literature, 1920–1965," *Journal of International Affairs* 20 (1966):152 ff., 159 f.

11 Deák, "Hungary," p. 396 f.

12 Macartney, *October Fifteenth*, 1:349 f.

13 I. T. Berend and G. Ránki, "The Hungarian Manufacturing Industry, Its Place in Europe," *Etudes historiques*. Publié par la Commission Nationale des Historiens Hongrois, 2 vols. (Budapest: 1960), 2:436.

14 Molnár-Pamlényi-Székely, eds., *Magyarország története*, 2:382.

15 George Mosse, "Introduction: The Genesis of Fascism," in "International Fascism 1920–1945," *Journal of Contemporary History* 1 (1966):21.

16 Ibid., pp. 21 and 24.

17 Hugh Seton-Watson, "Fascism, Right and Left," ibid., p. 192.

18 Berend-Ránki, "The Hungarian Manufacturing Industry," p. 446.

19 Mihály Kerék, *A magyar földkérdés* (Budapest: MEFHOSZ, 1939), pp. 344–48.

20 Macartney, *October Fifteenth*, 1:133, 179, 191; and Miklós Lackó, "A magyarországi nyilas mozgalom történetéhez (1935–37)," *Századok* 97 (1963):802.

21 Ibid., pp. 791–807. For a few samples of Szálasi's ideas, see Eugen Weber, *Varieties of Fascism* (Princeton: Anvil Paperback, 1964), pp. 92–96, 156–64.

22 Hungarian authorities refused passports to Jews at a time when Nazi Germany encouraged Jewish emigration. Cf. John Kosa, "A Century of Hungarian Emigration, 1850–1950," *The American Slavic and East European Review*, 16 (1957):509. For more information and references, see Randolph L. Braham, "Hungarian Jewry: An Historical Retrospect," *Journal of Central European Affairs* 20 (1960):5–15.

23 Cf. Docs. 65–70 in *Magyarország és a második világháboru*, Magda Ádám, Gyula Juhász, and Lajos Kerekes, eds. (Budapest: Kossuth, 1959), pp. 177–88.

Juhász, and Lajos Kerekes, eds., (Budapest: Kossuth, 1959), pp. 177–88.

24 Lóránt Tilkovszky, "A nyilasok törvényjavaslata a nemzetiségi kérdés rendezéséről," *Századok* 99 (1965):1247–58.

25 At the end of 1938, one could hear high school children shouting: "Ribbentrop/Pozsonyt lop" at solemn demonstrations organized by the authorities on the squares surrounding the Hungarian flag ("Ereklyés Országzászló") which was at half mast as a sign of mourning for the territories lost at Trianon.

26 György Ránki, *Emlékiratok és valósag Magyarország második világháborús szerepéről* (Budapest: Kossuth, 1964), pp. 17 f. Cf. Miksa Fenyő's excellent review of this book, "Clio, mint mindig, zavarban," *Irodalmi Ujság* (Paris) Jan. 15, 1965, pp. 6 f.

27 "Mert vétkesek közt cinkos aki néma" (*Jonás könyve,* III, rész.)

V
Poland

Henryk Wereszycki

Piotr S. Wandycz

A

Fascism in Poland

Henryk Wereszycki

The first question that the historian of the period between the two world wars has to ask himself is: was there really any fascism in Poland? Obviously, the answer to this question will depend on what we regard as fascism. If one considers that until the very collapse of interwar Poland, the opposition parties were legally active, that their papers and periodicals, as well as other journals totally independent of governmental inspiration, were freely published, that, although all strikingly antigovernmental utterances in the press were suppressed, it was still possible to express legally, both orally and in print, opinions combating the existing system of government, then one will have to admit that the authoritarian government that had existed in Poland since 1926 was *not* totalitarian. In fact, besides the legal opposition parties there were numerous other organizations, like the trade unions, whose membership reached several hundred thousand, whose activity was legal, and whose membership was not liable to persecution. On the other hand, it is incontestable that both the political and the social organizations controlled by governmental authorities were highly privileged. Thus one may define the system of government in Poland between 1926 and 1939 as semi-fascist. But within that system one can trace the constant and gradual evolution from a very moderate dictatorship, one conditioning and limiting the personal and political freedom of individuals and groups, to a more and more pronounced dictatorship, introducing rule by police measures.

However, the specific character of Polish fascism went beyond the police state. Compared to the fascist systems in other countries of contemporary Europe, the first important difference was the fact that the politico-military group that had come into power in 1926 did not, at first, have anything in common with fascist ideology. If classic fascist ideology consists of promoting extreme nationalism, in the negation of any kind of liberalism in the political sphere, we will observe that just this variety of fascism was promoted, not by the faction of Józef Piłsudski when it assumed power, but by the opposition, the extremist right-wing group. In a country where 30 percent of the population were not Polish, and one third of this figure were Jews, fascism would assert that these national minorities, the Jews particularly, were Poland's enemies and ought to be eliminated. Actually these views were not promoted by the leading group in Poland until the very last years of the interwar republic, and even then it was propounded with relative restraint, and against opposition from others in the government. It is true, nevertheless, that extremist nationalism was expounded and promoted by

85

certain right-wing political groups from the time of the establishment of the Polish state in 1919.

Certain of these ideas were gradually accepted by Piłsudski's camp, over a period of years. Acceptance accelerated after Piłsudski's death in 1935 when the ruling group, which had always depended on and referred to the authority of that "man of genius," suddenly faced an extremely difficult situation: the necessity of carrying on a dictatorship without an acknowledged dictator. It was only then that the government started borrowing arguments of fascist propaganda from its adversaries, the adherents of a truly fascist ideology. They did not accept them fully at any time, however, and thus, ultimately, what was known as Marshal Piłsudski's ideology, never clearly defined, cannot be regarded as truly fascist. If analogies are permissible, one could suggest that the policies formulated by General de Gaulle are rather similar to those promoted in Poland under Piłsudski's rule. These, as far as France is concerned, cannot be regarded as fascism.

To account for this specific feature of the Polish fascism or pseudo-fascism, one must go back to the time when the Polish state, restored after its century-and-a-half bondage, was beginning to rebuild.

It began in a historical moment when revolutionary tension was at its highest in Eastern Europe. To the east, the October Revolution was struggling for its existence in Russia; to the west, the German Reich was going through violent paroxysms of political and social revolution. The Polish state was structured while the Red Army was striving to take control of Poland, to provide a highway for the universal revolution —access to Germany, and introduction there of the socialist system. This was the essential condition for the scheduled communist rule in Europe.

Under these circumstances the political power of the working class in Poland was so strong that it was impossible for the state to take any action against it. On the positive side, assisting the establishment of the government was an extremely strong Polish tradition of fighting for national freedom. This struggle had been conducted by several successive generations with the greatest devotion. Moreover, the most ardent fighters for national freedom of the World War I generation were associated with the socialist movement and they nurtured the deep conviction that the social liberation of the working class was necessary not only for national freedom but also for the rebuilding of a Polish state that would justify the heavy sacrifices of all past generations. Thus when the foundations for the new state were laid the working class was granted far-reaching social privileges. The social assistance and legislative privileges it received were, at that time, more extensive than in any other capitalist country. All this, however, occurred in a largely agricultural country whose economic standards were low and obsolete. The technological development of industry was slight, and additionally, much of what industry there was had been devastated by war. Nor was agriculture modern, either in method or equipment. Thus the privileges granted to the working class were in striking disproportion to the economic basis of the country as a whole. The most modern social legislation was applied to obsolete economics, adding to the overwhelming difficulties that the parliamentary-democratic government established by the 1921 constitution had to face.

Another significant social problem was presented by the villages. Since two thirds of the population were rural and dependent on agriculture, a democratic constitution had to grant the peasants a decisive influence on the political and, above all, on the economic policy of the state. The rural population was divided by a deep class conflict: on the one side were the rich landowners and the well-to-do peasants; on the other, the masses of land-starved or even landless, peasantry.

The question of the land reform and the dissolution of the big estates became, therefore, a social issue of the first importance. It was in the wealthy peasant's interest that reform would enable him to purchase land; he would be able to consolidate his economic position and, as a result, his social position as well. On the other hand, the poor peasants strove for enforced division and the expropriation of the greater part of big landed property with subsequent distribution among the landless, for very little charge. On principle each of the political groups, even the representatives of the big estates, admitted the necessity for land reform. The example set by the Russian revolution was too close at hand and too instructive to make it possible, at least during the first years of independence, to avoid all change in the system of agriculture. Obviously, however, it was to the interest of the big landowners to support the program of the rich peasant-farmers because such a division of their estates would give them sufficient capital to invest, either in the technical improvement of any land they retained or in industrial enterprises. Thus the conditions were favorable for a coalition of the rich peasant-farmers and the owners of big landed property. It must be realized that the big landowners, with the lower middle class, were the main political supporters of the nationalistic camp during the generation before World War I. As a result, once a democratic constitution was introduced, the rule of a coalition consisting of the political right wing and the center was quite natural and expectable. But such a coalition meant a highly reactionary and right-wing social policy in Poland. Moreover, the only real and basic solution to the social problem was to industrialize the country, since even the most radical land reform would have been unable to solve the problem of overpopulation in the villages. Before World War I, the surplus village population found an outlet in emigration, either temporary—for the harvest time only—or permanently. The limitation of immigration by the United States had deep effects in the Polish villages. Tremendous capital was needed to turn Poland into an industrialized country, and around 1924 those in charge of the Polish economy expected to get these resources. They had managed to stabilize the currency to create favorable conditions for the allocation of foreign capital. Owing to German hostility towards Poland, however, the capital failed to come, for it was through German channels that capital from America and England was transferred to Poland. It was clearly against German interests to help Poland secure foreign capital, which would have helped consolidate the new state. The only way left was to build, with a proper fiscal policy, an industry out of the state's own resources. To this, predictably, the farmers and peasants provided most of the opposition. Once the Polish government had been established and once, as a result of the democratic system, it became dependent upon the big and medium-sized landowners, the government found it impossible to carry out an economic policy of industrialization. This by itself was enough to produce tendencies hostile to the democratic system of government and to favor the introduction of some kind of dictatorship.

Finally, the third extremely significant problem making it difficult to reconcile the democratic system to the needs of an economy in urgent need of modernization was the state's national composition. In 1921 Poland had incorporated in her eastern provinces areas inhabited by homogeneous masses of non-Poles, mostly Ukrainians and White Russians. While the White Russians, who had no state traditions of their own, reluctantly accepted the new state, the Ukrainians, led by politicians from Eastern Galicia, had strong political aspirations. In 1918–19 they fought Poland for their own state, having evolved since the last decades of the nineteenth century their own national institutions by taking advantage of the relatively liberal attitude of the Austrian state. As a result they did not wish to see the establishment of another state in areas they considered their own. On the other hand, at least two million Poles whom no Polish state could leave under Ukrainian rule lived in East Galicia. The result of this conflict was that the representatives of national minorities, who constituted an important force in the Polish parliament, did not really give their support to any of the successive Polish governments. Thus at no time did proper conditions exist for the creation of a government based on a strong and solid parliamentary majority, and the most important and difficult social and economic issues could be dealt with through parliamentary channels only with the utmost difficulty. This necessarily contributed further to the weakening of the whole political system, facilitated the formation and promotion of ideas tending towards nonparliamentary government, and made Poland liable to the lure of fascist tendencies.

The first fascistic measures were introduced by the right-wing circles around 1923, but earlier, the murder of the first president of the Republic, Gabryel Narutowicz, in December, 1922, was a result of extreme nationalistic tendencies. He had been elected president by the majority of the General Assembly in which representatives of national minorities sat also. This fact led to a campaign by the nationalists that convinced the assassin—a fanatic not associated with any organization—to commit his crime. These extremist nationalists later tried to make him into a sort of national hero, at a time when attempts were made to organize a conspiracy of a definitely fascist character. The plot was immediately discovered by the police and so did not lead to a formidable organization. Nevertheless, in 1926 the leader of the political right, Roman Dmowski, founded the "Great Poland Camp" organization. Based on the leader principle, it was noted for its extremely nationalistic and imperialistic ideology, but lacked a definite economic program. It was closely associated with youth organizations and had a particularly strong effect on the undergraduates.

The years 1925–26 brought an economic crisis to Poland. The newly introduced currency could not be supported, unemployment was spreading, and coalition governments were formed that were supported by markedly unstable majorities. The politicians, who gave their support to these coalitions, were conscious of the fact that the parliamentary system itself had been challenged. Fascism, which already had won in Italy, suggested a salutary solution in overcoming the overwhelming difficulties that the new state had to face in the economic and social fields. The young people as well as some groups of the intelligentsia, which for the last few generations had been very influential in Poland, were of the opinion that direct action, disregarding the parliamentary requirements, would solve the accumulating problems better and more effectively. On the other hand, those among the intelligentsia who had been most active in the struggle for independence and had actually won it were deeply attached to ideals of liberty, to complete liberalism. There was a distinct division on this question between left and right. The intelligentsia connected with the right wing was nationalistic and antiliberal, while those associated with the left wished to solve the social and national problems by reforms and by granting wide autonomy to other nationalities inhabiting Poland.

Around 1925 the whole political community was expecting a coup d'état, which, they were sure, would have a fascist character. It was not clear who would instigate it, Roman Dmowski or General Władisław Sikorski. Sikorski had been among the officers who had fought during the war with Piłsudski and others in the Legions, a military unit created in 1914 within the Austrian army, which, according to tradition, was to fight against tsarist Russia for a free Poland. But during the war a sharp conflict had arisen between these two military men and politicians. As early as 1916, Piłsudski began backing away from the Central European empires, whereas Sikorski faithfully stuck to the original conception. Later Piłsudski was put into a German prison, which eventually led to his coming into power in 1918. Sikorski favored the Central Powers to the very end of the war, but in 1919–20 he fought under Piłsudski's command and gave an excellent account of himself. Initially, at the time of the first internal tension associated with President Narutowicz's death, Sikorski, side by side with Piłsudski, attacked the right wing. But in the next few years their political paths drifted apart. The political right began supporting Sikorski against Piłsudski. There was a series of deep personal misunderstandings and differences of opinion between these two men when Sikorski, then Minister of War, opposed Piłsudski's views on the organization of the supreme military powers. It seemed that if there was to be a coup d'état, Sikorski would be its author.

In May, 1926, when a government backed by a wide coalition fell and a new government was formed that represented the right wing and the center, and was headed by Wincenty Witos, the leader of the rich peasantry, Piłsudski made his coup d'état. He, as the outstanding leader of the left, was supported by all the leftist parties, who saw in his attempt a counterattack against the threat of the planned fascist coup. He was backed not only by the political associations representative of the poor peasantry, but by the socialists, and even the communists. It was only a few months after that coup, which had put an end to the system of parliamentary government in the country, that it was possible to realize that Piłsudski, far from fulfilling the leftist postulates, was looking for support from the right, despite his lifelong antagonism to nationalistic groups and associations.

The first years of Piłsudski's dictatorship were years of relative prosperity. As a result the government was able to consolidate the currency as well as undertake some large-scale investments necessary for the economic stabilization of the new state. A modern port was constructed at Gdynia, formerly a small seaside resort, which was to make Poland independent of the hostile policy of the Free Town of Gdansk (Danzig), which up to that time had been the only Polish harbor. Furthermore a big plant for artificial fertilizers was erected to improve agriculture and to serve, in case of war, as the basis for the ammunition industry. The rules and regulations of the democratic-parliamentary constitutions of 1921 were formally respected. The only change was that in August, 1926, the president, a man devoted to Piłsudski, was legally granted markedly increased prerogatives. The general election of 1928 tremendously increased the power of the left, while weakening the position of the right and center. Yet it also brought into parliament a strong pro-government group that was awarded a dispropor-tionately large number of mandates due, incidentally, to a mild and formally legal pressure exerted by the administrative apparatus.

Thus until 1930 there can be no question of any fascist government in Poland. The government was authoritarian, in fact a dictatorship whose main supporters were the army and the bureaucracy, but which nevertheless respected, on the whole, the principles of a liberal and legal state.

It was only as a result of the great economic crisis and of the growing tension caused by the opposition from the left that the previous system was radically changed. In 1930 the president dissolved the parliament, while the leaders of the opposition, those of the left and center in particular, were illegally imprisoned. They were kept in prison during the next elections that, as a result of a now very definite pressure of the administrative apparatus, gave an absolute parliamentary majority to the government's candidates. After the election the imprisoned politicians were set free, but legal action was instituted against them; some went back to prison, some others went to live abroad.

This was the beginning of a real police rule. But still the formally valid constitution continued to be respected because the government's parliamentary majority was insufficient to change the constitution. The opposition was based almost exclusively on the left. The economic crisis resulted in a social upheaval: both workers and peasants went on strike, and there were some bloody incidents. The police repression became more and more drastic.

The fact that Hitler had taken over in Germany gave a violent impetus to the growth of fascist tendencies in Poland. It was striking, though, that these influences were spreading both within part of the government camp, which was disintegrating as Piłsudski's health worsened, and also in the ranks of the extreme right. In the governmental camp some deeply rooted socialistic and democratic traditions, deriving from the time when Piłsudski and his men on the eve of World War I had been preparing the military struggle against the tsarist rule, continued to survive. But there was also a rather large group of governmental politicians, particularly officers who had served in the intelligence division during the war, among whom could be detected a marked tendency to shake off all legality and, if necessary, to rule with an iron hand. These politicians were known as the colonels' group, and were obviously motivated by the example set by Italian and German fascism, although by no means adhering to the latter's extreme nationalistic or anti-Semitic ideology.

On the other hand, the right wing formed youth groups. Unimportant at first, then increasingly strong, these associations were looking for an opportunity to apply the methods and ideas promoted by Hitler. They were eager to take over the country and were opposed to the older right-wing politicians who still, to some extent, had remained true to the liberal ideology of their youth. This group of young men, who around 1934 had started on an open campaign of a distinctly fascist character, was led by Roman Dmowski. At first some steps were taken against them. They were even, for a short time, interned in the concentration camp established in 1934 at Bereza Kartuska, a place originally used for adversaries of the government, formerly communists or radical Ukrainian or White-Russian politicians.

Nevertheless, the anti-Semitic campaign was less and less opposed by the authorities. This became strikingly evident during the rows that usually took place at the beginning of the academic year at universities and colleges where, it was claimed, *numerus clausus* should be introduced for the Jewish students. These forces also asked that Jewish students be isolated in lecture halls. Although formally the authorities were against these measures, it was felt that their opposition was merely to save appearances.

Piłsudski's death, in 1935, quickened the fascistic tendencies. The government camp was in large measure supported by the great personal prestige of Marshal Piłsudski, and after his death it became imperative to find some broad social support for the government, which was torn by dissident forces. Some politicians wished to renew their former understanding with the left wing and to liberalize policies in general; others sought support from the right wing. Eventually, General Eduard Rydz-Śmigły was made Piłsudski's successor, and was soon converted to the idea of seeking support among the adherents of fascism. Agreements with young fascist politicians that had been formerly in opposition to the government were concluded. Finally, Rydz-Śmigły resolved to form a governmental party of fascist character, and the young fascist politicians were also captivated by the idea. But the action did not come easily, for within the government itself strong liberal traditions had to be overcome. Nevertheless, the evolution progressed distinctly although slowly towards the subjection of Poland —first to the doctrine, and then to the practice, of fascism. This tendency was greatly facilitated by the changed constitution which, in a semilegal way, had been introduced in April, 1935, or a month before the death of Marshal Piłsudski. The new election regulations included in that constitution were undemocratic in the extreme, and as a result the parliamentary elections held in accordance with the new regulations were boycotted by nearly all opposition parties, left as well as right. In 1938 all the indications were that Poland would soon become truly fascistic, but the change in the international situation, the suddenly revealed conflict with Germany, put the process in check. The government, realizing the threat from Hitler's Germany, discontinued its search for support in the community. Then the Second World War broke out, and the Polish state, created in 1918, fell and was subjugated by the enemy.

B

Fascism in Poland: 1918–1939

Piotr S. Wandycz

When Marshal Józef Piłsudski came to open a session of the Polish *sejm* on March 27, 1928, communist deputies greeted him with cries of "down with the fascist government." Police intervened and removed the shouting deputies from the chamber but the manifestation created a stir. The use of the word *fascist,* however, was not new. Polish communists had applied it two years earlier to the government overthrown by Piłsudski; they were to use it against their opponents in the years to come. Even the socialists did not escape being dubbed "social-fascists" in the 1930s, and the term—like the epithet *Judaeo-Communism* that Polish rightists applied indiscriminately to their democratic opponents—remained part of the political vocabulary. Its meaning was vague and loaded with emotion.

Who were the facists in interwar Poland? Can we use the word with any precision to describe a particular group or party?

After Piłsudski's coup d'état in 1926, Poland entered on a path leading toward dictatorship and an authoritarian regime. The Marshal was the strong man of Polish politics, and one is tempted to look first for analogies between him and Benito Mussolini. But such a search yields disappointing results. Both men shared a socialist background, and the march on Rome and the May events in Warsaw marked a new stage in the history of the two countries, but otherwise one finds only dissimilarities. Piłsudski was not a doctrinaire politician, and he avowed, quoting Goethe, that *die Theorie ist immer grau.* He had received power from practically all groups in the country in 1918, and officially from the hands of the *sejm*—when the first constituent *sejm* assembled—in 1919. Though ever more impatient with party politics, he tried to govern according to the laws of the land. When unable to adapt himself to the new constitution, he resigned in 1923 and went into seclusion—like de Gaulle, not like Mussolini.

The coup d'état of 1926 had no markings of a fascist revolution. Piłsudski struggled against a center-rightist government, and socialists and communists were on his side. A real or imaginary danger of a leftist takeover that would alarm the middle classes and prompt them to back the rightist extremists—as in Italy or Germany—was absent in the Polish political situation of 1926. A French journalist asked the Marshal point blank whether he was a supporter of fascism, and the latter replied: "I think that nothing like that could be introduced in Poland. People are patient but they must sincerely trust their leaders; they would not tolerate such use of force by small local organizations. No, this is not for us." Piłsudski made another remark about fascism, when he spoke of his coup d'état. He discussed the general crisis of parliamentary government throughout Europe, and asserted that a showdown was unavoidable. It came in Poland earlier and took a sharper form than in other countries, except in Italy, but Piłsudski saw the solution in strengthening the executive, not in introducing a new form of political, social, and economic organization.

The Marshal said on several occasions that he disliked governing through violence. He spoke of "the whip" that he refused to wield, and which he considered contrary to Polish traditions. But he wanted more power for the government and less for the omnipotent *sejm,* which he associated with all the evil practices in Polish political life. He attacked corruption, irresponsibility, and party politics. Having spent the best years of his life in relentless struggle against overwhelming odds, Piłsudski grew tired, impatient, and intolerant. A group of admiring followers that surrounded him accepted his word as gospel. It was a paradox of history that the Marshal assumed supreme rule over Poland when his forces were almost exhausted. And as is the case with many great personalities, his decisions were executed by little men, whose zeal outran their capacities.

No real political party came into existence to back the new regime; Piłsudski disliked parties, and his followers had no clear program. The Marshal had balanced the Right and the Left in the country, but introduced no new ideology. The interest of the state, variously interpreted and understood, was the magic phrase that concealed the weakness of economic or social ideas. The organization that stood behind him and strove to capture the majority in parliament bore the fitting name of Non-Partisan Bloc of Cooperation with the Government (BBWR) and its precepts were: maintain a strong executive, and cure the country's ailments. It included men of all walks of life and of many political orientations. If the democratic and leftist elements were originally predominant—Piłsudski and most of his followers came of a socialist or radical background—moderates and conservatives swelled the ranks of the organization.

In 1930 the government struck against the mounting opposition of the center and left parties. Their leaders were arrested, ill-treated, and sentenced to short terms of imprisonment. Some left the country. The regime, by this first act of overt brutality, succeeded in overawing political parties, and followed up its success by obtaining a parliamentary majority, which allowed it to pass an authoritarian constitution. A new electoral law, devised to operate against the opposition, met with a boycott of political parties. From 1935 on Poland had a colorless *sejm,* unrepresentative of major political trends in the country. More, it was now a dictatorship without a dictator, for the long ailing Piłsudski died in May, 1935.

The situation of the country was curious and tragic. Democracy had yielded to fascism, national socialism, or dictatorial regimes in many European states. Even in traditionally democratic France, Britain, and Belgium, such movements as the *Croix de feu,* Sir Oswald Mosley's blackshirts, and Léon Degrelle's Rexists attempted to win power. Spain became a battlefield. In the midst of European turmoil the Polish state had no clear bearings, and fascist victories and exploits abroad appealed to the imagination of some groups in the country. The government composed of Piłsudski's followers sought a wider basis for its rule. With the disappearance of BBWR, which had accomplished its purpose by introducing the 1935 constitution and which its leader, Walery Slawek refused to transform into a political party, there was need for a new ideology and a mass organization.

Two people came to occupy dominant positions in Poland in 1935: the President of the Republic, Professor Ignacy Mościcki, and the Commander-in-Chief, General Eduard Rydz-Śmigły. They naturally competed with one another. From May, 1936, Rydz-Śmigły began a political offensive. In a much publicized speech he announced the need of national consolidation, prelude to creation of a new political party. Two months later the general became officially "the second person" in the state. In November he was created Marshal of Poland. A good soldier and a talented individual but hardly a great statesman, Rydz-Śmigły sought, or was being encouraged to seek, the leading position in the state, vacated by Piłsudski's death. The new organization that appeared a few months later was destined to be his chief pillar of support.

In February, 1937, Colonel Adam Koc, a man close to the new marshal, officially announced in a radio broadcast the program of a new party, named the Camp of National Unity (*Obóz Zjednoczenia Narodowego*, shortened to OZN). The name of the movement indicated that it was to embrace the largest possible membership grouped on the basis of national solidarity, but its ideology was hazy and general. The OZN program accepted the authoritarian 1935 constitution as the foundation of state organization, and spoke of special prerogatives for the commander-in-chief. It put its emphasis on the consolidation and strengthening of the state. This stress was understandable in view of Poland's past and the double threat to the state from Germany and Russia. But it implied clear subordination of citizens' interests—social, economic, and political—to the omnipotence of the state. The program spoke of national consolidation, not of elimination of existing parties, but some historians believe elimination was implied. Catholicism appeared as the principal religion of the state, but the program favored religious toleration. It stressed private property and attacked the concept of class struggle. There was no original approach to economic and social problems, which on the whole received little attention. As for national minorities, the OZN was to respect their distinctiveness but seemed to favor economic struggle against the Jews although brutal attacks on the Jewish population were explicitly condemned.

All this was extremely vague. Socially and economically the program was conservative and it glossed over the real issues in the country. In contrast to BBWR, which made no differences between Polish citizens, the new party moved over to a nationalist position. Imprecise formulations were meant to attract various groups under the banner of OZN, and administrative pressure later swelled the ranks of the party. According to a prominent member of the government camp, OZN was based on three principles: nationalism, social justice, and organization.

The proclamation of Koc met with widespread criticism by the leading political parties. The Right from which OZN tried to steal the nationalist thunder was annoyed; the Left spoke of fascist tendencies of the new organization. There is no doubt that some fascist or pseudo-fascist overtones existed in OZN. The leader, his chief of staff, and sectional leaders were nominated, not elected. The party attempted to establish a cult of leadership; veneration for the dead leader Piłsudski combined with exaltation of the new leading figure, Rydz-Śmigły. OZN, unlike any fascist party, did not emerge spontaneously but was imposed from above. In essence it was a government party, an administrative formation, and its impressive membership—allegedly two million people joined within a week—hardly reflected a genuine enthusiasm of the masses. Apart from multiple political groups of small importance, entire social organizations and professional unions announced their desire to join. Among those who applied for membership were central boards of fire brigades and of post and telegraph officials, and the union of ex-army officers. The rank and file of these groups were rarely consulted by the leaders who proclaimed that their organizations joined OZN. No wonder that a wit said that OZN was based on two German philosophers—Kant and Nietzsche—their names in Polish slang mean "nothing" and "fraud."

The chief of the new party, Colonel Koc, naturally strove to attract the younger generation, and an organization called the Union of Young Poland (*Zwiazek Mlodej Polski,* ZMP) appeared. Its leader was a genuine fascist, Jan Rutkowski, and the youth movement aped fascist models: uniforms and fascist salutes, and a paramilitary discipline.

The name of Rutkowski was linked with a small but vocal fascist organization that had emerged in 1934, and with which Colonel Koc began to flirt at this time. This was the National Radical Camp (*Obóz Narodowo Radykalny,* ONR) and to understand its nature and character one has to go back to the middle twenties.

Among the great political parties of Poland, the National Democratic Party occupied a very important position. Its roots went back to the last decades of the nineteenth century, and it gradually evolved from a liberal-national to a militant nationalist movement. Its greatest leader was Roman Dmowski, an outstanding figure in Polish political life, and the most important antagonist and rival of Piłsudski. National Democrats, despite their undoubted influence and strength, did not gain power in postwar Poland. In 1926, after Piłsudski's coup d'état, Dmowski decided that the main task of the party was education of the younger generation in nationalist principles. Dmowski's great forte was doctrine, and in that respect he was the opposite of Piłsudski. The new organization that Dmowski called into existence—it was later dissolved by the government—was named Great Poland Camp *(Obóz Wielkiej Polski).* Its chief purpose was to form a cadre of future leaders of the nationalist movement in Poland. While the organization was not fascist it bore some marks of fascist influence. Dmowski founded it after a stay in Italy, where he observed and was impressed with Mussolini's experiment. One of Dmowski's close collaborators, S. Kozicki, was Poland's ambassador in Rome and he allegedly was interested in and sympathetic to fascist policies.

The Great Poland Camp was characterized, to quote Dmowski, by "principles of hierarchy, discipline, and personal responsibility of leaders for their sphere of activity." The central authority, called like its fascist prototype, "the great council," supervised nominated leaders on lower echelons. While not striving to introduce a replica of a fascist regime in Poland, the Great Poland Camp was to prepare the ground for a specifically Polish fascist-influenced version of a national state. Its activity was of great consequence for the National Democratic Party and it deepened the division between the "old" and the "young." The former remained true to the more liberal and parliamentary ideas, the latter veered toward totalitarian solutions.

In 1934 a group composed predominantly of young people broke away from the National Democrats, accusing them of opportunism and for failure to prepare to seize power in the state. It formed the National Radical Camp, ONR, which survived only for a few months. The government, whether acting in good faith or not, accused ONR of the murder of the Minister of the Interior. ONR leaders found themselves in Poland's only concentration camp, set up about this time, the notorious Bereza Kartuska. Their political organization was banned.

Freed from Bereza Kartuska, the National Radicals split into two groups, both engaging in illegal political activity. The nature of the split has never been fully explained but it apparently concerned tactics. The extremists favored a revolutionary takeover, prepared by violent methods. The group became known as ONR-Falanga, or just Falanga. Its leader was Bołeslaw Piasecki (at present head of the Pax organization in the Polish People's Republic), and one of his closest collaborators was Rutkowski. Falanga, which in spite of its illegal existence published several papers such as *Falanga* and *Ruch Młodych* and issued the National Radical Program in February, 1937. The document came close to fascist (even national socialist) models. It called for a complete political, economic, and social reconstruction of the country. Describing the state as the means of "historical strivings of the nation," it put all stress on the nation. There was room only for one political party, the "Political Organization of the Nation." Combining extreme nationalism with religion, the program stated that "God is the highest aim of man." Falanga demanded limitations of private property, and state control over the economic life. Its attitude toward national minorities was strongly anti-Semitic; it implied policies of Polonization of Ukrainians and Belorussians.

Falanga was a small but highly disciplined and effective organization. Its members belonged to the young generation—Piasecki himself was a student in his early twenties —and they were mainly concentrated in Warsaw. They represented a rebel group, opposed not only to the Polish realities of life, but also to the older nationalists. They believed in brutality and were notorious for anti-Jewish outbreaks. The militia of the Falanga attempted to use terror against political opponents, even against those who belonged to other national radical groups.

When at the turn of 1936 and 1937 Colonel Koc engaged in creating OZN and its youth branch, he turned his attention to Falanga. He was impressed by their discipline, military bearing, and obvious fanatical devotion to the Polish nationalist cause. As a result of political talks, Rutkowski and some Falanga members joined OZN's youth organization. Their objectives were clear. The Falangists sought to use the rich resources put up by OZN to further their own ends. While there were a few common ideas shared by OZN and Falanga, the program of the former was so vague that it could well evolve in a totalitarian and fascist direction. The honeymoon of Falanga and OZN was brief. It seems that while the original idea of OZN leadership was to collaborate with Falanga for tactical reasons—to weaken the rightist opposition to the government—genuine cooperation evoked strong protests. Ministers grouped around the president, and those Piłsudskiites who retained their democratic and leftist ideals could not stomach a common front with avowed fascists. There were rumors of preparations of a Falanga coup—a Polish St. Bartholomew's night—against the liberal elements in the government. Colonel Koc was forced to resign and General S. Skwarczyński became the new leader of OZN. Falanga replied by recalling Rutkowski from the OZN youth organization, which despite all its privileges never gained more than 26,000 adherents. The youth organization disintegrated.

Falanga went its own way. Its successes were so far limited, and its membership did not attain more than two thousand people. Violent and vocal—its somewhat theatrical mass meeting in a Warsaw circus was accompanied by all the fascist trappings—it never became more than an organization operating on the fringes of Polish political life. The same was true of the other national radical splinter groups. They made their biggest shows at universities and high schools where their hooliganism disrupted classes and terrorized Jewish and leftist students. On the eve of the war national radicals were torn by new divisions and splits.

Were there any connections between the Polish fascists and their Italian, Spanish, or German forerunners? There is no doubt that national radicals admired Italian and Spanish parties; their attitude toward national socialism was made more complex by the German-Polish antagonism. No evidence exists of actual collaboration. One of the founders of ONR, Jan Mosdorf, who died in the Nazi concentration camp of Oswiecim (Auschwitz), explicitly denied that ONR ever accepted any of the German advances. Piasecki and his followers fought against the Germans during the second World War. The extreme nationalism of Polish fascists and their undoubted sincerity—few if any could be accused of opportunism in the interwar period—make any links with the Nazis most unlikely. It was only after the war that Piasecki and several of his collaborators emerged in somewhat novel roles as staunch supporters of the present Polish regime. Others died during the war, went into exile, or, having abandoned the creed of their youth, moved away from political life altogether.

How important was fascism in interwar Poland? Numerically it could never compare with even lesser political parties in the country. Its membership was almost exclusively composed of very young people belonging to the intelligentsia. Neither Falanga nor the other group of ONR (usually called ABC after the paper of this name that it published) enjoyed any support among the peasants or workers. Unlike Italian fascism or national socialism, it had no mass following, nor did it seem to have any chance of gaining it. Polish conditions, political and economic, were not conducive to the growth of a strong fascist party. The bourgeoisie, which had given a helping hand to the rightist extremists in Germany and Italy, was sufficiently protected by the existing regime in Poland against the specter of a social revolution. The communist challenge to which the Nazis and fascists responded was almost absent. The only popular slogan of the national radicals that they shared with several large parties in Poland was anti-Semitism. It was characteristic of Polish conditions that this slogan was most catching in the towns, with their large Jewish population, and among the lower middle classes and intelligentsia. Economic competition provided a strong stimulus to anti-Semitism. There was also another aspect of the question. Given the specific Polish situation, high school and university graduates faced a genuine problem in finding jobs. This was especially true in liberal professions and medicine. The existing discontent could and was easily diverted against the Jews who were said to bar access to these professions. It is no coincidence that Polish fascists flourished at universities and that student corporations became the centers of anti-Semitism. Thus Polish fascists, although impressed more by Italian than German models (Falanga had some plans of establishing a corporate state like that of Italy) came closer to national socialists than to fascists in their anti-Semitism.

Polish fascism, operating on the margins of Poland's political life, was in many instances an artificial and imported product. Impressed by the rapid changes wrought by fascists abroad, influenced by fascist slogans, which appealed to youthful imagination, it could hardly be considered a solution for Poland's perennial problems. Nor was it a real sympton of the ailments of Polish society and system. Polish fascism went against the long tradition of Polish ideals of freedom, individualism, and toleration.

VI

Romania

Emanuel Turczynski

Stephen Fischer-Galati

A

The Background of Romanian Fascism

Emanuel Turczynski

The preponderantly village-oriented cultural and social structure of the Romanian people, which only recently led to the development of a genuine middle class, left a wide field of action to folk culture even in the realm of politics. Although this development did not become fully clear until the interwar period, its origins can already be found in the eighteenth and nineteenth centuries. Many of these causes, always present in latent form and visible on occasion in the early nationalistic movements and literature, finally became politically active in the 1920s in an ever increasing measure.

The nation-forming ideology of the Romanians developed in Transylvania and first became popular there and in the Banat. It crossed the Carpathian range slowly where it created the important ideological structure of the Romanians of Moldavia, Wallachia, and the Bukovina, an ideology which developed unevenly in the various regions and among the different social strata. This Daco-Romanism became the starting point of the Romanian national historical image whose basic elements were shaped and propagated with the help of the prestige of the Uniate clergy at first and later by that of the Orthodox priests. Novelists, poets, and historians developed and popularized this concept, but the process of creating a nation became politically relevant only as a result of the long-drawn-out fight for freedom and legal rights that the boyars of the principalities conducted against Turks and Greeks. These politically leading boyars and clergymen, influenced by imperialistic impulses, began as early as the Russian-Turkish war of 1768–74, with the help of Russians and Austrians, to agitate for a state autonomy along feudal and estate-based lines. This agitation finally led to the development of a national consciousness, chiefly as a result of Daco-Romanism and French influence, which was popular mainly among the boyars but finally reached other circles too. Although the Daco-Romanian ideal played an important role, the process of nation formation took a completely different path in Transylvania and the Banat. In these two provinces, where the Romanian nobility was unimportant, the role of the quasi-aristocratic leadership of Moldavia and Wallachia was taken over by educated clergymen during the first phase of the nation-formation process, which lasted roughly until 1830. In the Bukovina, where from 1775 the Romanian nobles, the Orthodox clergy, and the civil servants of Romanian origin carried greater weight than they did in Transylvania and the Banat, the situation of the Romanians was much more favorable than in any other land that they inhabited. For this reason nationalistic feelings developed much later in the Bukovina than in the other provinces.

101

Just as the social and cultural development differed from place to place, so did also the feeling of legality and the attitude toward state authority. This is another reason why national feelings developed differently in the various places and why this growing national consciousness meant different things from place to place. Language, religion, and folk culture were the important constant factors that finally permitted the concept of a unified nation-state to evolve in spite of century-long political separation. If these antinomies are considered and understood as background, then it is possible to explain the development of the national debates that, between the two world wars, led to the growth of right-wing parties with authoritarian and social reformist goals.

West of the Carpathians the political development differed from that east of these mountains. The following reasons for this should be kept in mind: Transylvanian Romanians reacted against the religious oppression of Calvinists, Lutherans, and Catholics; and the Greek Orthodox Romanian clergy of the Banat revolted against the Serb hierarchy. The Serbs had taken over the leadership of a religiously united but ethnically split population in southern Hungary, due to a legal position that was assured by the traditional ecclesiastic policy of the state. While the boyars in the principalities were able to further and broaden their economic and political preponderance in the eighteenth and nineteenth centuries, those in Crişana, Maramureş, Transylvania, and the Banat could not play any national or political role because they either lost all their political rights or became Magyarized. In Moldavia, although there was a serious danger of the Tatar, Armenian, Greek, and Albanian elements denationalizing the boyars, they were able, together with the higher clergy and the free peasantry, to create a state-maintaining structure. The extreme mobility of these boyars, forced on them by wars, social upheavals, frequent changes in rulers, and the depredations of robber bands, led to the establishment of strongholds or hideouts. These retreats existed in the cities of Hermannstadt (Sibiu), Kronstadt (Braşov), Lemberg (Lwow), and after 1775 in Czernowitz (Cernauti, Tschernowtze). Because of the frequent absence of leadership, the land became even more susceptible to foreign influences and the chasm, both cultural and spiritual, between the boyars and the masses of the peasant population grew deeper.

The takeover of the princely courts, chancelleries, and richly endowed monasteries by Phanariot Greeks, beginning during the last quarter of the eighteenth century, led to a steadily increasing anti-Greek attitude. The semiofficial sale of offices, corruption, and the practically limitless exploitation of the urban and rural population by foreign or domestic social climbers (*ciocci*) not only prevented the further development of a rudimentary state ethos, but also destroyed, by the end of the nineteenth century, all connections between the peasant and shepherd population and the state. In other words, the relationship between the taxpayers and the rulers was completely broken because two completely different groups were responsible for self government and defense on the one hand, and taxes on the other. Jurisprudence lost the respect that it once enjoyed, and a Romanian proverb, "Better a crooked deal than a just verdict," shows clearly how extensive and uncertain the legal process was and how the people felt about administration and justice.

In this period, and within the framework of a completely Orientalized way of life and a corrupt concept of justice, the Haiduk movement developed into an instrument of self-preservation and became an object of veneration. This development can be seen clearly in folk poetry in which the older and longer songs about heroes were replaced by Haiduk songs. Nevertheless, the locations in which these heroic deeds took place remained unchanged because, just as the Klephts in Greece and the Četniks in Serbia or Croatia, the Haiduks always spent the summer in the huge and deep forests. This is the origin of the special meaning and highly emotional feeling that *codru*, the Romanian word for virgin forest, acquired. In lyrical folk poetry, especially in the "Doina," in the heroic epics, and the Haiduk songs, and in most poetry since the middle of the nineteenth century, *codru* has been romantically idealized. Even on stage, in the second half of the nineteenth century, Haiduks and robbers were widely celebrated, and finally, since 1896, numerous German and Romanian novels have been published that deal in part with the war of liberation and in part with the life of the Haiduks. The following are typical: Karl Bleibtreu, *Ein Freiheitskampf in Siebenbürgen* (1896); Bucura Dumbrava, *Haiducul* (1908); Panait Istrati, *Présentation des Haidoucs* (1925). In all these songs, plays, narratives, and novels, the Haiduks were venerated in a manner comparable to that of the cowboy in modern American westerns, the only difference being that the Haiduks fought against foreign or local oppressors and not against Indians and badmen. Because of this attitude, the image of the Haiduk fights acquired a social connotation that was only partly justified.

Another and very important original source, besides the defense of religion and the worship of the Haiduks, was the growing rejection of foreigners in the public and commercial life of the nation. This rejection grew in proportion to the first latent, then openly aggressive xenophobia that became especially clear when religious considerations were added. One can assume that the action of Prince Stefan Rareş (1551–52), directed against the Armenians who accepted Luther's Reformation, was not based purely on religious considerations. Later the Greek-Romanian symbiosis broke down, more because of economic and social reasons than because of cultural considerations. This symbiosis overshadowed, during the one hundred years of Phanariot rule, the local and historical past of the principalities in such a way that the opinion could have been drawn erroneously that the Romanians were not a historic nation. Toward the end of the eighteenth and the beginning of the nineteenth century, the boyars first voiced their demand for the exclusion of Greeks from the administration and the church, although interventions aimed at the elimination of Greek merchants had occurred earlier. The growing influence of Russia and Austria, after the Russo-Turkish war of 1768–74, which facilitated the development by the principalities of a foreign policy independent of the Ottoman government, created a new problem. This problem was the issuing of letters of protection and privileges by the local governments to Russians and Austrians and later even to French and English citizens. In contrast, the legal position of the native artisans and merchants became relatively even more unfavorable so that social controversies often acquired ethnic and religious elements as well.

Between 1830 and 1881 the Romanian national movement was transformed from a spontaneous reaction against the imperial excesses into a movement that was state directed and ideologically firmly founded. Daco-Romanianism, which originated with Demetrius Cantemir but was first used as a political idea by the Transylvanian clergy, was combined in the principalities with the fourteenth-century Romanian myths of the establishment of states that had been propagated by the chroniclers from the time of Grigore Ureche (1590–1647). The historical consciousness was connected, with both the past of the people from those mythological days when they began their descent from the heights of the Carpathians into the plains of Moldavia and Wallachia, and with the language, which was considered the irrefutable proof of a Roman origin. Although these ideas were less important than the numerous social factors, they nevertheless played a significant role as a measure of the Romanian people's self-consciousness. The glorification of the Greek war of independence and the resistance against Russian despotism, which was intensified following the peace of Adrianople, introduced a new era into the national movement. Nationalism soon went beyond the circle of the educated, westernized boyars and began to influence the now rapidly growing middle class.

The ideals of liberty and social equality led a short life in Romania. The reaction against the liberal revolutionaries in 1848 cut this development short. "The misery, the laziness, or, more specifically, the degradation of people," which developed as a result of Oriental despotism and which Sulzer, Jean Louis Carra, and Dinicu Golescu criticized, were retained unchanged. Social barriers remained standing and with the creation of a national army, the opposition of the Levantine-Jewish merchant and artisan group to nationalism became even more obvious. The contrast was not as strong in Wallachia where the Sephardic Jews, often considered to be Greeks, had developed a very high culture. This prenationalistic anti-Semitism was, however, very strong in Moldavia. There the Ashkenazim, deprived both socially and culturally by life in Polish and Russian ghettos, tried to fill the gap in the Romanian social structure. The origin of this economically based anti-Semitism coincided with the growing immigration of Jews from the Russian districts of Podolia, as well as the large-scale influx from the Ukraine that occurred as a result of the ruthless Russian military service. In the Kiselev constitution (*Regulamentul organic*) which the Russians imposed on the Romanians, the legal position of the Jews was defined in a manner similar to that in force in Russia where, under the rule of Nicholas I, the anti-Semitic governmental policy had reached new heights. But while anti-Semitism in Russia had a chiefly religious basis, it was predominantly economic, social, and political in Moldavia and Wallachia. As early as 1844 the estate-controlled Diet (*adunare obştească*) introduced far-reaching discriminatory and restrictive measures that limited the economic expansion of Jews. For example, not only was it forbidden for Jews to buy property in certain sections of the cities, but they were also excluded from owning food or liquor stores. The decision of the executive branch of the government to ignore these resolutions of the Diet increased anti-Semitism even more than the government's efforts to eliminate the traditional practice of bribery. The liberalism of the revolutionaries of 1848 brought only ideological beginnings aimed at the realization of general freedom and equality. While these rights were supposed to extend to all ethnic and religious minorities, the tendency to exclude Jews, as an economic minority, from enjoying them proved stronger than the liberal principles.

The successive waves of Turkish, Greek, and Russian attempts to denationalize the Romanians created a very thorough xenophobia, which was never counterbalanced by state-erected legal barriers and seldom by an individual's conscience. A new addition to anti-Semitism was created by Austria, which unsuccessfully opposed the unification of the two principalities in 1859, because while anti-Semitism was directed against all Jews, it was primarily directed against Austrian and Russian subjects living in Romania. It is difficult to determine whether the anti-Russian feelings furthered only the Daco-Roman ideas or, to some extent, anti-Semitism also. In the case of the disturbances that occurred in connection with the drafting of peasants for military service-like guard duty, social motivations also played a part. The participation of Jews in these disturbances, as well as their participation in the liberation and unification movements, shows quite clearly that until 1858–59 anti-Semitism was directed only against those social groups (foreign citizens, mainly Austrian and Russian) that had collusive interests. The introduction of French culture among the higher social classes did not influence either the religious basis of folk culture or the Oriental civilization dominating the general way of life.

It is typical of this second period in the development of the national movement, which lasted approximately until 1881, that a haphazardly growing middle class joined the boyars as the propagators of a French-style nationalism, and that both nationalism and anti-Semitism were propagated jointly by the *Assemblée générale* (Parliament) in the years 1834–48, together with the princes and the administration. When George Dimitrie Bibescu ascended the throne in 1843 he dressed in a costume that was supposedly worn by Michael the Brave (Mihai Viteazul), and his country agreed to pay higher taxes to the sultan in exchange for the right to have a national flag. An Austrian diplomat wrote to Metternich in 1840: "It is regrettable when one observes how national pride counts for more than national well being." Both Prince Cuza and Prince Carol, who, as King Carol, ruled until 1914, came out for equal rights for Jews but were unable to influence the political programs of those who sat in the parliament. When pogroms brought foreign intervention, the Jewish question in Romania became an international issue, increasing the tension. The consequent orientation of Jews to political centers outside of Romania produced a certain polycentrism, which certainly did not help them in their fight for equality. It also produced an official state anti-Semitism that finally produced the most extreme forms of nationalism. When the signatories of the Berlin agreement, especially Bismarck, Andrássy, and Disraeli, intervened to enforce the equal rights paragraph of this agreement (1878), and insisted that Romania honor article 7 of its own constitution, which was designed to eliminate differentiation along religious lines and to give rights of citizenship to Jews who had lived in Romania for several decades, the result was contrary to what had been expected. Thus any chance for the assimilation of the Jews was lost in spite of the fact that the numbers of Jews in Romania were considerable and that in those days they played a very important part in the economic, cultural, and spiritual life of the country. Among these were the well-known philologist Lazar Saineanu, and Aurel I. Candrea, H. Tiktin, and Moses Gaster. Although Gaster was expelled from the country in 1885, he continued to produce works of great interest in the fields of Romanian folklore and literary history.

The Russian–Romanian–Turkish war of 1877–78, which not only permitted Romania to declare her full independence from the Porte, but also saw Russian troops fight under the supreme command of the young Prince Carol, introduced a new phase in the history of the Romanian state and national movement. The victory against Turkey, paid for in blood, the humiliation meted out by Russia, and the loss of Bessarabia, accelerated the transition from a somewhat moderate national consciousness to an integral nationalism. The proclamation establishing the kingdom and the festivities surrounding the coronation of the king, with a crown made from a captured Turkish cannon, increased the self-consciousness of the young nation. This new fervor expanded steadily among the Romanians in Transylvania, the Banat, the Bukovina, and even in Bessarabia, accelerating the trend that had been evident earlier. For example, in 1871, under the leadership of the Moldavian, Mihai Eminescu, a great celebration took place at Putna (belonging to the Bukovina at that time) to commemorate the four-hundredth anniversary of the famous monastery in that city. Romanians came to this celebration from all provinces and lands, thus demonstrating a feeling of unity. When, in 1875, a university was established in Czernowitz, to commemorate the hundredth anniversary of the Bukovina as an Austrian province, and when, at the request of the Romanians of the Bukovina, this university was created as an essentially German university, the Romanian nationalism in Moldavia was further inflamed by anti-Austrian propaganda. This anti-Austrian feeling grew even stronger after the proclamation of the Romanian kingdom. More important than the numerous attacks on the positive or negative administrative measures of the Austro-Hungarian government was the lopsided development of the historical picture through research and instruction, reflected especially by schoolbooks, and by an equally lopsided historical consciousness propagated by the highly emotional articles of the Romanian press.

From early in the nineteenth century the controversy regarding the continuous inhabitation of Transylvania by Romanians became increasingly important. Out of the supposedly continuous inhabitation came the claim of priority, which served to justify numerous political requests, mainly concerning Transylvania. The glorification of Roman ancestors, the victorious legions, and the cultural achievements of all Romance people introduced a romantic influence that, when fitted into the Levantine-Oriental way of life and a Byzantine-Orthodox folk culture, produced a curious cultural coating.

Poporănism and *Sămănătorism*, which led to the development of new directions in literature, produced, as had the *narodniki*, a rapprochement between the peasantry and the literary man whose previous orientation had been chiefly French and German. The value of folk culture and the misery of the peasantry were recognized and produced a gradual increase in cultural and social self-consciousness, but this recognition did not lead to either social reform or to any change in the administrative system. The result was only the development of a certain guilt feeling, but it did little to identify those primarily responsible for these miserable conditions. Instead the literature, and to a greater degree the press, gave a completely negative and distorted picture of Hungarians, Austrians, Germans, and Jews. For example, the image of Germany carried positive elements only in scientific and cultural circles, while the individual Austrian or German served mainly as a target for caricature. While among the first generation of writers (Alecu Russo, for example) the polyglot and polyethnic world around Romania was described with some respect for the idiosyncrasies of the foreigners in spite of the basically strongly nationalistic approach of the authors, in later writers we find only a negative evaluation of everything foreign, with the exception of France. This is important also for the development of anti-Semitism.

How closely Romanian and Russian anti-Semitism were connected becomes obvious when one remembers that, following an attempt on the life of Tsar Nicholas II in 1882, Romania, on Russian request, produced a law against nihilists, which facilitated the expulsion of Jews from Romania. Romanian official anti-Semitism thus merged with foreign influences and reinforced this component of nationalism. As a result, in order to weaken the strength of the anti-Semitic laws, corruption increased tremendously, so that the officials supplemented their often miserably low salaries by permitting the Jews to live under acceptable conditions. This habit of circumventing the law soon began to corrupt the national economy, giving additional impetus to economic anti-Semitism. When the Jews gained a little more influence in the national economy and when the Jewish workers, "in their quality as the largest segment of the enlightened and class conscious Jewish proletariat," joined the Social Democratic movement, even the *Liga pentru unitatea culturala a tuturor Românilor* (the League for the Cultural Unity of all Romanians), whose self-appointed task was to propagate Daco-Romanism among all social classes, changed and became increasingly anti-Semitic in its nationalism. Four years after this league was established, following goals outlined primarily by Nicolae Iorga, an "Alliance Antisémitique Universelle" (1895) was organized in Bucharest (Bucureşti). As a result, the national movement, whose goal had been to unite all Romanians in one country and culture, became more and more anti-Semitic, this time for cultural considerations. The economist and university professor, A. C. Cuza, who, together with Iorga, was one of the leaders of the political and economic anti-Semites, based his theoretical knowledge on the works of Edouard Drumont, who, by his book, *La France juive* (1885) and his journal, *La Libre Parole* (1886–1907) was the founding father of anti-Semitism in France. Cuza tried to create a national art and cultural movement and outlined his ideas in his book *Naţionalitatea în artă* (1908).

The constantly increasing struggle between Magyars and Romanians in Transylvania, Maramureş, Crişana, and the Banat, which was discussed in great detail by the Romanian press, inflamed national feelings even further and led to the sanctification of martyrs, beginning with Horia, Cloşca, and Crisan, and ending with the numerous dead who fought the national fight in Transylvania between 1848 and 1914. As a result, nationalism in Romania became a more popular movement, leaving the less interesting anti-Semitism to the bureaucrats and the middle class. Not until the Russian Revolution of 1905 and the revolt of the Romanian peasants in 1907 did an agrarian anti-Semitism become firmly established among the people at large, because at that time an anti-Semitic hate campaign was also organized among the peasants. Even at this stage foreign interventions, like those of Georges Clemenceau and Luigi Luzzati, produced no results. To the same degree in which the situation of the Romanians in Transylvania and the Banat deteriorated as a result of Magyar terror in political and cultural fields, so grew the hostility of the Romanian party leaders and army toward Austria-Hungary. The great enthusiasm for war that was manifest during the second Balkan clash was channeled, after the outbreak of the war in 1914, into anti-Austro-Hungarian manifestations, not a difficult diversion, given the strength of the French cultural propaganda. This reinforced old hatreds, including those against Germany that stemmed from the intrigues of the railroad speculator, Dr. Bethel Henry Strousberg, and those against Jewish capitalists who, in the Romanian mind, were transformed into the main supports of Austria. The rather extensive freedom of the press was directed toward agitation for nationalism and when Romania finally entered the war in 1916, numerous organized hunts and brutal excesses were inflicted on the citizens of the Central Powers. The absence of a tradition honoring the law and the lack of a bourgeois legal background became obvious both in word and deed. Even the economic and cultural contacts of the Bessarabian Jews with Germany, due to the generally cosmopolitan and liberal outlook of the Jews, earned them the label of "defeatist" in some Romanian circles.

The military collapse of Russia and the dissolution of the Habsburg monarchy gave the victorious powers a chance to enlarge Romania and to give her the borders that the Daco-Romanian ideology demanded. The population of Great Romania amounted, after the unification of all Romanians, to sixteen million people, but of these

30 percent belonged to either ethnic or religious minorities. Consequently, Romania was transformed from a nation state into a nationality state and faced a whole series of new problems. The cities of Transylvania, the Banat, Crişana, Maramureş, the Bukovina, and Bessarabia had a non-Romanian majority. The political goal of unification of all Romanians had been achieved, but the antinomies which it created were very difficult to overcome. The Romanian-Magyar controversy was only increased by the *nem, nem, soha* (no, no, never) of the Magyars, and even the relationship with the Jews and Germans acquired new cultural, political, and social aspects after the acquisition of the Bukovina, Transylvania, and Bessarabia. According to both Romanian and German public opinion, the Russian revolution, as well as the revolt of Béla Kun in Hungary, was the result of Jewish action, and a leading role was still being played by Jews in Russia and in the Ukraine. Even the Ukrainian minority in the Bukovina was now included among the ethnic groups whose presence was resented because of Ukrainian plans that advocated the partition of the Bukovina according to both confessional and territorial lines. The Ukrainians, who were bilingual and belonged to the same church to which the Romanians belonged, could avoid the pressure of the authorities by switching nationalities, but the differences between the Romanians on one hand and the Magyars and Jews on the other could not be solved this easily. While the number of Magyars decreased due to the voluntary or forced emigration of a large segment of the Hungarian intelligentsia, the Jewish element increased and became nationally more conscious as a result of the annexation of the Bukovina. This development sharpened the Romanian-Jewish antagonism. This became even more obvious when the Jewish editors of some Romanian newspapers reacted quite sharply to anti-Semitic attacks. The result was that in wide circles of the Romanian people, but especially among the half-educated and the university students who opposed assimilation, Romanian nationalism acquired a chauvinistic and economic anti-Semitism, a populistic tinge.

The largely increased bureaucratic apparatus, which was almost completely changed each time the government changed, increased the tax load and produced a new sign of social prestige. Because of this prestige everybody had a new goal: they wanted to become state employees and for this reason joined one or the other of the political parties. The number of those going to school increased rapidly, producing an intellectual proletariat and thereby adding considerably to the ranks of the dissatisfied. The blame for this inadvertent development was ascribed to the foreigners, especially the Jews who happened to be successful in economic life. Because the optimistic expectations that had been attached to the unification of all Romanians in one kingdom were not realized, unrest grew and accelerated the search for solutions to national problems. The politically inexperienced younger generation, disappointed by the programs of the parties and the activities of the government, searched for new ideas, preferably simple ones that corresponded to their naive views. With these idealized and simplified concepts they were helpless in the face of the very complicated social and ethnic problems of the nation, meanwhile rejecting democracy because its misuse by experienced politicians stripped it of all value in the eyes of these youngsters. The facts that controversies can be solved without radical measures, that compromise is useful, and that evolution needs time, could not even be discussed. Total domination by authority and excessive centralization, as well as the absence of self-governing institutions, produced catastrophic results after the victorious war. The authorities declared war on the minorities because among these, especially the Germans and Jews, they found themselves face to face with well-organized institutions, based on organically developed and generally well-proven conventions, which are typical of the cohesion of religious and ethnic minorities. In order to regulate the various professions, the baccalaureate examination was made more difficult and candidates were required to prove their citizenship. Although the constitution of 1923 finally granted equal rights to Jews, citizenship papers were checked meticulously to ensure that later émigrés into Romania did not profit from the 1923 constitution. As is often the case in the history of nationalism, inferiority complexes developed which people tried to conceal with bravado, thus laying an important sociopsychological foundation for the subsequent reaction.

The political leadership was not able to create a state ethos and just as in the period of the Ottoman-Greek condominium, neither the peasantry nor the rapidly growing bourgeoisie felt any identity with the state. For this reason patriotism and national consciousness were not connected either with state or governmental loyalty, but were partly pure abstractions and, in part, loyalty to the dynasty. The failure of the Liberal Party to solve the country's social problems facilitated a shift toward the right (Junimea), thus demanding a strong hand and refuting the pseudodemocracy of the political parties. Under these circumstances the Greek Orthodox clergy, the estate that sponsored the national movement in the eighteenth and nineteenth centuries and protected its moral integrity more effectively than the others, began to gain new respect. This was particularly the case in the rapidly growing cities of Transylvania and the Banat, which were originally inhabited by large ethnic and religious minorities but were now rapidly gaining an Orthodox Romanian population that was moving in from the countryside. The national Romanian leading element began to include, primarily in Transylvania and the Bukovina where Ottoman tradition, and consequently corruption, was the weakest, a large percentage of sons of clergymen and teachers. These people began to create a family tradition facilitated by the clergy who, in the provinces, held the primary position in the social scale of values. Teachers and priests soon assumed responsibility for advising the peasants on political and social questions of daily life such as elections. The growing attempts of the local administrators and the boyar polyarchy to influence elections and the frequent falsification of election results added to this trend. There remained little room for the free expression of the will of the people who became more and more reluctant to cast their votes as a consequence.

In 1928, Iuliu Maniu's National Peasant Party succeeded in gaining 80 percent of the popular vote without cheating. When the party subsequently failed to introduce needed reforms and also opened the borders of the land to foreign capital, strongly anti-Semitic, social revolutionary and, in general, more radical trends in the Romanian Front that Dr. Alexander Vaida-Voevod had established began to emerge, even in Transylvania. The Peasant Party, and especially Maniu, whom the king secretly labeled "idiot," lost the respect of the younger generation. The royal house lost prestige because of King Ferdinand's vacillation and eventual death, and the subsequent excesses of Prince Carol, who first renounced the throne only to return triumphantly as king. As a result the political situation became as difficult as the economic had already been.

If one wished to analyze the forces that contributed first to the creation of Romanian right-wing parties and then to their conversion to totalitarianism, one must consider both the glorification of an agonized way of life and the willingness to give one's life for a cause. This attitude, which was already politically important before the emergence of Corneliu Zelea Codreanu, became, as far as he was concerned, identified with his education in a military high school. Up to a certain point this can be accepted if one thinks of his *führer* personality, which had such a basic influence on the attitude of his followers. One cannot overlook the agonized way of life that the name Codreanu itself illustrated, because the *codreni* belonged to the border guards who, like the *plăieş*, had protected the land for centuries against the incursion of Tatar and Turkish bands.

The ideological attitude of later generations was also influenced by the respect that the younger revolutionaries of 1848 accorded students who were willing to defend their honor with arms, thus stemming, although only provisionally, the Levantine propensity for quarrel and intrigue. In his comedy, *Boieri şi Ciocoi* (The Boyars and the Social Climbers), Vasile Alexandri lauded anti-Semitism and excoriated the corruption and lack of integrity of social climbers. He showed as preferable to them the generation of young boyars who had adopted a way of life in which both dueling and brotherly cooperation deserved respect. The Romanian student organizations and fraternities, first in Vienna and then in Czernowitz, who wore specific colors and indulged in duels, included numerous Moldavians. The principle of absolute honorable satisfaction, almost universally accepted at the universities of Vienna, Prague, and Czernowitz before and after the First World War, by the young of Czech, Polish, Romanian, Jewish, and Ukrainian origin, was not popular at Iaşi, Bucureşti, and Cluj. This rejection was due to the social background of the students at these universities, which made the acceptance of the Central European mentality and a state-based code of honor impossible. Nevertheless, the ideology of the fighting students, as well as fraternity life, had a lasting though indirect influence on the form and spiritual content of the national Romanian student organization out of which the Iron Guard grew. This specific code of honor was accepted in the eighteenth and nineteenth centuries in all German-speaking universities, and also influenced, to a lesser degree, the young people in the non-German borderlands of East and Southeastern Europe. It has been excellently described by the German-Baltic historian Reinhard Wittram:

> To defend one's self against all slights, to demand satisfaction under all circumstances, became one of the strictest demands of the unwritten Baltic code. Whoever accepted a slight without insisting that the violated order be reestablished was not taken seriously any longer.

Out of the merger of these often misunderstood traditions, judged only by their outward appearances, and the romantic Haiduk life and veneration of the Daco-Roman past, arose a willingness to fight that regarded dying for the nation an honor. Old stories, such as the death of the Dacian King Decebal at Sarmisigetuza, were brought up as examples. Even the motive of the ballad "Miorita" became, much more often than in the past, the center of philosophic and poetic verse. Consequently, dying for the nation gained a chiliastic halo, explainable only through the mysticism of Orthodox piety, until heroic death was equated with sanctity because it contributed to national unity.

Under these circumstances it was much easier for Codreanu, than it had been for Cuza before him, to create a mass movement with radical-national and social-evolutional aims. Iaşi proved to be an ideal breeding ground for this movement because Moldavia bordered on less nationalistic Bessarabia and the Soviet Union, and because the high percentage of Jews among the city's population, which also included many socialists and communists, pushed the Romanian youth toward reaction under the influence of false nationalistic slogans. Examples found in neighboring countries reinforced this tendency and the following should be remembered: in Hungary the radically nationalistic student organizations that organized in the openly anti-Semitic "Turul" Association; in Bulgaria the introduction of voluntary labor service; and, in Poland, the glorification of right-wing, semimilitaristic, voluntary associations. The Polish legions, which in part were incorporated into the Polish army, and with whose help Piłsudski defeated the much stronger Red Army under the Soviet Marshal Tuchacevskii, made a tremendous impression on northeastern Romania. Codreanu's description of the beginnings of his political, semimilitary activities, and of his fight against communism in Iaşi, shows clearly how the romantic memory of the Haiduks and the myths of the *Freicorps* merged. The manner in which Codreanu reacted to the excesses and slights of the authorities, and especially to maltreatment by the police, shows that in the generation of students to which he belonged a new moral code was developing. This code represented the beginning of a spiritual and moral reaction against the Oriental way of life, and was directed against corrupt Romanian politicians more than against Jews because the Jews were able to protect themselves in acceptable and strictly legal ways. The Jews had several other advantages: they had their own communal life with Zionistic-nationalistic organizations; they were experienced in democratic and parliamentary action; they were represented in all political parties, and even enjoyed the sympathies of the Orthodox hierarchy when religious and charitable issues were involved.

To oppose the existing political parties with an effective program, more clearly nationalistic and anti-Semitic, something specific had to be created. In other words, the new program had to be more than aggressively nationalistic because the programs of the other political parties included virulent chauvinism. It had to be conservative and nationalistic. The road to this development led through Codreanu's own inner conversion, which took place while he sat in jail during the winter of 1923–24. Up to that moment, according to his own writings, icons did not impress him. But after that date, with the selection of the Archangel Michael as both the symbol and the very name of his youth organization, he consciously embarked on the development of religious nationalism, a road that the student organization of Iasi had already discovered in 1920. The "Association of Christian Students" (1922) developed into a totalitarian, right-wing, nationalistic organization whose goals included social reform and, as time went on, a stronger and stronger political anti-Semitism in which the economic and cultural aspects predominated. The irrational aspect, the religious mysticism, and the organization along lines of a clerical order, attracted a rapid growth of sympathizers and party members.

What followed has been described in numerous up-to-date works and will be discussed by Professor Fischer-Galati. Thus I was able to limit myself to those other aspects of Romanian nationalism that I felt were relevant. Future research will have to answer the question as to whether this development represented a religiously founded national movement or a rebirth or reawakening of the Orthodox church, including some rudimentary nationalistic aspects. It is equally questionable, although it is often assumed to be the case, that the Iron Guard was the result of the work of one man. It is quite possible that concepts of this movement emerged out of a collective willingness to move in a given direction. Perhaps all that was needed was someone to activate and direct this widely held tendency.

B

Fascism in Romania

Stephen Fischer-Galati

The role and rule of Carol II in Romanian history remain a subject of continuing controversy. Condemned by most critics as a forerunner of fascism and a betrayer of the country's democratic potential and tradition, Carol has also been characterized by his defenders as the man of the hour, who realistically faced and solved the problems and challenges of the thirties.[1] Unquestionably Carol lacked confidence in and had little respect for the democratic process. In this regard his attitude was similar to that of his father Ferdinand and, for that matter, of the entire crowned dynasty of the Hohenzollerns and the uncrowned of the Brătianus. His political philosophy, if he had one, was that of dynastic authoritarianism: the King was the ultimate source of political decision and the initiator of meaningful political action. It is a matter of conjecture whether these views were based on deep-rooted suspicions and contempt for Romanian politicians; a desire to avenge the humiliations inflicted upon him by his political persecutors, the Brătianus; or an exaggerated confidence in his own abilities. It was probably a combination of all three. In any case, his attitude toward Iuliu Maniu and the National Peasant leadership that recalled him from exile was not one of gratitude. It is not that he found any intrinsic incompatibility between Maniu's alleged democratic sentiments and policies and his own royal authoritarianism; rather he clashed with Maniu's authoritarianism and views on the role of the monarchy.

Maniu favored controlled democracy in a constitutional monarchy; Carol clearly relegated the Prime Minister to the position of executor of the King's decisions. The break between Maniu and the monarch, regarded by most historians and politicians of Romania as the end of the "democratic experiment" and a steppingstone to totalitarianism, was the consequence of the clash between parochial and "modern" authoritarianism rather than between democratic and antidemocratic forces. Maniu's resignation, technically over the issue of Carol's extramarital relationship with Magda Lupescu, was far more revealing of the true nature of interwar Romanian politics and political mentality than the problem of public morality allegedly involved. The King's unwillingness to take a back seat to the Prime Minister and to follow the National Peasants' political course was the true cause of the rupture. It is nevertheless significant that morality became an issue in a country racked with immorality and that Madame Lupescu was of Jewish origin. Maniu knowingly raised the Jewish issue in his search for political support from those who would turn against the King because of the monarch's betrayal of the nationalist (to them anti-Semitic) tradition. The oft-quoted view that this tradition had been "democratized" during Maniu's regime and, therefore, that Carol's "dismissal" of the National Peasant leader was directed against both the national-Christian and democratic inheritance is untenable.[2] In fact, Maniu's denunciation of Lupescu, Carol, and royal authoritarianism, facilitated and perhaps paved the way to the eventual establishment of totalitarian fascism in Romania. The reestablishment of "directed democracy" a la Brătianu, this time under the monarch himself, was the first major step in that direction.

Carol cannot be personally charged with the failure of directed democracy by 1938. The internal pressures, generated by nationalists and the international economic crisis, and the external pressures exerted by fascist Italy and Nazi Germany initiated —more than any action by the King—the "monarcho-fascist" dictatorship. It is fair to say that the King fought for the perpetuation and, later, preservation of his political philosophy and state in the thirties against heavy pressures and heavy odds. It was under Carol's direction that Nicolae Titulescu became minister of foreign affairs, and he sought reconciliation of Romania's differences with the Soviet Union in vain. Also under Carol's guidance, reconciliation was sought with conflicting forms of Balkan nationalism and chauvinism with a view toward establishing a "zone of peace" in the Peninsula. Furthermore, Carol encouraged the enlightened rule of Ion Duca, the Liberal premier eventually assassinated by members of the fascist Iron Guard. Of course, there were also negative aspects to the monarch's rule. He relied on a narrowly based and essentially corrupt political coterie for advice. He appeased the right when advantageous to his political interests and persecuted the left in the same spirit. He failed to fulfill the desiderata of the peasantry because of the agricultural crisis generated by the Great Depression and because of a desire to accumulate the available national wealth for his personal enrichment and that of his camarilla. Still, at least until 1937, he was able to maintain a degree of political equilibrium that did not require the abandonment of "parliamentary democracy" in favor of "royal dictatorship."

It has been a subject of debate whether Carol's dictatorship, formalized in 1938, was preventive—an effort to avoid a fascist dictatorship by the Iron Guard—or a deliberate move based on the conviction that stronger forms of political control had become necessary in 1938 because of the rapid deterioration of the internal and external balance of power. In all probability the King's action was ultimately determined by his belief that the establishment of a fascist dictatorship by the Iron Guard—with external fascist support—was a distinct possibility after the last "free" parliamentary elections in December, 1937, failed to provide his hand-picked prime minister, Gheorghe Tătărescu, with the 40 percent of the votes required to insure reelection. The power of the nationalist right and of the reformist ideas of the social-revolutionary, ultranationalist Iron Guard, which had been minimized by students of the Romanian political scene from the time of the assassination of Duca in 1933, became apparent four years later and forced the de facto termination of "monarcho-democratic" rule. Fascism as the solution to Romania's political and socioeconomic problems was an ever present danger since the time of the exoneration of the Legion of Duca's murder. Also, this verdict illustrated that Romanian fascism was compatible with the country's political tradition and mores. In fact, the Guardist movement had a uniquely Romanian character, essentially different from its western equivalents and even from Carol's dictatorship of later years.[3]

Henry Roberts, the eminent student of interwar Romanian politics, has distinguished four elements of international fascism that were in one form or another recognizable in the Romanian movement.[4] In order of growing significance, Romanian fascism represented "the death rattle of capitalism," a national chauvinist manifestation, a form of dictatorship plus hooliganism, and an expression of anti-Semitism and racial glorification. Of these, the first element is the least significant. Capitalism, identified in Romania with urban, Jewish-dominated ownership or control of the banking, commercial, and industrial network was roundly attacked by the followers of Romanian fascism. But historically the target of their attacks had been the Jewish arendaş—the *locum tenens* of the absentee landlord of pre-World War I years. The forerunners of the anticapitalist fascists of the interwar era were the agrarian, anti-Semitic populists of the early nineteenth century, the followers of Constantin Stere.[5] As glorifiers of the peasant and opponents of his exploitation by the then most powerful capitalist figure, the Jewish "corporation," the populists assumed the role of friends of the "masses" and defenders of their interests. But the "masses" were generally equated with the peasantry even after the "second emancipation" of 1917–21 and the socioeconomic reorganization of the village after World War I. The industrial "masses" never enjoyed the same privileged position as the rural in fascist ideology. The distinction between agrarian and industrial capitalism remained valid throughout the interwar years: Guardists were friends of the peasant and their anticapitalism bore that stamp. Industrial capitalists were tolerated perhaps because they were the principal financiers of the fascist movement whose doctrines had little effect on their industrial empires. Guardist anticapitalism combined the populist and anti-Semitic strands. The success of Romanian fascism was as much a consequence of mass reaction to socioeconomic proposals by the Guardist leadership as of popular acceptance of anti-Semitic slogans and policies.

It is noteworthy that all Romanian "fascists" advocated populist doctrines at one time or another in varying degrees. Populism was vociferously expounded by members of the Iron Guardist movement led by Corneliu Zelea Codreanu, but even the exclusively anti-Semitic LANC (League of National Christian Defense) headed by Professor A. C. Cuza initially sought the support of the peasantry in its struggle against the Jewish entrepreneur and merchant—the League's scapegoat and alleged exploiter of the Romanian peasantry. Cuza abandoned the peasant in the twenties—he considered them satisfied by the agrarian reform—and concentrated on the Jew, now the enemy of all Romanians. Codreanu's Legion of the Archangel Michael and its activist political section, the Iron Guard, remained dedicated to the peasants' cause, and thereupon split with the Cuzists. Thus, while the Cuzist movement only spouted invectives against the Jew, Codreanu was developing a complex socioeconomic and political philosophy, which in the early thirties became the doctrine of "pure" Romanian fascism.[6]

In this doctrine anticapitalism remained a cornerstone. But since the peasants were unresponsive to Codreanu's appeals as long as the National Peasant Party was still regarded as the representative of their political interests, Codreanu's men concentrated temporarily on the Jew and his alleged friend and the peasant's enemy, the communist. It was during the early years of Carol's reign that the Guardist "anti-Judaeo-Communist Christian crusade" assumed clear expression. To Codreanu and his associates the King represented betrayal of true Romanian values as evidenced by his association with Magda Lupescu, appeasement of Jews in general, a search for reconciliation with the Soviet Union, and a basically unfriendly attitude toward Mussolini's fascism. Maniu's replacement by men of lesser nationalist orientation and particularly the appointment of the "pro-Jewish" Duca regime, which eventually outlawed the Legion, provided a basis for testing the strength of nationalist anti-Semitic and anti-communist sentiments among the population at large. The assassination of the Prime Minister was that test and the minimal consequences of that criminal action convinced Codreanu that national vindication was not a lost cause.[7]

It is a misinterpretation of the events of the early thirties to equate the Legionaries' actual power with the results of the popular elections held in that period. Official tallies reflected a falsification of actual results and the continuing allegiance of voters sympathetic to Codreanu's cause to more established parties offering programs superficially similar to the Guards. Any meaningful appraisal of the actual strength and following of the Legion of Archangel Michael became possible only after the establishment by Codreanu of a formal political party, *Totul Pentru Ţară* and publication of its program in 1934. The Guardists' power was by no means negligible.[8]

The development of that power after 1934 was intimately related to the broad dissatisfaction with existing economic conditions prevalent among the Romanian peasantry and the unemployed or frustrated urban intelligentsia and bureaucracy. The Great Depression aggravated the perennial instability of the Romanian economy, and few valid economic solutions could be offered by the monarch or the National Liberal government then in power. It would be erroneous, however, to assume that economic problems alone accounted for the success of Codreanu's legionaries. *Totul Pentru Ţară* promised palliatives and even solutions for the general *malaise* that engulfed Romanian society in the mid-thirties. The traditional corruption, inaction, and ineffectualness of the political establishment and the prevalent social injustice and immobility seemed particularly oppressive and detestable at a time of growing economic insecurity. Codreanu held out national rejuvenation, moral rearmament, and, above all, a national Christian social and moral crusade against all betrayers of what the Legionaries believed to be the true national historic legacy. In specific terms the Legionaries identified that legacy with the supremacy of the Christian Romanian peasant and his supporters and friends. The peasant, led by the Guard, would develop a Romania for the Romanians over the dead bodies of Judaeo-Communists and all other exponents of non-Christian, non-Romanian, political, and socioeconomic philosophies. Judaism was the plague of Romanianism; it had to be eradicated. The Jew was the mortal enemy of the Romanian and Romania's progress; he had to be expropriated, destroyed economically as well as physically. The Jew professed or was in sympathy with anti-Christian communism; that faith had to be extirpated also. To cleanse Romania and Christendom of the Jew and his allies and reorganize society according to the principles of Christianity, as interpreted by Codreanu, was the "Captain's" goal and his party's political program.[9] In terms of Roberts' criteria and definitions, only anti-Semitism could be identified as an integral component of Guardist fascism in 1934. The Legionaries had no monopoly on chauvinism, hooliganism, and notions of dictatorship. Chauvinism was not an indispensable part of their political philosophy; their ideas on dictatorship were still poorly defined; hooliganism was held in abeyance. An element of idealism and Christian mysticism pervaded the movement. But this was to change under the impact of domestic political reaction against the potentially explosive doctrine of the Guardists and of the rapid progress recorded by fascism in Germany, Italy, and Spain.[10]

The transformation of the Guardist movement from an idealistic, politically immature, Christian, reformist crusade into the brutal, hooliganistic, and fanatically anti-Semitic one it became occurred after its expectations were frustrated by the political forces associated with Carol II. Between 1934 and 1937 the Legionaries concentrated on preaching rural reform and anti-Semitic doctrine while they also condemned the mores of the political establishment. Their moderation was partly owing to the belief that accommodation with Carol was possible since he and some of his industrial friends lent financial and, occasionally, ideological support to Codreanu's team but mainly because they expected the eventual conversion of the masses to populist fascism. And they had good reason to believe the latter as the reception of Legionaries in the village was generally responsive and frequently enthusiastic.[11] The Guardists were also welcomed by the clergy—anxious to participate in Christian reform—by schoolteachers, students, and disgruntled intellectuals and bureaucrats who for one reason or another believed in moral rejuvenation and, in any event, were anti-Semitic. The extent of the penetration of the village and the effectiveness of the Guardist movement in the country at large was underestimated at the time by all political parties except those concerned with the attitude of the peasantry. By 1937 the National Peasant Party, the Plowmen's Front, and the latter's ideological ally, the disorganized Communist Party, alone recognized the depth of Guardist influence. Characteristically, their reactions differed: the dominant conservative wing of the National Peasant Party sought an *Ausgleich* with the Legion in the common political struggle against the National Liberals and their patron, the King; the communists and leaders of the Plowmen's front responded by intensifying their heretofore empty campaign against fascism.[12] The responses of these political groups, particularly the National Peasants', gave more direction to the fascist movement in the crucial months immediately preceding and following the ill-fated election of December, 1937, and establishment of the "monarcho-fascist" dictatorship of Carol II in February, 1938, than Carol's own increasingly sharper reaction to Guardist successes and the activities of the Legion's foreign friends, Hitler, Franco, and Mussolini.

Ideological and financial contacts between the Romanian fascists and their counterparts elsewhere were surprisingly limited in the early thirties.[13] Mussolini's flirtations and subsequent engagement to Romania's revisionist neighbors, Bulgaria and Hungary, did not entail the establishment of any meaningful relations with Codreanu and his associates. If anything, the Legionaries were as opposed as the monarchy to these Italian policies, regarding them as unjust and anti-Romanian. The Legion also appears to have been immune to the doctrine of Italian fascism. Similarly, Hitler's assumption of power in Germany and initiation of his political and economic penetration of Romania did not involve the Iron Guard. On the contrary, the Guardists were shunned by Berlin, which preferred orderly action through the King to working through illegal and untested ideological sympathizers. It is not improbable, however, that funds were made available to the Guardists for pursuit of anti-Semitic and pro-German propaganda and it is now known that the foreign activities of the Legionaries were largely financed by the Nazis, chiefly through German underwriting of the expenses incurred by Romanian volunteers in the Spanish Civil War. But the sums expended by the Germans on Romanian fascists in Spain were apparently no larger, and most likely smaller, than those spent by the Russians on the Romanian communists who joined the anti-fascist forces in the conflict.

Significantly, the Spanish Civil War provided the Iron Guard the political-military experience and ideological exposure to militant fascism that was to place the Legionaries in direct and mortal combat with the national and international forces of "Judaeo-Communism." The crusading spirit that developed during the war affected the entire movement following the return of the veterans of the confrontation between the totalitarian right and left. Similarly, the anti-fascist cause was fought with greater conviction and deliberation by the defeated communist returnees. It was not by accident that the first major clash between the fascist and communist crusaders occurred in the regional elections of 1936, with both sides vying for the support of the masses for their respective reformist plans. The accompanying verbal and physical battles between the members of *Totul Pentru Ţară* and those of the communist-dominated Popular Front were further proof of the growing threat of fascism in Romania. The communists and their sympathizers preached against the dangers of organized and disorganized fascism in a futile attempt to discredit the Guardists with the peasantry and the working class.[14]

The struggle for the allegiance of the masses was unequal because the left was overpowered and outnumbered by the right. But once the struggle was joined, the right benefited from the assistance of those who opposed communism as well as of those opposed to monarchic rule. The inroads made by the Iron Guard in the villages and among the population at large in 1936–37, with the blessings of those seeking common action by all dedicated to "Romanianism," were extensive. When translated into concrete terms in the national election of December, 1937, they were the difference between victory and defeat for directed democracy.

The official results of this last so-called "free" Romanian election resulted in the defeat of the National Liberal government, which was unable to muster the minimum 40 percent of the vote required to insure its continuation in power.[15] The defeat was ascribed to the unexpected size of the Guardist vote, reported as 16 percent of the ballots cast. It is conceded by contemporary political observers that the actual fascist vote was well above that percentage. In fact, the King's decision not to proclaim the National Liberals winners but instead to hand over the government to the right-wing coalition of Octavian Goga and A. C. Cuza was a clear reflection of his realization that the country was leaning toward the extreme right. The appointment of the Goga-Cuza cabinet was a stopgap measure in anticipation of the establishment of an outright royal dictatorship. The King's maneuver of December, 1937, revealed his great political acumen and also his shock over the extent of Guardist penetration into the society at large. It would be erroneous to assume, as some analysts of the Romanian fascist movement have done, that the size of the Guardist vote merely reflected the anti-Semitic sentiment of the Romanian population. That this was not the case was amply proven by the failure of the Goga-Cuza electoral coalition to obtain more than 9 percent of the total popular vote or to stay in power for more than a few weeks on the basis of their purely nationalistic and specifically anti-Semitic program. The success of the Guard, as Carol realized, was based on the broad support it received from the village and urban bureaucracy and intelligentsia and on the electoral alliance that it concluded with the National Peasant Party earlier in 1937. Even if the majority of the peasantry did not vote Guardist, enough votes were cast to insure defeat of the National Liberals. It has been suggested, with much validity, that the National Peasant leadership knew that it could not muster a majority on its own strength and therefore decided to collaborate with the Iron Guard on the assumption that the combined vote would force the King to accept the popular mandate and summon to power a National Peasant coalition and perhaps an actual National Peasant government. This thesis is apparently correct.[16] The corollary interpretation that the virulence of the opposition, the Guard's in particular, increased when Carol upset their plans first by appointing the unrepresentative Goga-Cuza regime and then by assuming dictatorial powers himself also appears to be correct. The monarch's decision to substitute monarcho-fascism for legionary-fascism of the populist-Guardist variety forced an immediate and far-reaching modification of tactics, policies, and alignments by the "betrayed" Guard and its political supporters. After February, 1938, a life and death struggle began between the King and the Iron Guard during which the very character of Romanian fascism was profoundly altered.

The royal dictatorship, "monarcho-fascist" as it has been characterized by its detractors, had few of the characteristics ascribed by Roberts to fascist movements. It was not anticapitalistic, it was only moderately anti-Semitic and chauvinistic, and it contained no elements of racial glorification or hooliganism. It was, however, a dictatorship that "borrowed" the essential tenets of Guardist philosophy: nationalist socioreformism and national renaissance. The abolition of political parties and the establishment of "collective democracy" under the leadership of the King in the *Frontul Renaşterii Naţionale* (The Front of National Rebirth) was designed to diminish the power of the Iron Guard and its supporters who had successfully advocated national rebirth and social reform. Carol's dictatorship was unquestionably an immediate reaction to Guardist successes in 1937; however, it was a poor substitute for the militant idealism and reformism of Codreanu and his associates. The failure of Carol's policies was ultimately due to his inability to destroy the Guard as a political force in Romania —it was not due to his inability to gain the support of politicians who had flirted or collaborated with the Iron Guard, nor can it be said that he was unsuccessful in retaining the allegiance of the dissatisfied peasantry. He had, on occasion, executed pro-peasant policies. His foolhardy decision to execute Corneliu Zelea Codreanu and the "Captain's" closest associates in November, 1938, "while trying to escape" and subsequent attempt to carry out a policy of mass extermination of Legionaries strengthened rather than weakened the determination of the Romanian right to rid itself of Carol at all cost. And, for the first time, the fascists secured the support of a Nazi Germany dissatisfied with the monarch's wavering foreign policy. Forced underground, the survivors of the purge assumed the role of martyrs and avengers of the dead. Between 1938 and 1940, they became the executioners of Carol's "accomplices," hooligans and assassins dedicated to the physical annihilation of their mortal enemies —Jews, communists, and royalists. In the process they abandoned their idealism and plans for nationalist social reform in the village, the factory, and the bureaucracy. The Romanian fascists lost their original political identity and with it their political *raison d'être*, between the fall of 1938 and the summer of 1940, when the Guard defeated its archenemy, Carol II, and finally gained power.

The struggle for power between Carol and the Guard was deceptively uneven before 1940. If Carol had the upper hand in 1938, it was because the Germans were not ready, before Munich, to impose their dictates on Romania. Their interests were sufficiently safeguarded, although superficially and temporarily, by the Carolist dictatorship and the efficiency of the King's major-domo, Armand Călinescu. Nevertheless, the Germans and their sympathizers in Romania were not out of touch with the remnants of the Legion, which to them represented a lever and alternative to the "monarcho-fascists." After the Anschluss, and increasingly after Munich, the balance of power began to shift in the direction of the Guard. Carol's dictatorship was suspect because of his refusal to proclaim himself overtly in favor of Germany. The fact that Carol succumbed to German economic pressures in March, 1939, and accepted the onerous Nazi-Romanian economic agreement of that month did not satisfy the aggressive and suspicious German leadership or the "rejuvenated" Guard. The royal dictatorship was increasingly threatened during the second half of 1939, particularly after the Ribbentrop-Molotov agreement ushered in World War II. Carol, still anxious to maintain Romania's neutrality, became to the Germans increasingly more expendable and certainly *de trop* for the Legionaries. In September, 1939, as Poland's defeat was recorded, the Guard assassinated Călinescu in cold blood. The assassination was a challenge to the royal dictatorship, and even the public execution of the assassins did not deter the Legionaries from portraying themselves as martyrs and as saviors of the Romanians from Carol. Defections from the King's to the Guard's cause were slow, at least on the surface, until the "Judaeo-Communist conspiracy" was finally and fully "exposed" in June, 1940. The seizure of Bessarabia and northern Bukovina by the Soviet Union during that month vindicated the Guardist cause. And as France also lay prostrate before the superior German armies, the Legionaries appeared as the champions of true militant Romanianism, defenders of the interests of Romania against bolshevism and Judaism, avengers of treacherous royalism, rectifiers of all ills afflicting Romanian society and politics. In fact, however, reform was no longer part of their program; revenge, power, extermination of the Jews, destruction of the Bolsheviks and all other opponents of their plans for unlimited control of the country had become their only credo. In September, 1940, when the Germans had cynically given northern Transylvania to Hungary and the Bulgarians had secured southern Dobrudja with Germany's support, monarcho-fascism came to an inglorious end. Carol barely escaped alive; most of his followers joined the Guardists, and his son, now King Michael, entrusted power to the Iron Guard and the pro-Guardist military leaders headed by General Ion Antonescu. A new crusade, anti-communist, anti-Semitic and anti-all opponents of the Guard was initiated under the "new" Iron Guard led by power-hungry men like Horia Sima and other "betrayers" of original legionary goals.[17]

The triumph of legionary-fascism was short lived. The Guardists came to power late, at a time of major international crisis on the eve of the entry of the German forces of occupation into Romania, and had little time to carry out their program. They disrupted the country's economy and engaged in acts of hooliganism and crime against their enemies and so were forcibly removed from power in the bloody revolution of January, 1941. That revolution was totally devoid of the reformist idealism that had permeated the movement in the thirties. It was an unprincipled bloodbath engaged in for political survival. The hooligans were defeated by the forces of order headed by the Guard's ally, Marshal Ion Antonescu, and supported by the German High Command. But the decimation of the Guardists did not mark the end of fascism or of the Guardist movement.

Antonescu ruled the National Legionary State, which he and the Guard had established in September, 1940, as a fascist military dictatorship.[18] His dictatorship, however, differed from that of his predecessors and of contemporary European counterparts in significant respects. He adopted many of the corporatist features characteristic of Carol's regime and sought the support of traditional conservative political groups and of responsible Legionaries for the pursuit of an anti-communist and nationalist crusade of his own. It is noteworthy that Antonescu rooted out all manifestations of hooliganism and did not claim the racist and anti-Semitic Guardist legacy. His reformist tendencies were closer to Carol's than Codreanu's, concentrating, albeit for military purposes, on the modernization of agriculture and industry. His crucial error, inherent in the *raison d'être* of his dictatorship, was in focusing the national effort onto the pursuit of an anti-Russian, anti-communist, military campaign. He thus was the forerunner of the explicitly anti-Bolshevik orientation that became the fascists' trademark after World War II. Antonescu's de facto repudiation of anti-Semitism and hooliganism was not endorsed, however, by the Guardist leaders in exile in Germany or Spain until after the final débâcle of the Third Reich. At that time only Sima and his retinue reassumed the position of social reformers bent on "liberating" Romania from communism. The revamped fascists enjoyed more than a modicum of success until their political successors, the Romanian communists, assumed anti-Russian positions themselves and carried out, as Romanian national communists, the social reforms that had been anticipated by Codreanu and initiated by Carol and Antonescu. As nationalist social reformers, the fascists may be regarded as the communists' immediate predecessors. Therein lies their primary historic significance and, for that matter, also that of their successors.

FOOTNOTES

1 The best analysis of the Carolist period remains Henry L. Roberts, *Rumania: Political Problems of an Agrarian State* (New Haven, Conn.: Yale University Press, 1951), pp. 170–222.

2 Roberts, *Rumania*, pp. 130–86, contains an excellent discussion of these problems.

3 On the Iron Guard and Romanian fascism in general consult the excellent study by Eugen Weber, "Romania," in *The European Right*, Hans Rogger and Eugen Weber, eds. (Berkeley; University of California Press, 1966), pp. 501–74.

4 Roberts, *Rumania*, p. 223.

5 On populism and Stere's ideology consult Roberts, *Rumania*, pp. 142–56.

6 Codreanu's political philosophy is contained in Corneliu Zelea Codreanu, *Pentru Legionari* (București: Editure Miscării Legionare, 1937). The program of the Legion of Archangel Michael is available in an English translation in Stephen Fischer-Galati, *Twentieth Century Europe: A Documentary History* (Philadelphia: Lippincott, 1956), pp. 137–40.

7 See in particular Weber, "Romania," pp. 547–48.

8 Weber, "Romania," pp. 544–45, provides valuable data.

9 Fisher-Galati, *Twentieth Century Europe*, pp. 137–40.

10 In addition to Roberts' and Weber's studies consult Lucrețiu D. Pătrăşcanu, *Sub Trei Dictaturi* (Bucareşti: Forum, 1945) a stimulating analysis of Romanian politics in the thirties.

11 Weber, "Romania," pp. 541–43 contains excellent illustrative material.

12 Stephen Fischer-Galati, *The New Rumania: From People's Democracy to Socialist Republic* (Cambridge, Mass.: Harvard University Press, 1967), pp. 10–16.

13 See in particular Andreas Hillgruber, *Hitler, König Carol und Marschall Antonescu; die deutsch-rumänischen Beziehungen, 1938–1944* (Wiesbaden: F. Steiner, 1954) with excellent bibliographical references.

14 Valuable data and bibliographical references in Ion M. Oprea, "Lupta P.C.R. impotriva fascizarii tarii si a razboiului antisovietic," *Studii* 15, no. 6 (1962): 1723–34.

15 Roberts, *Rumania*, pp. 191–92.

16 This interpretation, best set forth in Pătrăşcanu, *Sub Trei Dictaturi*, appears to be more valid than Roberts' in *Rumania*, p. 191.

17 An excellent discussion of these problems in Roberts, *Rumania*, pp. 223–35.

18 Antonescu's views are clearly expressed in his public statements contained in Ion Antonescu, *Generalul Antonescu către Ţară, 6 Septemvrie 1940–22 Iunie 1941* (Bucureşti: Luceafarul, 1941).

VII
Yugoslavia

USTASHI PARTY EMBLEM

Dimitrije Djordjevic

Ivan Avakumovic

A

Fascism in Yugoslavia: 1918–1941

Dimitrije Djordjević

The emergence of fascist trends and ideas in Yugoslavia between the two wars displays the characteristics of a specific phenomenon: the general internal and external factors that affected the development of the Yugoslav state from 1918 until 1941. In order to provide a full explanation of this phenomenon one must understand the domestic and external circumstances that influenced the formation of Yugoslav political movements in general.

I

The two main issues that played a dominant role in the political life of Yugoslavia between the two wars were national and social. The national question was the consequence of the separate courses that the political, social, and cultural life of the Yugoslav peoples took until their unification in 1918. In their past, Yugoslavs lived under the political rule of several states and were exposed to the influence of two distinct civilizations—eastern and western. Economically, Yugoslavia was unevenly developed. The most advanced regions until 1918 were those which had been under the strong influence of Central European and Mediterranean economic forces. The most backward were the areas that remained under the rule of Ottoman feudalism until that time. Hence the differences in the development of Yugoslav society. For example, the big estates dominated in the northern parts of the country, small peasant holdings were the rule in Serbia, tribal customs in Montenegro, serfdom in feudal Macedonia and in parts of Bosnia and Hercegovina. As a result of these many influences, differences appeared in the political institutions of the various Yugoslav peoples. Serbia succeeded in gradually building a free and independent state on the foundations laid by its revolution at the beginning of the nineteenth century. Montenegro followed a similar process. As a result both, but particularly Serbia, exerted strong influence on the development of the entire Yugoslav liberation movement. Among the Yugoslavs living under the Habsburg monarchy, national emancipation assumed the form of a struggle against Vienna and Budapest for political autonomy, whereas in the Ottoman Empire it had a revolutionary character.

In 1918, Yugoslavs brought this variegated historical heritage into the newly formed common state. This heritage lay at the root of the chief political conflict in Yugoslavia and focused on the question of whether the state system should be centralistic (unitaristic) or federal. Serbian political circles, considering Yugoslavia to be a kind of extended Serbia, were in favor of centralism, arguing that Serbia made the greatest contribution to the unification of Yugoslavs by her role in World War I. On the other hand, in Yugoslav regions that had been a part of Austria-Hungary, federalist ideas were strongly favored as a means of national affirmation. The conflict between centralism and federalism in the Yugoslav movement had already become evident during World War I and became the main issue in the political life of Yugoslavia between the two wars. This conflict is of great importance for the study of the subject we are discussing today: centralistic concepts, in the struggle for the maintenance of Yugoslav unitarism, resulted in restrictions imposed on parliamentarianism and in the introduction of dictatorship. On the other hand, federalism, in its extreme forms, turned into state separatism. Both of these trends contained the seeds of totalitarianism. Centralism attempted to resolve the national crisis by nonconstitutional means; separatism sought the support of fascist ideologies and powers (Italy and Germany) that advocated the revision of the peace treaties, and thus also the revision of the entire state structure of Yugoslavia.

The second cause of the internal crisis of Yugoslavia between 1918 and 1941 was social. The disparate economic developments in its various regions made the emergence of a unified Yugoslav middle class impossible. Big capital showed a tendency to cooperate on an all-Yugoslav scale, but the smaller capitalists (who were predominate in number) retained a narrow, regional character, even in their transactions. On the whole, Yugoslav capital remained decentralized and exposed to the strong infiltration and influence of foreign capital. The peasants, who comprised the majority of the population, suffered from the agrarian crises that caused upheavals on a world-wide scale between the wars, from low productivity, and from a shortage of technical equipment and capital. Industrial development was too slow to absorb the surplus of labor that came from the villages, but it was significant enough to lead to the formation of a working class that was exposed to the effects of the domestic and international economic crises as well as to the influence of great ideological movements in twentieth-century Europe: the October Revolution in Russia, the development of the international labor movement, and the great world crisis of the 1930s.

The sharp division into left and right wing political movements at the expense of the center was typical at this time throughout Europe and was accompanied by a deepening internal national and social crisis. This division was reflected in Yugoslavia, a country subjected to the increasingly aggressive designs of the Central European and Mediterranean fascist powers. However, when examining the appearance of fascist tendencies in Yugoslavia, it should be borne in mind that fascism never took deep roots in the country. Several political and social circumstances account for this lack of enthusiasm. Centralism and unitarism, which advocated rightist ideas in dealing with the national question, came into conflict with the revisionist aspirations of the fascist powers and with the separatist tendencies of fascism's Yugoslav exponents. The national emancipation of Yugoslavia took place during the nineteenth century in opposition to German and Italian designs on Yugoslav territories.

Anti-German feelings were particularly strong in Serbia, whose political circles were the main forces of national unity because Serbia had to bear the brunt of the

German *Drang nach Osten,* directed against Southeastern Europe during the first two decades of the twentieth century. In addition, the social forces that would have been most likely to become exponents of the fascist ideology were rather weak in Yugoslavia. The aristocracy and the big landowners, the main conservative forces in Austro-Hungary, were eliminated in the Yugoslav regions of the Habsburg monarchy during the stormy days at the end of World War I. Financial and industrial magnates, who provided support for fascist concepts in the rest of Europe, were a thin stratum in Yugoslavia, which had a low level of economic development. On the contrary, the Yugoslav middle class, in the stage of an intensive accumulation of capital, demanded economic liberalism, which was most in keeping with their level of development. The working class took antifascist positions and neither did the peasant population show an affinity toward the fascist ideology. The freedom-loving traditions, born in the process of liberation struggles, uprisings, and revolutions in the Balkans of the nineteenth century, and the traditional spirit prevalent on small private farms that predominated in Yugoslavia were antithetical to fascism. Officers of the Yugoslav army supported the authoritarian regime introduced on January 6, 1929, and while some Yugoslav officers of high rank were fascinated by the German military machinery, the army as a whole did not possess pro-fascist sympathies. This climate of opinion was the result of the traditional ties born out of the alliance with the anti-German coalition during the First World War. This mood was further strengthened by the revisionist aspirations that the fascist powers displayed toward Yugoslav territories. The mood of the army was clearly manifested in the military coup of March 27, 1941. For all these reasons, fascism could only find a stronghold in national separatism or in the extreme anticommunism of the upper sections of society and some youth (student) circles. On the whole, fascism was isolated from the masses and lacked influence on their political affiliations.

II

A major role in the appearance of fascist concepts in Yugoslavia between the two wars was played by external factors. With regard to her links with other countries, Yugoslavia was not in a favorable position. Among the great powers, she enjoyed only the full support of France, at least until 1935. Until 1940 Yugoslavia had no diplomatic relations with the Soviet Union; relations with Italy were tense until 1937. The same state of affairs prevailed with respect to Austria and Hungary as well, because of their revisionist aspirations and because of the more imaginary than real threat of the restoration of the Habsburg dynasty. Relations with Bulgaria were strained (after the death of Alexander Stamboliiski) because of Macedonia, and with Albania because of the Kosovo region.

Regardless of authoritarian policies at home, Yugoslav foreign policy, within the framework of the Little Entente and the Balkan Pact, followed a Francophile and anti-fascist line until 1935. The strengthening of the influence of fascist Italy and Nazi Germany, which became noticeable everywhere in the Balkans in 1934–35, the hesitation of the western democracies, anticommunism and fear of the Soviet Union, together with the threat presented by national separatists—drove the conservative Yugoslav political circles closer to Rome and Berlin in the period between 1936 and 1938. The unsettled national question was an important element in the new line adopted by Yugoslav foreign policy. The Croatian question became part of the struggle of the great powers for Yugoslavia in the years preceding World War II. The Western European powers, whose resistance to the German economic penetration in the Balkans grew increasingly weak, largely supported the centralism of Belgrade. The Axis powers, Italy and Germany, on the other hand, supported national separatist elements, turning them into a means of pressure on the Yugoslav government, and into a weapon wherewith to break Yugoslavia when the time came to change the status quo in Southeastern Europe. In this manner, Yugoslavia was surrounded by a network of separatist organizations, like the Ustaši of Ante Pavelić in Italy, Austria and Germany, the *vrhovists* of Ivan Mihailov in Bulgaria and Macedonia, and the Kosovo-Albanian committees in Albania and Italy, all of which were supported by fascist powers. The problem of national separatism, provided, among other things, one of the motives that induced the government of Milan Stojadinović to draw closer to the Axis in the endeavor to induce the fascists to withdraw their support from the Ustaši separatists. On the other hand, the unsettled national question, especially Croatian dissatisfaction with the policy of centralism became part of the struggle between Italy and Germany for supremacy on the Adriatic. As much as Italy may have wished to see Yugoslavia divided she hesitated to provoke her collapse in fear of eliminating the barrier that Yugoslavia presented to the German penetration southward, into the sphere of influence of Italian imperialism. The Italian-German threat also induced the Croatian nationalists, headed by Dr. Vladko Maček, to seek an agreement with the centralism of Belgrade in 1939. The contacts that Maček established with Italy and Germany in 1939 were strategic moves to bring pressure to bear on Belgrade rather than serious attempts to solve the Croatian question outside the boundaries of Yugoslavia.

The policy of relying on fascist powers, practiced between 1935 and 1938, met violent resistance from Yugoslav public opinion. The general deterioration of international relations and the beginning of World War II were reflected in Yugoslavia's attempt between 1939 and 1941 to maintain a neutralistic foreign policy and to avoid taking sides with any of the countries at war. This attempt was doomed to failure for a number of internal and external reasons. The mood of the people was democratic and anti-fascist, yet neutralism was impossible, because a total war was spreading. The Anschluss of Austria in 1938, the Italian occupation of Albania in 1939, war with Greece in 1940, and the arrival of Germans in Romania and Bulgaria made Yugoslavia an island in a fascist sea. The capitulation of Yugoslavia, which took the form of joining the Tripartite Pact on March 25, 1941, was revoked by the violent resistance of the army and masses of the Yugoslav people, who overthrew the government on March 27. By this act Yugoslavia entered the war against the Axis powers.

III

When examining and assessing fascist tendencies in Yugoslavia between the two wars, three phenomena deserve special consideration. These are the regime introduced after the abolition of parliamentarism on January 6, 1929; the emergence of nationalistic organizations with unitaristic or federalistic programs; and, the appearance of movements with explicitly fascist ideologies.

The internal political life of Yugoslavia between 1918 and 1941 went through three stages. The first stage covered the period from the unification in 1918 until the introduction of royal dictatorship on January 6, 1929. The second stage was the personal rule of King Alexander which lasted until the proclamation of the new Constitution of 1931, which was granted by the King. Political relations in the first stage developed within the framework of the parliamentary system set up in 1921 by the Constitution of Vidovdan, with certain restrictions, such as the banning of the Communist Party and the prohibition of the Croatian Republican Peasant Party. During the second stage, all political organizations were banned, and political power was transferred to the King, the army, and the civil servants. Political freedoms in the third stage were somewhere between those permitted during the preceding two phases, while parliamentarism remained restricted.

In the period of parliamentary rule, political life was characterized by the activities of political parties. Political affiliation was determined on the basis of national and class criteria, in the struggle for centralism, federalism, and social reform. With the exception of some all-Yugoslav parties (Democratic, Radical, Social-Democratic and Communist, until its prohibition in 1920), those remaining were formed on a narrower national basis (Croatian Peasant Party, Slovene People's Party, Yugoslav Muslim Party). The existence, side by side, of so many parties and the balance of power politics, which was the result of this state of affairs, necessitated the formation of coalition cabinets, which were torn by internal dissension and burdened with the question of national unity. In the period from December, 1918, until January, 1929, Yugoslavia went through twenty-four changes or reconstructions of the cabinet.

The regime of January 7, introduced in 1929 by the abolition of the constitution and the prohibition of political parties, is treated in modern Yugoslav historiography as the monarcho-fascist dictatorship. The King's dictatorship between 1929 and 1931 contained many of the characteristics of the personal absolutist regimes of Serbian nineteenth-century rulers. The fascist features in it can be found in the proclamation of the principle of order and discipline, in the emphasis on the political leadership of the King (the slogan "The King and the people"), in the stress laid on the authority of the state, in centralism and in anticommunism. The regime introduced on January 6, however, was declared to be temporary, justifying national unitarism as the unavoidable means of preserving national unity (the proclamation of Yugoslavia, instead of the Kingdom of the Serbs, Croats, and Slovenes, as it was called until then). The active participants in the introduction of the regime of January 6 were, in addition to the King, the army and civil servants, also the dissidents of various political parties (Democratic, Radical, Croatian Peasant Party, and the Yugoslav Muslim Organization and of the Slovene People's Party, headed by Mgr. Anton Korošec). The attempt at introducing corporativism into the new constitution was rejected. That constitution, proclaimed by the King in 1931, introduced again, although only to a limited degree, the representative system. During the King's dictatorship, Yugoslav foreign policy retained a Francophile line. The signing of the Balkan Pact in 1934 was directed against German and Italian aspirations in the Balkans. Finally, fascist Italy was directly involved in the preparations for the assassination in Marseilles, which took place in 1934 and in which the head of the regime of January 6, King Alexander, lost his life. Some recent Soviet publications claim that the participation of Nazi Germany in that act of terrorism has also been proven. All these factors lead to the conclusion that the dictatorial regime introduced in Yugoslavia between 1929 and 1931 is best described as a Balkanic variant of personal absolutism based on the support of the army, civil servants, and the centralistically inclined upper stratum of society.

The regime that followed the proclamation of the Constitution of 1931 gave rise to new types of political parties. These parties formed to supply parliamentary support to the cabinet. Among the new parties were, for example, the Yugoslav National Party (JNS) and the Yugoslav Radical Community (JRZ) headed by Milan Stojadinović and Dragiša Cvetković. The general strengthening of external fascist influences—from Germany and Italy—in the Balkans gave rise to fascist tendencies not only in the foreign policy of the Stojadinović cabinet in 1935–38 but also in internal manifestations —the election of a leader, party uniforms, and the setting up of state trade unions. However, as already mentioned, these tendencies did not get a firm footing among the masses, and the impression given by some of the uniformed formations was operetta like.

Another phenomenon bearing upon our subject is the establishment of a larger number of nationalistic organizations that did not adopt a fascist ideology, but which made use of fascist methods of terrorism in their political and national struggle.

The appearance of nationalistic organizations was closely connected to the conflict between centralism and federalism, which comprised the substance of their programs. Unitarism was the foundation for a number of organizations, such as the Organization of Yugoslav Nationalists (ORJUNA), Yugoslav Action, the Organization of National Students (ORNAS), the Patriotic Youth Front (POF), the Yugoslav Academic Club (JAK) and, to a lesser extent, a large number of national organizations like the Popular Defense, the Union of Četniks, the Society of Reserve Officers, the Federation of Volunteers, the Yugoslav Sokol Confederation, the Adriatic Guard, the Yugoslav Matica, and so on. For the most part, these organizations supported the government in carrying out its centralistic policy.

Along with them, more narrowly nationalistic organizations also sprang up, mostly with federalistic programs. Those were the Croatian National Youth (HRNAO), the Slovene National Youth (SLONAO), the Muslim National Youth (MUNAO), the Organization of Bunjevo Nationalists (ORBUNA), the Organization of Catholic Nationalists (ORKAN), and so on. The Serbian Nationalistic Youth Organization (SRNAO) supported the radical party.

The political coloring of all these organizations was nationalistic. The activities of the unitaristic all-Yugoslav organizations were mainly directed against communists, federalists and separatists. The ORJUNA, founded in 1921, called for a crusade against Italian revisionism in Dalmatia, Istria, and Slovenia, and considered itself the successor of the prewar Yugoslav National Youth, especially in its aspirations toward a Great Yugoslavia, which would also incorporate Bulgaria. ORJUNA denied that it was a fascist movement, claiming to be a national organization without explicit political aims. Yet, the influence of fascism was undeniable in the semimilitary units of the ORJUNA, in the military discipline of its members, in methods of physical violence in the struggle against their opponents, and in the centralization of leadership.

The so-called Yugoslav Action, founded in 1930 to support the basic concepts of the regime of January 6, was even more rightist in its policy. The presence of fascist ideas is explicit in its program: antiparliamentarism, corporativism, anticommunism, and a planned economy. The supporters of that movement also denied any links with fascism, claiming to be a nonparty organization, whose aim was to defend Yugoslav unity from revolutionary, social, and narrowly nationalistic movements. Although originally founded in order to propagate the ideas of the regime of January 6, the Yugoslav Action organization soon came into conflict with that regime and was banned in 1934. The same fate was shared by the Slovene semimilitary organization, Union of Slovene Soldiers (BOJ), which started its activities in 1929 by supporting the dictatorship, joined the opposition later, and which was banned in 1934.

Fascist methods of struggle, physical clashes with opponents, were accepted by organizations founded on more narrowly nationalistic principles, who fought both among themselves and against the unitarists. Among these, the Serbian National Youth (SRNAO) was the exponent of the Radical Party, the Croatian Youth accepted the ideas of the Peasant Party of Stjepan Radić, and the Muslim Youth was part of the Muslim political organization. The conflicts between them were particularly strong in the Vojvodina, Croatia, Dalmatia, and Bosnia. All of these nationalistic organizations were banned in 1929.

The third group within this context consisted of explicitly fascist organizations with corresponding programs and methods of action. They were political and terrorist organizations—the *Zbor* movement, the Ustaši and Macedonian separatists.

The *Zbor* movement was formed in 1935 from rightist elements of the Yugoslav Action, the Slovene organization *Boj* and from a Serbian group centered around the newspapers, *Zbor* ("Convention"), *Otadžbina* ("Native Country"), and *Budjenje* ("Awakening"). *Zbor* was organized on the leadership principle with a strict hierarchy. The fascist program based on a corporative system did not gain popular support. In the elections of 1935 and 1938, *Zbor* did not win a single seat in Parliament (in the first election it gained 0.86 percent and in the second 1.01 percent of the total vote). After failing to gain national support, *Zbor* began forming task groups to fight against the labor movement and the middle-class parties. An open conflict developed between it and the government of M. Stojadinović, and its leader, Dimitrije Ljotić, was arrested. As German influence grew, the activities of *Zbor* expanded, especially in the direction of anticommunism and anti-Semitism. After a violent clash between rightist and leftist students at Belgrade University in 1940, and especially following the deterioration of relations with Italy after the bombing of Bitolj on November 5, the government of Cvetković-Maček prohibited *Zbor* and ordered the arrest of its members on the charge of preparing a coup d'état to introduce fascism. The party continued its activities underground until the war broke out in 1941.

Terrorist organizations with fascist ideologies, directly relying on Italy and Germany, were formed among the separatist Croatian emigrants. Taking advantage of the revisionist aspirations of some of Yugoslavia's neighbors, these organizations grew in the Italy of Mussolini, in the Hungary of Horthy, and in the Bulgaria of Boris. Ante Pavelić, who was later to become the head of the Ustaši quisling Independent State of Croatia, began, in 1929, to organize the Ustaši movement by linking separatist elements who lived abroad and by establishing contact with all anti-Yugoslav movements, for example with Macedonian separatists in Sofia. In this manner, Ustaši camps and centers were formed in Italian cities, Verona, Bovegno, Brescia, Borgo Val di Taro, San Demetrio nei Vestone, as well as in Vienna and Graz (from where they were later transferred to Janka Puszta in Hungary), in Berlin, and other places. All these were training centers for terrorist activities and assassinations to be undertaken in Yugoslavia. They were financed first by Italian and later also by Hungarian fascist circles. The Ustaši terrorists conducted a series of attacks with explosives on trains, railway stations, police barracks, and larger public gatherings. The assassination of King Alexander in Marseilles was the joint action of the Ustaši and the Macedonian separatists. The Ustaši separatists sought to gain the support of fascist elements in Croatia, taking advantage of the general dissatisfaction provoked by the centralist policy of the Belgrade government. In 1935, the Labor Legion was founded in Zagreb, becoming the nucleus of the subsequent Task Force for the Liberation of Croatia. The Ustaši also enjoyed the support of the student pro-fascist association, August Senoa, and of the organization, Crusaders *(Krizari),* which was founded immediately before the war.

Two currents can be distinguished among the Ustaši—one was fascist under the domination of Italy, and one Nazi, subject to German influence. Both groups used the Axis powers to exert pressure on Yugoslavia and to blackmail its authorities. This division was an expression of the struggle taking place between Italy and Germany for supremacy in the Croatian region and on the Adriatic. After the Yugoslav-Italian agreement, signed in 1937, prohibiting the activities of the Ustaši in Italy, they were withdrawn to Sicily, and were not used actively again until Italy's attack on Yugoslavia in 1941. The Ustaši group in Germany, headed by Dr. Branimir Jelić, maintained contacts with Alfred Rosenberg, with the *Aussenpolitisches Amt,* the *Abwehr,* the GESTAPO and the S.D., giving excellent service especially to the German intelligence. Suppressed at the time of the Yugoslav-German rapprochement during the Stojadinović government, the Ustaši organization was again active on the eve of the German attack on Yugoslavia, and took an active part in destroying this state in 1941.

The Ustaši activities developed parallel to the action of the Macedonian separatists concentrated around the *vrhovist* committees of the Internal Macedonian Revolutionary Organization (IMRO), headed by Todor Aleksandrov, Alexander Protogerov, and later by Mihailov. After World War I, a split developed in IMRO between the *vrhovists,* who demanded the dissolution of Yugoslavia and the accession of Macedonia to Bulgaria, and the federalists, who advocated the idea of an autonomous Macedonia within a Balkan Federation. The internal conflicts in the organization resulted in violent armed clashes, while the spearhead of their action remained directed against the communists and federalists. The right wing organized the infiltration of terrorist units into Yugoslavia to perpetrate sabotage and assassinations (in 1922 alone 11 units of that kind were sent over to Yugoslavia). The agreement reached between Mihailov and Pavelić was the expression of the association of anti-Yugoslav fascist movements abroad.

IV

This brief survey is presented in the hope that it conveys an idea of the complex character of the emergence of fascist tendencies in Yugoslavia between the two wars. At the root of the internal Yugoslav crisis lay unsettled national and social problems, aggravated by external influences, which provoked rightist deviations, and some fascistic traits both in the conflict between centralism and federalism and in the suppression of the social discontent under the slogan of anticommunism. In the increasingly bitter struggle between the right and the left wing, the middle class center lost its bearings, gradually moving to the right. In the internal conflicts, democracy was sacrificed by the use of coercive measures. These measures were used both in the political struggle between nationalistic organizations and by the personal regime of 1929. In spite of this, and partly because of this, fascist ideology did not find a political and social footing in Yugoslavia. Hence its appearance in pure form was confined to extremist separatists, a small, insignificant minority of youths and middle and upper middle class people. The exponents of fascism in Yugoslavia, encouraged by the external fascist forces and by their growing aggression against the Balkans, became increasingly aggressive on the eve of World War II. Their ideas, however, never grew deep roots among the Yugoslav peoples. The truth of this assertion is best supported by the unanimity with which Yugoslavs rejected the Tripartite Treaty on March 27, 1941, and by the determined mass resistance that the peoples of Yugoslavia offered to the fascist forces of occupation during the war, in the period between 1941 and 1945.

BIBLIOGRAPHY

Apostolov, A., "Strui, vlijanija, organizacii i partii vo periodot na sozdavanjeto na Kralstvoto SHS," *Glasnik na Institutot za Nacionalna Istorija* 6, nos. 1–2 (1962): 61–95.

Avramovski, Ž., "Izveštaji Ulricha von Hassela o putu u Boegrad i Zagreb," *Historijski Pregled* 2 (1963): 136–46.

Bartulović, N., "Od revolucionarne omladine do ORJUNE," *Istorijat jugoslavenskog omladinskog polkreta* (Split: E. Desman, 1925).

Bauer, E., "Italien und Kroatien, 1938–1945," *Zeitschrift für Geopolitik* 26 (1955): 112–22.

Biber, D., "Ustaše i Treči Rajh," *Jugoslovenski Istorijski Časopis* 2 (1964): 37–54.

Bitoski, K., "Za položbata na makedonskata emigracija vo Bulgarija medju dvete svetski vojni," *Glasnik na Institutot za Nacionalna Istorija* 6, nos. 1–2 (1962): 97–194.

Boban, Lj., "Oko Mačekovo pregovora s grofom Čanom," *Istorija XX veka - Zbornik Radova* 6 (1964): 302–55.

Ciano, G., *Diario,* vol. 2 (Milano: Rizzoli, 1946).

Čubrilović, V., *Istorija političke misli u Srbiji XIX veka* (Beograd: Prosveta, 1958), pp. 534–71.

Čulinović, F., *Jugoslavija izmedju dva rata,* vol. 2 (Zagreb: Jugoslavenska Akademija, 1961).

Dinev, D., *Političkite ubistva vo Bulgarije* (Skopje: Ilinden, 1951).

Gligorijević, B., "Organizacija jugoslovenskih nacionalista (ORJUNA)," *Istorija XX veka - Zbornik Radova* 5 (1963): 315–99.

"Srbska nacionalna omladina (SRNAO), *Istorijski Glasnik* 2–3 (1964): 3–37.

"Politički pokreti i grupe s nacionalsocijalističkom ideologijom i njihova fuzija u Ljotičevom 'Zboru,'" *Istorijski Glasnik* 4 (1925): 35–83.

"Napad ljotičevaca na studente Tehnickog fakulteta u Beogradu u oktobru 1940 i rasturanje Ljotičevog 'Zbora,'" *Istorijski Glasnik* 2 (1963): 52–82.

Hoptner, I. B., *Yugoslavia in Crisis, 1934–41* (New York–London: Columbia University Press, 1962).

Horvat, J., *Politička Povjest Hrvatske, 1918-1929* (Zagreb: Izdanja nakladnog zavoda, 1936).

Horvat, R., *Hrvatska na mučilištu* (Zagreb: Hrvatska tiskara, 1942), pp. 432–34, 521–23, 618–26.

Keršovani, O., "Nove generacije i njihova pokreti," in *Zbornik - Generacije pred stavranjem* (Beograd: Grupa na socialnu i kulturna akcije, 1925), pp. 117–37.

Masleša, V., "Fašizam i agrarne države," and "Fašizam i zadrugarstvo," *Dela* 1 (1954): 193, 202.

Miličević, V., *Der Königsmord von Marseille. Das Verbrechen und die Hintergründe* (Bad Godesberg: Hochwacht, 1959).

Milovanović, N., *Od Marseljskog atentata do Trojnog pakta* (Zagreb: Epoka, 1963).

Ribar, O., *Politički zapisi,* vol. 2 (Beograd: Prosveta, 1949).

Stojkov, T., "O stvaranju bloka narodnog sporazuma," *Istorija XX veka - Zbornik Radova* 6 (1964): 245–301.

Volkov, V. K., *Germano-Jugoslovenskie otnošenia i razval Maloi Antamte, 1933–1938* (Moskva: Nauka, 1966).

B

Yugoslavia's Fascist Movements

Ivan Avakumovic

The study of fascism in Yugoslavia presents a number of problems. Some of these have a specifically Yugoslav origin, others can be attributed to the same factors that make the study of fascism elsewhere in Europe so complicated. To begin with, much of the basic data is not available. The Italian archives which are extremely important for the study of the Ustaši movement are closed to scholars. The information at our disposal is literally scattered over three continents. Some leading Ustaši publications in the early 1930s appeared as far apart as Argentina and the United States. Secondly, much of the evidence is highly suspect. Fascists, whether Yugoslav or not, are not known for their dedication to the pursuit of truth and this applies as much to what they wrote in the 1930s as to the memoirs and apologias they produced after 1945.

In the third place, the history of interwar Yugoslavia is complex. After 1918 parliamentary government based on coalition cabinets and frequent elections prevailed until the shooting of the Croat leader Stjepan Radić in the Parliament building in 1928. This incident produced a complete deadlock and provided King Alexander with a pretext to suspend the constitution and dissolve parliament and all political parties (January 6, 1929). For almost six years Yugoslavia was run on authoritarian lines in an effort to develop a strong feeling of national solidarity among the different national groups inhabiting Yugoslavia. In the process the press was censored and a number of opponents of the regime were arrested or interned. Power rested firmly in the hands of the King, who selected most of his collaborators from among politicians active in the previous decades. The failure of King Alexander's domestic politics was evident even before the Yugoslav economy experienced the full impact of the Great Depression and the Bulgarian-Macedonian terrorists removed him from the Yugoslav scene in 1934. The regents who governed the country during the minority of King Peter II (1934–41) reestablished some but not all of the civil liberties that Yugoslavia had enjoyed in the previous decade. They also succeeded in coming to terms with the representatives of the largest Croat party, the Peasant Party. The formation of a broad coalition government on the eve of the Second World War failed to unite Yugoslav opinion in the face of growing pressure from Berlin and Rome. The invasion of Yugoslavia in April, 1941, and the events that occurred under the German occupation revealed the differences that separated one Yugoslav from another and enabled the native fascists and communists to emerge from the political underworld.

The remaining major problem facing the student of fascism is to determine who was a fascist, who was pro-fascist, and who was merely authoritarian in the traditional sense of the term. On that question differences of opinion exist just as they do, for instance, among students of fascism in France. In Yugoslavia there are two borderline cases. One is King Alexander's dictatorship or personal regime, which in the 1930s the communists defined as "military-fascist." After they came to power they used the term "monarcho-fascist." However, the communists were unable to agree on this definition. In 1947 one of the leading officials of the Agitprop of the central committee of the Communist Party of Yugoslavia, R. Zogović, argued that it was a mistake to talk of "monarcho-fascism" because, after all, under that regime the works of Marx, Engels, and Lenin were published legally and sold openly.[1] Zogović's thesis can be buttressed with other arguments. No political party, let alone a mass movement, forced the King to suspend the constitution in 1929. For the first three years of his dictatorship no political parties existed. After 1931 several of them had a legal existence, including the Socialist Party of Yugoslavia. At the same time Yugoslavia had close relations with France and Czechoslovakia, while those with Italy were bad, far worse than during the 1920s when the Yugoslav government began to subsidize Italian anti-fascists in exile.[2] Under these circumstances, it is possible to relegate King Alexander's regime to the category of authoritarian government, similar to King Carol's regime in Romania from 1938 to 1940.

Another source of controversy is the character of Milan Stojadinović's government from 1935 to 1939. It was a coalition government based on a wing of the Serb Radical Party, the Slovene Catholic Party, and the Muslims in Bosnia. The Prime Minister displayed increasingly strong pro-Axis tendencies, expressed admiration for Hitler and Mussolini, provided his youth organization with green shirts, and liked to hear crowds chanting "*Voda! Voda!*" the Serbo-Croat equivalent of "*Duce, Duce.*"[3] Although after Anschluss, Stojadinović's sympathies were definitely pro-Axis, he was unable to introduce a system of government similar to that in Germany and Italy. He faced strong opposition from the democratic parties as well as from the genuine fascist groups. The latter considered Stojadinović an impostor who was prepared to adopt some of the trappings of fascism to improve his own position at home and abroad. In several ways Stojadinović's approach to politics resembled that of Gömbös' in Hungary.

As in other European countries, fascism in Yugoslavia can be considered as a response to three major problems. First, it was a response to the challenge of communism, which was a mass movement on Yugoslav soil in 1919-20. Second, it was a response to the failure of liberal democracy and of the various Yugolsav governments in the 1930s to provide solutions that would inspire the educated youth throughout the country. In a society in which few found politics as practiced in the interwar period particularly edifying, fascism seemed to offer alternatives to at least some intellectuals and semi-intellectuals who, while opposed to the existing order, were unwilling to fight it under the auspices of the illegal Communist Party of Yugoslavia. Finally, fascism was a response of those Croat circles who were convinced that the very existence of the Croat nation was seriously endangered by the political, economic, and cultural policies of successive Yugoslav governments.

In the 1920s Yugoslavia possessed in ORJUNA (*Organizacija Jugoslovenskih Nacionalista*) an organization that had several fascist characteristics. Its objectives were the creation of a strong feeling of Yugoslav solidarity and the strengthening of the young Yugoslav state. ORJUNA spokesmen claimed that the existence of Yugoslavia was gravely endangered by Communist and Croat Peasant Party agitation and by the intrigues of several of Yugoslavia's neighbors, in particular Mussolini's Italy. To attract attention and gain a following, ORJUNA engaged in street fighting, demonstrations, bombastic propaganda, and occasional strikes in factories that were owned by foreigners. Its leaders were a group of young Yugoslav intellectuals, mostly Croats from Dalmatia. Several of them were marginally successful playwrights and minor poets who saw themselves as Yugoslav D'Annunzios, the same D'Annunzio whose exploits in Fiume were well known along the eastern shores of the Adriatic.

Although the leaders of ORJUNA were eager to create an organization independent of the established political parties, they never succeeded in emancipating themselves from certain politicians like Svetozar Pribičević, who aided them in one way or another. When these politicians left the government, ORJUNA lost the support of the authorities and most of the influence it had exercised previously. Even at its zenith it lacked cohesion and faced the competition of two similar organizations, HRANAO (Croatian National Youth) and SRONAO (Serbian National Youth). However, these organizations differed from ORJUNA in their approach to the nationality question. Unlike ORJUNA they did not advocate the creation of a Yugoslav national consciousness. On the contrary, they stood for what they considered to be the Croat and Serb national traditions. Both organizations claimed to represent what was best in the youth of the two respective nations and both campaigned against the merging of the Croat and Serb national identity in an all-embracing Yugoslav nationalism. ORJUNA lost ground to both HRANAO and SRONAO though neither of these two organizations had a mass following and though both faded before the end of the 1920s.[4]

After the dissolution of ORJUNA in 1929 its leaders dispersed. One of its chief ideologists, N. Bartulović, became editor of a monthly financed by the Freemasons, several of whom had taken a paternal interest in ORJUNA in the early 1920s. Although during the Popular Front days Bartulović appeared more than once on the same platform as the communists, they shot him in 1943. Other ORJUNA leaders and militants joined Second World War movements as diverse as the Četnik, Communist, and Ustaši, while the former head of ORJUNA who had the grandiloquent title of "Great Leader" became Tito's first ambassador in London.

It was not until the 1930s that two truly fascist movements emerged. Founded by Dimitrÿe Ljotić and Ante Pavelić, these movements promoted the Yugoslav contingent to the ranks of European fascism. Ljotić came from a well-known Serb family. Like many other Serb intellectuals of his generation he studied at the universities of Belgrade and Paris and had a good war record. In the 1920s he played a minor role in the leading Serb political group, the Radical Party, and was active in the cooperative movement in his native town. As Minister of Justice in the early 1930s, he created a minor sensation when he resigned after a few months because the king refused to follow his advice by introducing the corporative system. In 1935 he formed his own political party with a program that resembled in some ways that of Charles Maurras' Action Française.[5] Ljotić insisted that the Yugoslav state be maintained at all cost and that no concessions be made to the leaders of the Croats until they favored a unitary as opposed to a federal Yugoslavia. Abroad, Yugoslavia was to follow a policy of strict neutrality. According to Ljotić the U.S.S.R. presented the main threat to the future of Yugoslavia because of Soviet world-wide ambitions.

Ljotić's party did poorly in the parliamentary elections in 1935 and 1938, polling only about 30,000 votes. It was only in Smederovo, Ljotić's native town, that he won considerable support partly because his family was well-known, partly because Ljotić was an efficient organizer of the local winegrowers' cooperative, and partly because he had the reputation of being incorruptible and God-fearing. Unlike all other Serb political leaders in the interwar period, he was a regular churchgoer. This was considered so unusual that when the Yugoslav government looked for a reason to have him jailed they decided to have him arrested as a religious maniac and shipped to a lunatic asylum. In the end he was sent to an ordinary prison, where he wrote his autobiography.

The majority of Ljotić's followers were Serbs, although he had a sprinkling of supporters among Slovenes and Croats from Dalmatia. His representative in Zagreb, Dr. Lenac, defended Tito in court. Ljotić's nucleus consisted of a group of young intellectuals, students, and some young priests of the Serb Orthodox church. The public at large considered him peculiar because it was very difficult to determine what he really wanted, and because most Serbs associated him with Nazi Germany and fascist Italy. This did not help his cause, especially when the leading Beograd liberal daily *Politika* produced evidence that Ljotić was in touch with Nazi circles associated with Alfred Rosenberg that intended to establish in Yugoslavia an export-import firm through which the Germans could subsidize Ljotić's party. Both the Germans and Ljotić were made to appear foolish when it was discovered that the intermediary between Berlin and Ljotić was a Jewish businessman whom Béla Kun had sent as his secret envoy to Zagreb in 1919. Naturally, the irreplaceable A. Diamantstein had changed his surname to Dragić before the fascists utilized his talents.

Under the German occupation of Yugoslavia, Ljotić's followers became the most reliable German auxiliaries and policemen in Serbia. Several thousand of them were armed by the Wehrmacht, on whose side they fought well in spite of their former talk about the need to preserve the Yugoslav state and avoid foreign entanglements. Ironically, they suffered heavier casualties in the struggle against Draža Mihailović than against Tito. When the Soviet army and Josep Tito's partisans entered Serbia in 1944, the Germans evacuated Ljotić and his group to Istria where they stayed until the final advance of Tito's troops toward Trieste. Then they fled so quickly that Ljotić was killed in a car accident on April 23, 1945.

In retrospect, Ljotić's party was anemic compared to the Croatian Ustaši movement, which stemmed from the mid-nineteenth century. The Croat fascists regarded Ante Starčević, a lawyer who founded the Croat Rights Party in 1861, as their forerunner. He had demanded an independent Croatia that would be part of a Danubian confederation under the Habsburgs. The Emperor of Austria was to be crowned in Zagreb as King of a Croatia that would embrace Bosnia, Dalmatia, and Hercegovina. He considered the Serbs and the Jews who lived in Croatia as aliens who had settled on purely Croat soil and who, moreover, were instruments of Magyarization. Hence they were not entitled to the same civil rights as the Croats. Thus the Croat Rights Party became the first political party in Yugoslavia to advocate discrimination against the Jews.

Starčević had the support of many intellectuals, a segment of the lower middle class, and a number of workers whom his followers organized into special workers' associations to fight the budding Marxist movement. The party itself underwent a number of changes and splits until 1918.[6] By then it was fairly discredited because many of its leaders had supported the Austro-Hungarian war effort. Even in the 1920s the party vegetated, never gaining more than two seats in the Yugoslav Parliament. Neither collaboration with the much stronger Croat Peasant Party nor opposition to it improved the Croat Rights Party's electoral performance.

In the late 1920s its leader was Dr. Ante Pavelić, the son of a building contractor who, as a law student at Zagreb University, joined the successors of Starčević before 1914. After the First World War he was elected municipal counselor in Zagreb and then represented that city in the Yugoslav Parliament. There he acted as the spokesman for those Croat circles that attributed all the national ills to the Serbs and to the failure of the leaders of other Croat parties to use the correct tactics and raise the appropriate issues in the struggle for an independent Croatia.[7]

As Croat dissatisfaction with the Yugoslav state increased, Pavelić's popularity in Zagreb increased. Soon after King Alexander suspended the constitution, Pavelić created the illegal Ustaši movement, which was organized in a military style, and advocated armed struggle to achieve Croat independence. Early in 1929 Pavelić went abroad and after being received with open arms by Mussolini and irredentist circles in Budapest and Sofia, he established his headquarters in Italy. As long as Italo-Yugoslav relations were bad—and they were until 1937—he could rely on Mussolini's support. Italy provided shelter for the Croat fascists who at one stage numbered approximately one thousand. They were housed in special military camps and supplied with uniforms, arms, and money. Some Ustaši were smuggled back into Yugoslavia to engage in sabotage and attempts to murder their Croat and Serb opponents. In 1932 a revolt was planned, but it was limited to an attack on a village gendarmerie station. Italian financial support enabled Pavelić to start a major propaganda campaign in the West. Its objective was to show the extent of Croat dissatisfaction in Yugoslavia and the threat the Serbs presented to European peace. This was combined with recruitment drives among Croat immigrants in western Europe, and Latin and North America.

Pavelić's prestige among those who favored the establishment of an independent Croatia increased rapidly when the Ustaši planned the murder of King Alexander in Marseilles. It seemed to many that at last the hour of Croat independence had struck. In the end, Pavelić was charged with murder in a French court and sentenced to death *in absentia*. Mussolini, however, refused to extradite him because Italy was deeply implicated in the preparations for the assassination.

The signing of an Italo-Yugoslav friendship treaty in 1937 forced Pavelić into political hibernation. One of the concessions that the Yugoslav negotiators obtained from Mussolini was the internment of Pavelić and the disbandment of the Ustaši camps in Italy. Ustaši exiles were shipped to the Lipari Islands, while Pavelić devoted his enforced leisure to writing a novel—earlier he had dabbled in poetry—and to compiling a Croat dictionary purged of all Serbianisms.

In Yugoslavia his followers tried to enliven the Ustaši spirit by publishing several newspapers and periodicals, and by forming or infiltrating a number of Croat clerical,[8] cultural, professional, and youth organizations. Others preferred to agitate within the Croat Peasant Party, which by the 1930s had won overwhelming support in the Croat countryside and considerable sympathies among large sections of the Croat middle class and workers. The support that the leaders of the Croat Peasant Party received from these Ustaši and pro-Ustaši intellectuals was subject to strong reservations. They felt that the Croat Peasant Party leadership was insufficiently aggressive in the struggle for a Croatia independent of Belgrade. More than once fascist and pro-fascist elements in the Croat Peasant Party called for a more radical national program and more violent tactics in the struggle against Yugoslav authorities. To the chagrin of the Ustaši, Dr. Vladko Maček, the leader of the Peasant Party, vacillated. His retiring disposition and the ratio of forces in Yugoslavia prevented him from acting decisively either for or against Ustaši wishes. Armed revolt was impossible and the expulsion of camouflaged fascists from the Croat Peasant Party was never seriously considered. Such a step would have narrowed the popular basis of Maček's party, which prided itself on representing the entire Croat people.

By exploiting Croat grievances and the growing weakness of the Yugoslav administration, the Ustaši contributed to the radicalization of Croat public opinion in the 1930s. Their influence in and out of the Croat Peasant Party increased when two events in 1939 provided them with additional arguments. The breakup of Czechoslovakia and the proclamation of an independent Slovakia seemed a portent of things to come in Yugoslavia. In addition, the Ustaši argued that the entry of the Croat Peasant Party into the Yugoslav government had not improved the lot of Croats. Prices were rising and Croats were mobilized to defend the frontiers of Yugoslavia against enemies that the Ustaši felt were imaginary. To them the real enemy was not abroad but inside the country: the Serb and the Jew had to be fought. Riots, a few cases of sabotage and bomb-throwing, and a mutiny or two in the Yugoslav army were the landmarks of Ustaši agitation. Their day came with the German attack on Yugoslavia in April, 1941. Some assisted the invading forces, others greeted the advancing German motorized units with flowers. A proclamation of the central committee of the Communist Party of Yugoslavia described the Ustaši behavior during those days as "the most shameful blot in the history of the Croat people."[9] The Ustaši thought it was their finest hour. Pavelić returned from exile and an independent Croat state existed at last.

Few outside Pavelić's entourage realized how heavy the price of independence would be. Most of Dalmatia was surrendered to Mussolini, and there were large-scale massacres of Serbs and Jews. After more than half a million Serbs and Jews had been killed, the Ustaši movement had followers in all areas inhabited by Croats. With German assistance Pavelić raised an army of two hundred thousand soldiers in 1944. They fought well and retreated slowly; Zagreb fell to Tito a week after Hitler's suicide.

The student of fascism in Yugoslavia is struck by the fact that the native fascists displayed repeatedly the same characteristics as fascists elsewhere in Eastern Europe. Liberal democracy, communism, and the Jews were attacked with the same arguments and the same viciousness as elsewhere. The solutions that the different brands of fascism in Yugoslavia advocated were also similar: a strong state based on the rule of the elite, social peace through a system of corporations, protection of private property, and control of big business. Christianity as interpreted by Ljotić and Pavelić was to be one of the pillars of the new order.

As in other parts of Europe, fascism began as an urban movement. It made little impact in the countryside until the disintegration of the Yugoslav state enabled the victorious Ustaši to recruit a substantial number of supporters in the poor, mountainous parts of Bosnia, Hercegovina, and Lika. It was the Ustaši from Hercegovina who provided Pavelić with the best armed units in the struggle against Mihailović and Tito.

The leaders and the bulk of the fascist militants were young intellectuals and students who were a representative cross section of the educated youth. This is as true of the followers of Ljotić as of the followers of Pavelić. Some were poor, others were middle class, while a few came from the best-known Croat families (e.g., Kvaternik, Lorković). The available evidence does not permit us to say with any degree of precision whether the students in one discipline were more likely to go fascist than in others. At Zagreb University the Ustaši were the largest student group in 1940. They won 15 percent of the votes in the elections held in 1939–40, and their main strength was in the faculties of law, agriculture, and veterinary science. Elsewhere the followers of Maček and Tito had a slight majority. At Belgrade University the communists were strongest in the law faculty. They polled 7 percent of the votes in a student election early in 1941—while in the 1930s the student council in the engineering faculty was dominated for a time by Ljotić's supporters.

The fascists had some working-class support, a fact that the communists will be the first to admit. The minority of workers sympathetic to the fascists consisted mainly of those who were not unionized, in particular young workers and apprentices. Many of these youngsters joined the fascists to find excitement in an otherwise drab life. The Ustaši were more successful among Croat workers than Ljotić was among Serbs. The only exception occurred when the fascists decided on a showdown at Belgrade University in the autumn of 1940. Before they tackled their rivals, the followers of Ljotić hired several workers from the municipal slaughterhouse who were paid to beat up the communist students.

The relative weakness of fascism in interwar Yugoslavia can be attributed to several factors. First, the fascists were handicapped because the public associated them with Italy and Germany. Opposition to fascist Italy was the one issue which large segments of Yugoslav opinion agreed upon, for Italy was the heir of Venice, the hand behind the London Treaty of 1915, the oppressor of the Croat and Slovene minorities in Istria, and the great hope of the irredentists in Budapest, Sofia, Tirana, and Vienna before Hitler came to power. Moreover, Mussolini's imperial ambitions were considered out of proportion to Italy's real strength and the courage of her soldiers.[10]

Equally damaging to the fascist cause was the existence of other political parties closer to the outlook of the average Yugoslav. Though some non-fascist politicians were occasionally prepared to give the benefit of the doubt to this or that, fascist group and they were prepared to talk to some of the fascist intellectuals, no non-communist party in Yugoslavia engaged in a systematic campaign to unmask native fascism, and no politician was prepared to treat the fascist groups as equal partners. This is as true of those who were democrats as of those who, like Stojadinović, favored close relations with the Axis. As a result, the fascists remained on the fringe of Yugoslav politics until the German and Italian armies brought them to the fore in 1941.

The issues raised by the fascists in the 1930s were not sufficiently distinct and attractive to gain much support. The fascists thundered against nepotism, corruption, and manipulation of election results, they shed tears over the plight of the various social classes, they promised shortcuts to greatness, affluence, and peace, only to find that nearly every politician in opposition said the same thing. Even when they called for the defense of the Yugoslav state as Ljotić did in the 1930s or advocated the establishment of the independent Croatia that the Ustaši demanded, the fascists were not alone. All Serb political parties opposed the break-up of Yugoslavia, and every Croat politician who sought a hearing or votes in the 1930s had to insist that the Croats be masters of their own house.

Two other issues the fascists raised elsewhere could not be exploited successfully in Yugoslavia. Anti-Semitic propaganda paid few dividends, partly because the Jews were a tiny minority, less than one-half of 1 percent of the total population of Yugoslavia, and partly because many of the Jews, especially those in pre-1914 Serbia, were well assimilated. It was only in Croatia that a tradition of anti-Semitism existed. The Ustaši exploited it to the limit of the possible, even though the wives of several Ustaši leaders were half or quarter Jewish—a matter of concern to Himmler's envoys in wartime Zagreb. The other issue that failed to generate widespread enthusiasm was the fascists' demand for a legislature based on occupational representation. Once again, others had preceded them. The Slovene Catholic Party had advocated such an institution long before Engelbert Dolfuss came to power in Vienna; so had the Serb Agrarian Union, a moderate left-wing organization, since 1920.

Finally, it is significant that the range of fascist agitation was severely restricted by police action. The Ustaši were illegal throughout the 1930s and were treated by King Alexander as the primary enemy of the Yugoslav state. Ljotić's party was not banned until the autumn of 1940, but throughout its legal existence it was subject to administrative pinpricks: fines, arrests, prohibition of meetings, confiscation of an occasional issue of their newspapers and so on. Those Ustaši who plotted insurrection and assassination were often betrayed by informers, a common occupation, for which there was no shortage of recruits, in and out of fascist ranks. Under these circumstances it is understandable that the fascists were more successful at the universities, where police counteraction was not very effective. The existing autonomy of the universities, which successive Yugoslav governments generally respected, enabled young fascists and communists to conduct their activities almost undisturbed within university walls.[11]

Paradoxically enough, the weakness of native fascism diverted attention from the potential danger domestic fascists represented in conjunction with the military, political, and economic power of the Axis. It took the German invasion of Yugoslavia and the establishment of Hitler's New Order in the Balkans to show the peoples of Yugoslavia the capabilities of their compatriots once they were in power.

FOOTNOTES

1   R. Zogović, *Primjer kako ne treba praviti "Primjere Knjizevnosti"* (Beograd; Kultura, 1947).

2   The former Italian Prime Minister, Francesco Nitti, was among those who received financial assistance from Yugoslavia.

3   Stojadinović's opponents retaliated with "Djavo, Djavo" (Devil, Devil).

4   For a communist study of ORJUNA and SRNAO see the following articles by B. Gligorijević: "Organizacija jugoslovenskih nacionalista (ORJUNA)," *Istorija XX veka - Zbornik Radovi* 5 (1963): 315–99, and "Srbska nacionalna omladina (SRNAO)," *Istorijski Glasnik* 2–3 (1964): 3–37.

5   For a selection of Ljotić's articles and speeches, as well as his statements before and during the Second World War see, inter alia: *Govori i Članci* (Munich: Iskra, 1948); *Svetska Revolucije* (Munich: Iskra, 1949); *Iz Moga Života* (Munich, 1952).

6   One of Starčević's most prominent aides was Joseph Frank, whose followers are known in Croat politics as "Frankovci." They provided the nucleus of the Ustaši with whom they virtually merged in the 1930s.

7   Some of his speeches and articles dealing with this period were published in A. Pavelić, *Putem Hrvatskog Državnog Prava* (Zagreb: Velebit, 1942).

8   A dispassionate study of the impact of the Ustaši ideology and slogans on the Catholic clergy of Croat extraction remains to be written. V. Novak's *Magnum Crimen* (Beograd, 1945)

provided an ideological justification for the campaign against the Catholic Church in the early years of Communist Yugoslavia.

9 *Dokumenti Istorije Omladinskog Pokreta Jugoslavije* (Beograd: Istorijsko Odelenje Centralnog Komiteta Narodne Omladine Jugoslavije, 1954), vol. 1, no. 4.

10 The extent to which Yugoslavs, right, left, or center, Serb or Croat, looked down on Italians as soldiers can best be understood in the light of the often asked question: "Why did the Italians adopt the Fascist salute?" The answer to this question is: "Because during the First World War they got tired of raising both hands."

11 In a number of instances Ustaši and communist students at Zagreb University collaborated in organizing demonstrations and riots against the state and university authorities. See I. Avakumović, *History of the Communist Party of Yugoslavia* (Aberdeen: Aberdeen University Press, 1964).

VIII
Conclusion

Conclusion

Peter F. Sugar

This volume was devoted to six states that, in spite of differences in size, official language, level of economic development, degree of national satisfaction or dissatisfaction, had one characteristic in common: they all began their interwar existence as the heirs or successors of the Austro-Hungarian monarchy. Consequently they all faced common problems of which the most important were: the need to establish a national currency, to reintegrate their economic systems, to face the problems of multinationality and/or minorities, to establish "democratic" form of government, and, in the temporary absence of dominating super powers, to attempt to fit their states into the family of nations.

States other than those we have surveyed also faced some of these problems in post-World War I Europe, and all over the continent a relatively small variety of solutions were put to the test by leaders of governments, opposition parties, revolutionaries, military men, and representatives of other professional interest groups. All these solutions departed, to a smaller or larger degree, from the "traditional" prewar approaches to state-wide problem solving; in the search for "new" approaches to old issues there was the hope that the new headaches would be cured, too. One of these new, European-wide approaches was fascism.

Just as with all the many other movements, ideologies, solutions, and panaceas in history, fascism has its roots in the centuries that preceded—in this case the interwar period—in which it became a fully articulated and prominent movement. Like all others, this movement underwent changes even during the relatively few years during which it was of primary importance and it had to adjust to local conditions in the various parts of Europe. Our twelve authors were asked to investigate what features of the fascism manifested in Eastern Europe differed from those observable elsewhere and what common characteristics these local manifestations had that could be tied, at least to some extent, to their common Habsburg inheritance.

The voluminous literature dealing with fascism recognizes that the fascist movement, associated primarily with Mussolini's Italy and Hitler's Germany, had followers all over Europe including the countries we studied. These followers were nationals of these states and were fascists. They recognized either the Italian Duce or the German Führer as their master, sang their praises and often consciously imitated their methods, ideas, and goals. These people are well known to those who studied the movement, and while their names appear in these pages, they are not the primary focus of our authors'

147

interest. The authors were interested either in the truly "native"—as opposed to imitative—causes, manifestations, and aims of fascism or in the locally rooted reasons that made certain people in the Successor States accept fascism either out of conviction or because of opportunistic considerations. This was the special and specific purpose of these essays. For this reason neither the authors nor I attempted to define fascism nor to differentiate between it and its close relative, national socialism. This was simply taken for granted, and the twelve essays show that in spite of the authors' differing national origin, a basic common understanding of which movements were truly fascistic existed among them.

Out of this common understanding emerged the first shared aspect of our countries' fascism. Our authors differentiated very carefully between autocratic and totalitarian regimes. In this volume we do not find, as we do in some others, especially those written in the late 1940s and early 1950s, such diverse people as Engelbert Dollfuss and Arthur Seyss-Inquart, King Carol II and Corneliu Zelea Codreanu, Admiral Miklós Horthy and Ferenc Szálasi, Milan Stojadinović and Ante Pavelić all lumped together as "fascist." While all authors clearly recognize the distinction between what was the political right prior to 1914 and what Eugen Weber called the "new right," they very carefully differentiate between the various manifestations of this "new right."[1] Expressions like "clerico-fascism," and "monarcho-fascism," are used with great care and often even called unsatisfactory labels. It becomes evident that while each writer considers all manifestations of the "new right" as antidemocratic and autocratic, each reserves the fascist label for those movements that they consider totalitarian, almost unanimously in the sense of Hannah Arendt's explanations.[2] As a result we have not only a very fine tacit definition of fascist movements in the Successor States, but a careful delineation of the first truly "native" aspect of the history of fascism in parts of Eastern Europe.

Before the outbreak of the Second World War only three fascist movements were able to attain power—the Italian, the German, and for a short period the Romanian. When Mussolini "marched on Rome," riding comfortably in a train during the night of October 29, 1922 to assume power—whether we consider his move to be a coup d'état or a revolution—he displaced a democratic government. In no way was his road made easier or the population prepared for the drastic change by a transition period of autocratic, rightist-oriented government. The same is true of Hitler's *Machtergreifung.* Whatever one may think of the behind-the-scene power and intrigues of the circle around President Paul von Hindenburg and the other irregularities on the German political scene, one cannot speak of an autocratic dictatorship in Germany before January 30, 1933. It was the democratic process that permitted Hitler's party to gain the needed number of seats in the *Reichstag* and to become the largest single party in this legislative body, making the takeover of power possible. If the short-lived government of the Octavian Goga–A. C. Cuza cabinet can be called fascist, and this might be questioned, then we see the third fascist takeover prior to World War II occurring under quite different circumstances in Professor Stephen Fischer-Galati's chapter. In this case the road was clearly paved by totalitarian rule.

The fact that our states, during the years under discussion, developed a trend leading from true or nominal democracy to various forms of autocracies might furnish a clue to the understanding of another feature in the history of the Successor States' fascist movements. It has often been noted that while these states developed their own varieties of fascist parties fairly early in the post-World War I years, and that while several of these had a relatively strong early appeal, they did not gain power prior to the years of the Second World War, when German influence helped them to achieve their goal. On the other hand, the epithet *quisling* is applied much less often to those Eastern European fascist leaders who came to power with German help during World War II than it is to their Western European counterparts. I believe that our authors have given us a clear explanation of these two apparently contradictory phenomena.

Whenever a Western European found himself in the extreme right wing of the "new right," he had little choice but to start his own movement, recruit his own followers, and dream of staging a coup or winning enough followers to come to power quasi-legally. In these countries, with their strong liberal, socialist, and conservative traditions and relatively high economic development, this was a hopeless task, and these men came to power with foreign help, on occasion with enemy help, and, consequently, in the eyes of their contemporary countrymen and the historian they played the role of quislings. In Central Europe, Italy, and Germany, where these traditions were weaker and parliamentary practices less truly democratic, the chances of fascist leaders were better and they could use the democratic machinery to their own advantage. Both Mussolini and Hitler were legally called to power by the constitutional heads of their respective states, although the process was a form of blackmail and was anything but democratic or parliamentarian. Here Western and Eastern European tradition blended.

In Eastern Europe the situation was different. At first power fell into the hands of those segments of the population that already held power under the Habsburgs, usually the men of the "old right." They were violently opposed to socialism in any form, and their adjustment to the democratic requirements of the early 1920s was insincere and nominal at best. Yet the forces opposing them were stronger after 1918 than they were prior to 1914, resulting in a progressive polarization of political life. The "old right," transformed by stages into a "new right," allowed those who represented the extreme, fascist wing of the new to ride with the tide, waiting for their day to come. Thus they could either remain in the ruling or local majority parties (Gömbös and Imrédy in the Party of National Unity, Pavelić's followers in the Croatian Peasant Party, Tuka in the Slovak People's Catholic Party), they could find a place for themselves in the new parties that the leaders of autocratic dictatorships created to give themselves the appearance of popular backing (Jan Rutkowski and the *Obóz Zjednoczenia Narodowego*), or they could expect the dictators to cooperate with them (the Goga–Cuza experiment) or at least look tolerantly at their activities. They did not have to attack from without, they could subvert from within. In the 1930s, especially, the trend seemed to go in the direction that suited them: from autocracy to totalitarianism. Taking the line of least resistance, letting the autocratic regimes prepare the field, they had to do little more than wait, using the time to make their views and goals clearer and clearer. By the time their fleeting moments in power came, they were known at home and abroad as bona fide home-grown fascists who saw in fascism the salvation of their country. They had cooperated with fascists in other countries, had backed the autocratic regimes, pushed their countries' rights more and more towards the extreme. The foreign powers who helped them were not enemies, but allies. It is, therefore, hard to look at them as quislings in the strict sense of the word. What is more significant is the explanation this state of affairs supplies to the question of why they did not take power earlier. They did not have to; they could wait until those already in power shifted far enough to the right. They did not need more drastic or dramatic methods for gaining their ends, for those who inherited power from the Habsburg administration had no choice, given their background, training, and sympathies, but to hand power over to those on the right of them when they were forced off the political scene.

The consideration of background, training, and sympathies permit the analysis of a few other features that, while present to some degree in other states, played a disproportionately large role in the development of fascism in the Successor States. Most authors discuss the role played by the bureaucracy and the teachers, and, in one way or another, all wrote about religion. All Successor States had swollen bureaucracies. In some, especialiy Austria and Hungary, this resulted from the necessity to find employment in a small state for the civil servants of a large country. In others, jobs had to be given to faithful fighters who helped to create the new, transformed, or enlarged states, and in all of them jobs became part of an elaborate spoils system. What is important about these people is their attitude and self-image: they did not consider themselves civil servants but functionaries; they were not fulfilling duties, serving the people, but were functional parts of a powerful government apparatus (although admittedly, but hopefully only temporarily, on a relatively low level) dispensing favors. They has a vested interest in their positions, for the position brought status as well as a livelihood, and this status, in their eyes, was both important and exalted. Any egalitarian trend was as abhorrent to them as an elitist trend was to their liking, for an elitist trend—such as fascism—would raise them, along with the party and state, to the pinnacle of the social scale. They considered themselves superior people and gladly joined forces with movements that claimed to be open only to superior beings, whatever criteria they might use to establish claims to superiority. Holding key positions on every level in an overly extensive administrative set-up, these bureaucrats were an invaluable asset to the fascists in Eastern Europe. Nothing of similar magnitude can be found elsewhere on the continent. Once again, we see the Austro-Hungarian heritage. Anybody familiar with the Habsburg state will easily recognize in this short description of the bureaucracy's attitudes those of the K. u K. establishment.

Professor Fellner's description of the Austrian university professors' attitude during the interwar period can be applied with equal validity to those in Hungary, Regat Romania, and even Serbia. Rightly or wrongly, the Slovaks accused the Czech teachers working in their elementary and secondary schools of a similar approach. In all countries instruction on every level was narrowly nationalistic, filled with self-praise and hero worship. This approach to the past is a feature of fascism, and the connection between this movement and the teachers was not too difficult to establish. The honorable exceptions, which we can find in every country, only confirm the rule. Education was also, in many respects, similarly nationalistic and narrow in countries outside our region. Yet the pro-fascist influence of the schools was not as strong as it was in our states. The pluralism found in true democracies permits the balancing of influences wielded by state-supported establishments, including the schools. Furthermore in the Successor States the interwar years produced a great extension of mass education, with teachers reaching a large number of young people whose parents had little if any education and who, therefore, were more prone to accept the views that their scholar children were taught than to contradict them with knowledge of their own. Nor did the problem of multinationalism and minorities color the approach of teachers to history elsewhere to the degree that it did in our six countries. Here the difference is in degree, not a purely "native" Eastern European background phenomenon, but even this difference in degree is highly significant.

Neither Hitler nor Mussolini can be accused of religious bigotry. Hitler never made his peace with the churches, and the first fascist program in Italy included the nationalization of church property. Neither the Italian nor the German movement had a "Christian" goal, and by the time the Spanish movement produced one, the Eastern European programs were fully worked out. Our twelve essays make quite clear that the Eastern European fascist movements included, almost without exception, the creation of a "corporative-Christian" state in their final goals. In each of our essays we find references to religion, organized churches, and the clergy. If in the case of schools the difference is only in degree, and in the case of the corporative half of the future fascist state's description we clearly deal with imitation, it is something very "native" when we deal with the religion-church-clergy triad as a factor in fascist development.

The three components of this triad must be strictly separated. Nobody familiar with the history of Central and Eastern Europe will be surprised to learn that religion played an important role in the fascist developments of the Successor States even if only in a negative sense. Orthodoxy became the sign of their identity to Romanians and Serbs during the long years of Ottoman rule; the Catholic-Orthodox schism created the first, and perhaps the strongest, element that helped to differentiate Serb from Croat; the House of Habsburg made Catholicism a symbol of its rule, into a basic element of its establishment; to the Slovaks and Poles their religion was almost synonymous with their ethnic or national identity for centuries, while the Czechs, at least after the writings of Palacký, saw their Hussite heritage and religious liberalism as the hallmark of their civilization and cultural superiority. In the long centuries of alternately overt or covert anti-Semitism, Christianity meant, if nothing else, a differentiation from the Jews. The historic significance of religious identity is, of course, not exclusively an Eastern European phenomenon, but in Eastern Europe it survived into the twentieth century.

In the multinational eastern empires ruler and ruled often followed different creeds, making the ruled cling to their faith more tenaciously the more they became conscious of their ethnic-national identity. When the Ottoman Empire began to disintegrate, the states that took its place—in our case Romania and Serbia—started with official state religions and gave the clergy very important functions. Obligatory religious instruction in the Successor States survived World War I, just as the close connection between church and state did, and continued to inculcate in the young the belief in a divinely sanctioned (if not ordered) and highly structured sense of values. The educational institution at large, about which we have already written, reinforced this religious instruction by continuing to stress the close contact between church and national history, also by teaching the value of a highly ordered society (so dearly valued by the bureaucracy that controlled the schools), and by offering few alternatives. All this occurred in states where (with the exception of Czechoslovakia) the highly structured empires were replaced, not by democratic, pluralistic societies but by much weaker, equally structured administrations that tried to assure the survival of pre-1914 values. In these pre-1914 days a basic variation of the "Gott und Kaiser" slogan summed up the demands made on the people's basic loyalties but with declining adequacy as time passed. When the war destroyed not only the emperors, but practically all the old values and beliefs, when the surviving members of the ruling elements failed miserably to maintain their values and themselves in power, it would have been too much to expect the divine half of the old slogan to retain its old validity.

The old values were dead, the highly touted but basically untried new panacea of democracy quickly proved inadequate; new problems appeared before the old were solved. Quite naturally people looked for new solutions, but like their leaders, they too were captives of their backgrounds and especially their training. This did not permit them much leeway, or much individuality. It was much easier to attempt simply to pour new wine into old bottles. They looked for a new highly structured alternative. They rejected the various forms of Marxism, which were often called a form of secular religion, because they either believed what they were told about it in school or press, or because their background and training, their status consciousness made it unappealing to them, or because, after the early 1920s, they believed that it had failed. Fascism, another laic religion, as Professor Fellner and several of our other authors pointed out, offered an easy answer to those who were looking for a movement that offered answers and appeared to be familiar, at least in its hierarchial structure. It had the additional attraction of catering, in one form or another, to the mildly or violently anti-Semitic prejudices of the majority.

The Eastern-Central European region was not the only one in which numerous "lights had failed," where people were looking for a new star over a new stable, but in this region the number of possible alternatives was smaller, the habit of independent thinking less developed, and the influence of religious training stronger than it was further to the west. This created the psychological framework for this curious transference of loyalties that not only our authors but the fascist leaders of Eastern Europe also recognized. While only two movements, the Slovak and the Romanian, went so far as to pick religious symbols for their movements (the apostolic cross and the Archangel Michael), all of them recognized the value of stressing the connection. Thus emerged the corporate-Christian plank of their program in which Christian stood for nothing that any traditional, conscious, or thinking Christian would have recognized. Here we have a truly "native" feature of Eastern fascism.

The organized churches should not be confused with what was said about the influence of religion. The number of leading bishops, theologians, and other policy makers who, like Theodor Cardinal Innitzer, sympathized with the extreme right, at least temporarily, was small, and the churches as organizations never came out openly on the side of the fascists. On the other hand, they seldom opposed them, overtly trying, in most cases, to find ways of accomodation in order to maintain their organizations and other interests intact. This too was significant. Given the psychological climate just discussed, the willingness of the churches to coexist with fascism, and the temporary stands taken by some leading figures within the church organizations (well publicized by the fascists), was of significance for the spread of fascism.

Apart from the churches and their leaders, there were few persons of significance among the rank and file. Men like Hlinka and Tiso, both of whom were clergymen and important right-wing political leaders, were not too numerous, and while many priests, popes, and ministers had fascist sympathies as individuals, many others took a different stand. Professor Avakumovic's remarks that the role of the Croat clergy during the rule of Pavelić needs investigation can be extended to include the clergy of all the Successor States.

Together religion (and to a lesser extent the attitudes of the organized churches), the schools, and the bureaucracy gave East-Central European fascism a base from which to operate that was important, extremely influential, and in its composition and significance very different from what we know about fascism in Western Europe. If the army is added to these three organizations, it makes a power structure solidly rooted in the state organizations that explains, once again, why the fascists of Eastern Europe —unlike those in the West—could operate within the existing system and could wait for their moment in the sun.

It is true, not only in our region, that demobilized veterans, who could not readjust to civilian life and who found in army structure and party armies the answer to their problems, were an important element in the creation of fascist movements. In several of our states the officer corps of the regular army, not only the reservists and veterans, were involved in the movement. While the Hungarian Szeged group is our best example, the regime of the colonels in Poland illustrates the same trend, and it existed in other states as well. These military men traveled the same road followed by politicians. They began with their old pre-World War I standards, supported the social status quo, the prestige of their profession, moved further to the right when the polarization of political life occurred, supplied or supported the autocratic dictators, and slid more and more toward fascism and totalitarianism. To see how important the political orientation of these men was, one has only to realize that in all states, even where it was officially forbidden by the peace parties, every young man served in the army or at least in paramilitary organizations directed by the officer corps. Indoctrination could be carried out in the army even more overtly than in the schools, and the views of the officers made a deep impression, especially on the peasants and other recruits with a low educational level.

Once the importance and influence of various official, state-supported institutions (bureaucracy, schools, army, and so on) and their tendency to support the extreme right becomes clear, it is not surprising that most of our authors (but not all), reject such standard explanations for the rise of fascism as economic dislocation and the Great Depression. It also explains their image of the social composition of the movements' followers. Because these followers operated within the establishments they attracted both a wider and a more exalted following than the petty bourgeoisie, the "riffraff" that are usually mentioned as the first supporters of fascist movements. Besides entire groups of civil and military servants, there were students, professional people, and in a few instances even workers and peasants involved. This is not a clearly "native" phenomenon, but once again a shift in emphasis that would not be too significant in itself, but must be noted as an important part of the total picture.

There are two more features associated with the German version of fascism, if we consider national socialism as simply a totalitarian form of the interwar "new right" movements, that show interesting variations in the essays included in this volume: racism and anti-Semitism. If we think of men like Georg von Schönerer, we could call this a "native" contribution to the fascist movement at large, and could explain it in terms of the minority problems and the multinational character of the old Habsburg Empire. Doing this would be neither novel nor really significant. It is more important to realize that the Szeged men in Hungary, the followers of Goga in Romania, important statesmen like Dmowski in Poland all developed a racist approach to politics either before the First World War or soon after, and included it in their political programs years before Hitler made it "popular." The anti-Semitism of these men was racist in conception, but several of our authors make references to anti-Semitism that can be explained as manifestations of xenophobia, of religious conviction, or of a desire for economic reform. Codreanu, for example (unlike his successor as leader of the Iron Guard, Horia Sima) made it quite clear that he was interested in saving and/or reestablishing the old, noble, pure Romanian spirit and was welcoming into the movement (or in his projected Romania) anybody who manifested this spirit. Jews were not likely to have this approach to life, but if they did they were acceptable. Without going into detail and repeating what our two authors dealing with him said, we can see that Codreanu's anti-Semitism would shock any pure racist, and his movement never enjoyed (while Codreanu was alive) the sympathy of Mr. Hitler. Outside Eastern Europe we are not faced—when dealing with Nazi-type movements—with the necessity of differentiating between racist and non-racist anti-Semitism and between the various versions of the non-racist variety. Admittedly, it made little difference to the Jews why they were persecuted, but the different reasons are real to a scholar interested in local, "native," variations of a European-wide phenomenon.

This curious racist versus non-racist approach to anti-Semitism and other aspects of fascism (for example, chauvinism) is, to some extent, the result of the Austro-Hungarian inheritance. Hungarians in Hungary and Poles in Galicia (and for that matter also in Russia's Polish provinces) represented the old ruling element in their respective territories and could dream of a day when they would administer them as independent states. Looking ahead to these days, but also assessing what they saw around them, they discovered numerous people of other nationalities who had the same dreams of at least cultural independence. They were fully conscious of the minority problem that the Austro-Hungarian state was unable to solve, foresaw similar problems emerging in the states they hoped to build, and could not accept either the multinational structure or the Habsburg methods of dealing with it for their future "national" states. Because the other nationalities used basically the same arguments to further their own goals, this old ruling element could not reject them and turned, instead, to the justification used when they were privileged nationalities in Austria-Hungary: historical superiority and tradition. They practiced Magyarization and Polonization as a result, but were never able to accept their converts fully. Converts were not original believers. From here the step to racism is very small. The trend was stopped short by the outbreak of the Second World War in Poland, but reached its tragic, but logical conclusion in Hungary and in Croatia where the Ustaši consciously imitated much of what they learned during their long association with the Magyars in the Habsburg monarchy. While Goga and Sima followed this line in Romania, they never really mattered when they faced people like Codreanu or Antonescu respectively. Unless the number of Jews was too small to make anti-Semitism a really useful slogan, anti-Semitism was used as a focus for the hostility that was felt, basically, toward the politically or economically important elites that survived from Habsburg days in the Successor States. The Jew became the xenophobic, religious, and economic scapegoat on whom the population vented its feeling of revenge for the long centuries of economic and political oppression that preceded World War I. That the Jew had little to do with this oppression did not matter; the fact that he was "different"—just as the oppressors had been—did. It was not entirely due to Hitler's policy and henchmen that the Hungarian Jews (once the Nazis achieved power in that country), and their Polish and Croatian coreligionists suffered relatively more than did their Czech, Serb, or Romanian fellow victims. This had something to do also with the conviction, motivation, and zeal of both the persecutors and those much too few people who opposed them.

This summary of the findings of all or most of our authors must end by repeating something that is certainly obvious by now to all readers. Not only the racism, but even the nationalism of the Eastern European fascists had to include "exclusions and reservations," with which their Western European counterparts were not saddled. Some of these were anything but "native" in origin. When our fascists preached nationalism and racism, even in such ethnically fairly unitary states like Hungary, they had to admit that they were not the only "master race." It would have been very difficult to move against the German minorities in these countries while more or less imitating Hitler and accepting financial or other substantial aid from him. These Germans were permitted to organize their own Nazi movements and could not be curbed even when they asserted their superiority in comparison with the local "master race," or when they claimed what amounted to extraterritorial rights within the framework of the highly centralized, "purely" national state that the fascists proposed to erect. This nationalism and racism with reservations, an almost ridiculous contradiction by definition, was something specifically Eastern European, if not "native" to the fascist movements of the Successor States.

Germany retarded the full flowering of certain Eastern European fascist movements in yet another manner. To use only two examples, Polish fascism never developed fully and the Czech variant practically never got off the ground because it was very difficult to be an extreme nationalist, or even a racist, let alone a fascist, when it was Nazi Germany whose plans and appetites were obviously the greatest danger to the very survival of one's state. Eastern Europe produced several curious social and political phenomena in its long history, but anti-fascist fascism was something even the people living in this part of the world were unable to manufacture. They had to be content with a quasi-fascism that, like all other inept imitations, lacked the dynamics to appeal to the large masses who were looking for easy, all-inclusive answers. Thus, all the cases discussed in this book are, in a sense, examples of fascism with reservations (on the theoretical plane), once again a ridiculous contradiction which is made more ironic because it was forced on these movements by the existence of the most powerful of the fascist states which the people in the Successor States often admired in spite of themselves.

Yet these were not the only contradictions within Eastern European fascism, and a few others had "native" causes. The multinationality inherited from the Habsburg Empire by Yugoslavia and Czechoslovakia created, as those authors who discussed these states pointed out, another kind of contradiction: the anti-state national movements. We can exclude the fascist movements of the Sudeten Germans. Here we have the reverse of what was so familiar to Eastern Europe in the pre-World War I days. Germans living in border areas adjacent to German-speaking states behaved like minorities, and it is not surprising that they finally accepted or were forced to follow the ideology that became dominant in these states. In this context the inability of Czech and Slovak, or Serb and Croat fascists to cooperate is significant. They were unable to create a Czechoslovak or a Yugoslav movement, and their appeal was localized and fragmented. We get manifestations of local patriotism, local nationalism, which would make sense if they had been aimed from the outset at the destruction of the existing state complex. Yet this did not occur until very late, when this solution was virtually imposed on them from the outside. At the beginning these movements represented simply contradictory solutions to the reorganization of the existing states based on the denial of the theory on which the existence of these states based the basic sameness of their "ruling nationalities." In this manner these people justified the claims of their enemies (basically Germans and Hungarians) whose pretensions they opposed and whose demands they ridiculed and denied. Czech, Slovak, Serb and Croat fascists opposed those who advocated dissolution of Czechoslovakia and Yugoslavia, therefore support of dissolution was impossible even though this is what the fascists would have liked. The result was another typically Eastern contradiction: the extreme right had to champion states it did not like, yet create localized movements whose existence was the greatest danger to the survival of the countries that they, at least officially, supported. The Eastern European fascists brought their past into their present and were left with no future.

Fascism was a European, if not a world-wide, phenomenon. It is, therefore, extremely easy to study its most important and powerful manifestations, generalize on the basis of these studies, and endow—based on these findings—the entire fascist movement with more unity and uniformity than it really possessed. It was the intention of those who cooperated in the production of this volume to show that in the Successor States we could reveal significant variations on the general theme. I cannot speak for the authors, even less for the readers, but my reading of those twelve studies convinced me that there was enough that was "native" in the fascist movements of the Successor States to create them even without the examples and prestige of those in Italy or Germany. In other words, I believe that these states would have produced something that, without Mussolini's choice of labels for his party we would possibly not have called fascist, but which, in their essence and numerous manifestations, would have amounted to nearly the same thing. What the existence of fascism in Italy and Germany did was to make the emergence of the movements we studied in the Successor States easier, but it did not create them.

What I just ventured to say about potential fascist proclivities in the Successor States might easily be true of other regions of the world. Even in the case of our states much remains to be done because papers prepared for oral presentation at a conference can only scratch the surface of the mountain of problems presented by the study of these fascist movements. Fortunately, others have already begun, since we held our conference, to dig into this mountain.[3] If our efforts will achieve nothing but the encouragement of a few other miners, we will have accomplished our task.

FOOTNOTES

[1]Hans Rogger and Eugen Weber, ed., *The European Right: A Historical Profile* (Berkeley and Los Angeles: University of California Press, 1966), pp. 1–28

[2]Hannah Arendt, *The Origins of Totalitarianism* (New York: Meridian Books, 1968), pp. 389–459

[3]Miklós Lackó, *Nyilasok, Nemzetiszocialisták* [The Arrow Cross, National Socialists] (Budapest: Kossuth Könyvkiadó, 1966); N. M. Nagy-Talavera, *Green Shirts and Others; A History of Fascism in Hungary and Rumania* (Stanford: The Hoover Institute, 1970)

Index

47-48, 66-68, 75, 127; as
secular religion, 18;
Slovak, 51-52, 57, 59-60,
152; social basis of, 7,
21; and Social
Darwinism, 18; as social
revolution, 48; and
social status, 150; stages
of, 4, 6, 9; strength of,
77; and students, 153;
Sudeten-German, 52-59;
support for, 141; and
teachers, 18-19, 116,
150; with reservations,
155; Yugoslav, 127, 141
Fatherland Front, 27, 34;
and Mussolini, 32
Feder, Gottfried, 67
Federalism, Yugoslav, 126,
128-130, 133
Federation of Volunteers
(Yugoslavia), 130
Fellner, Fritz, 150, 152
Ferdinand I, King of
Romania, 109, 112
Festetich, Count Sándor, 77
Fey, Emil, 32-33
Fischer-Galati, Stephen, 111,
148
France, 31, 93, 106, 119,
127; anti-Semitism in,
107
Franco, General Francisco,
7, 116
Frank, Karl H., 54
Freemasons, 137
French influence in Romania,
104
Friedrich, Carl, 15, 18
Frontul Renaşterii Naţionale,
118
G
Gajda, General Radola
(Rudolf), 48-51, 60-61
Galicia, 154
Gaster, Moses, 105
Gdansk, 89
Gdynia, 89
Gentry, Hungarian, 66, 70
German, education, 18;
fascism, 48; occupation
of Eastern Europe, 5;
students in Prague, 53

German-Hungarian relations,
71, 80
German-Polish relations, 87,
97
German Technical University
of Prague, 53-54
Germany, 31, 34, 65, 69-70,
74, 78, 86, 90-92, 94,
113, 115, 118-119,
126-128, 130, 132, 136,
138, 148-149, 155-156
Geschichte der
Österreichischen
Republik, 21
Gestapo, 132
Goebbels, Joseph, 53
Goethe, Johann W., 92
Goga, Octavian, 111, 148,
153-154
Goga-Cuza Regime, 117-118,
149
Golescu, Dinicu, 104
"Gott und Kaiser," 151-152
Gömbös, Gyula, 68-70,
74-76, 78-79, 136, 149
Graz, 131
Great Britain, 93
Great Depression, 17, 48, 54,
58-59, 69, 71, 76, 78, 90,
113, 115, 135, 153
Greater German Peoples
Party (Austria), 29
Great Poland Camp; see
Obóz Wielkiej Polski
Greece, 102, 128
Greek-Romanian symbiosis,
103-104
Greek War of Independence,
104
Greeks in Romania, 103-104
H
Habsburg Empire; see
Austria-Hungary
Haiducul, 102
Haiduks, 102-103, 110, 111
Hájek, Jiři S., 47
Héjjas, Iván, 79
Heimwehr, 21, 30-31, 33-34;
in Austrian Cabinet,
31-32; dissolved, 34; and
Italy, 32; and Mussolini,
33
Henlein, Konrad, 52, 54, 58,

61; flight of, 58
Himmler, Heinrich, 142
Hindenburg, President Paul
von, 148
Historiography, 80; Austrian,
16, 22; and fascism, 71;
German, 16; Romanian
105-106
Hitler, Adolf, 17-18, 30, 32,
48, 58-61, 68, 75, 80, 90,
116, 136, 140-142,
147-149, 151, 153-155;
and Catholic Church,
18; and Hungary, 69;
Machtergreifung of, 16
Hlinka, Msgr. Andrej, 51-52,
59, 61, 152
Hlinka Guard, 59
Hlinka Party; see Slovak
Peoples Party
Hlinka Youth, 59
Hodáč, František, 51
Horia (Ion Ursu), 107
Horthy, Admiral Miklos, 65,
73, 75, 77-78, 131, 148
HRNAO; see Croatian
National Youth
Hungarian, imperialism, 80;
irredentism, 59-60, 66,
73; nationalism, 65-66,
67, 73; revisionism, 67,
69-70
Hungarian-Romanian
controversy, 108
Hungarian Soviet Republic
(1919), 66, 73-74
Hungarist Ideology, 78
Hungary, 35, 110, 116, 119,
127, 150, 153-155;
anti-Semitic legislation
in, 71, 75, 79;
anti-Semitism in, 66,
69-71, 73-74; civil
service in, 66-67;
Communist Party of, 68,
76; conservatism in, 67;
corporativism in, 68-69;
democracy in, 65;
foreign policy of, 169;
gentry in, 66, 70; and
Hitler, 69; Jews in, 77;
liberalism in, 68, 75;
military of, 66, 68-69,